Books by James P. Cannon

Socialism on Trial (1942)
The Struggle for a Proletarian Party (1943)
The History of American Trotskyism (1944)
America's Road to Socialism (1953)
Notebook of an Agitator (1958)
The First Ten Years of American Communism (1962)
Letters from Prison (1968)
Speeches for Socialism (1971)
Speeches to the Party (1973)
The Socialist Workers Party in World War II (1975)

1935

James P. Cannon As We Knew Him

BY THIRTY-THREE COMRADES, FRIENDS, AND RELATIVES

Introduction by Jack Barnes

PATHFINDER PRESS   NEW YORK

Edited by Les Evans
Copyright © 1976 by Pathfinder Press, Inc.
All rights reserved

Library of Congress Catalog Card Number 76-25382
ISBN: 0-87348-474-6 (cloth); 0-87348-500-9 (paper)
Manufactured in the United States of America

First Edition, 1976

Pathfinder Press, Inc.
410 West Street
New York, N.Y. 10014

Contents

Introduction

by Jack Barnes

This is a book of reminiscences by people who knew and worked with Jim Cannon at various times during the last fifty years. It is not the biography of him that will one day be written by historians of the American working class movement. And it is not a substitute for what Jim, in his own books, had to say about the meaning of a revolutionist's life and the building of a Leninist party in America.

The title of the book is appropriate. It is "James P. Cannon As We Knew Him," not "James P. Cannon As He Was." The two who knew him best and longest—his companion of forty years, Rose Karsner, and Vincent Dunne—died before Jim did, and could not contribute to this volume. Few of the others, apart from his immediate family, were on close personal terms with Jim—he was much older than most of the contributors.

In their correspondence with the editors some of the contributors said that in writing about Jim they found that they were really writing about themselves. But this tells us something about Jim too, although in a roundabout way. After all, these writers— political associates, former comrades, and relatives—all had their lives touched or shaped by Jim Cannon and the party he led and they are in part the kind of people they are because of his influence.

What comes through most clearly in these articles is Jim Cannon as a politician and public figure. The private man is more elusive. But this is not necessarily a defect. While Jim

JACK BARNES was born in 1940. He joined the Young Socialist Alliance in 1961 and became its national chairman in 1965. He first met Cannon in 1963 and saw him often in the late 1960s and early 1970s in Los Angeles. He has served as national secretary of the Socialist Workers Party since 1972.

Cannon was a complex personality he saw himself above all as a revolutionary politician and that is how he will be judged by future generations.

This collection does shed light on Jim Cannon as a principled man. It confirms something I had observed in my own association with Jim in the last ten years of his life—that there was no *secret* political Cannon. There is a popular image of political leaders that comes from the backroom practices of capitalist party politics: that it is considered smart to say one thing publicly and keep your real reasons private for discussion only with your close associates. This book shows that people— and some of the contributors no longer share Jim's views—do not remember Jim saying one thing privately and something else publicly.

As a young leader of the Socialist Workers Party I worked with Jim from about 1965 on, and met with him whenever I was in Los Angeles. One thing I discovered was that there was no discrepancy between his private advice and his public writings. Initiation into the leadership did not consist in being taught inside tips or secret leadership techniques.

What we talked about were the big political questions of the day and the internal life of the Trotskyist movement nationally and internationally. One of the weaknesses of the reminiscences collected here is that they do not adequately reflect Jim Cannon's internationalism as I saw it, his concern with the world movement, with the international repercussions of American events, and his consistent conscious attention to these questions. During his last five years, whenever I would see him he wanted above all to talk about political developments in the Fourth International and the strategy required to strengthen it. This was a dominating concern for him. And he drew here on his immense personal experience, which went back further in the leadership of the international communist movement than anyone else alive in the Fourth International.

Jim Cannon must be measured as a Leninist and an internationalist. Here he made an outstanding contribution to the world Marxist movement and thus to the socialist future of humanity. He drew together that irreplaceable nucleus of the future mass party of the American workers and their allies. Jim built a party. He gathered together the first nucleus and inspired and trained it. And he left behind an organization that aspires to lead the coming American socialist revolution.

It is not far-fetched to record Jim Cannon as the greatest American Leninist of the mid-twentieth century, or even as the best builder of a Bolshevik-type party anywhere in the world after the death of Leon Trotsky. Cannon not only did it but he wrote about what he did so that his experience could be used by others, both in the United States and in the rest of the world.

Many of the anecdotes in this book help to dispel a common caricature of Leninism fostered by Stalinism. One of the things that comes through in this book is Jim's patience, his appreciation of each individual won to the revolutionary party.

Jim's ability to hold together a cadre where so many others had failed was not only owing to his talent for sizing up a political situation and knowing what to do about it, but to his appreciation of the human material of the party. He was violently opposed to any tendency to write people off because of passing disagreements, incidental mistakes, or personal weaknesses. Long ago he learned the hard way not to make any hasty or subjective decisions about what a cadre might ultimately contribute to the movement.

Jim's concern with drawing out the best efforts of his comrades is reflected in these reminiscences. This is an aspect of his *political* personality. Most of the people writing here felt that he did care about what happened to them and was concerned about each individual cadre. This did not reflect softness on his part but was an essential characteristic of what he said he had learned from the Bolsheviks.

One of the jobs of a leader is to find out what people can do and to get them to do it. That means looking for all kinds of unsuspected talent in people who come to the movement. It also means protecting people when they can't handle some job, because of lack of experience or distaste for an assignment. Personal incompatibility must never be permitted to affect judgments on this. Jim told me that he learned this from Trotsky.

I never talked to him extensively about the very early days of the American Trotskyist movement, when the party was brought to the point of split by differences between Jim and Shachtman. But he did give me copies of Trotsky's letters of 1933 advocating a halt to the fight and urging Jim to place the unity of the movement above his political dislike of Shachtman. It was this objectivity about personalities, learned by Jim from his teachers after making errors, that he was especially anxious to pass along. He felt that this was a particularly difficult acquisition for younger leaders, usually coming to be appreciated only after decisiveness or "toughness" had been learned.

Of course Jim did not always succeed in living up to the standards he tried to set for himself and for the movement. He would acknowledge this occasional human discrepancy without giving an inch on how things ought to be done, sometimes advising his co-workers, "Do as I say, not as I do."

Jim was always going to do more than he could actually accomplish. He wasn't as well organized or as self-disciplined as a Lenin or a Trotsky. But even if he didn't finish all the projects he started, he called our attention to things that should be done and many of them, such as the ones he talks about in his *Letters from Prison,* should still be done. Jim knew that his enthusiasm ran ahead of his performance. This was sometimes aggravating to his colleagues, but he did do quite a bit.

The authors of these recollections are of many ages and backgrounds. Some are members of the Socialist Workers Party. Some are not. Some knew Jim for many years. Some had met him only recently. There is no one still living of his own generation and outlook able to add the special dimension of a close and contemporary friend. Not everyone who worked with Jim over the years chose to write something for this collection. Therefore this is a partial record.

Many of the contributions were written or given as speeches a few weeks or months after Jim's death in August 1974. Some of these have been abridged for reasons of space. Not all of the contributors are professional writers—the majority in fact are not—but each had something to tell and they told it in their own way.

The sequence, with the exception of the two opening selections by Joseph Hansen and George Novack, which make general assessments of Jim Cannon's political career, is roughly chronological, based either on when the writer first met Jim or on the period they chose to recall. The editors have supplied a note for each article telling something about the author's relation to Jim. The collection closes with the piece by Reba Hansen, who was for many years Jim's secretary in the national office of the SWP. Apart from those who are no longer here, Jim probably told Reba more about his early life than anyone else, and through her, told us as much as he was willing to about the way he saw himself personally.

January 1976

Joseph Hansen

Jim's life was so bound up with the life of the generation I belong to that it is difficult to speak about him briefly. The mass of material, particularly the flood of memories, is simply too great. I will confine myself to making only a few observations about his development as a revolutionist and his achievements.

At the age of eighty-four, after sixty-six years of service in the revolutionary socialist movement, Jim's mind was still sharp and lucid. He followed world events closely, kept up with the current literature of the radical movement, remained on top of developments in the Socialist Workers Party and the Young Socialist Alliance, and was keenly interested in the affairs of the Fourth International, holding strong opinions on the current differences being debated in the world party of the socialist revolution.

His advice and judgments will be sorely missed. They were always advanced with complete objectivity and with the interests of the movement as a whole uppermost in his considerations.

Jim was born in Rosedale, Kansas, on February 11, 1890. The family, of Irish background, was an ordinary one except for politics. His father was a socialist and a partisan of the *Appeal to Reason,* a socialist journal of wide circulation and great

---

JOSEPH HANSEN was born in 1910. He joined the Communist League of America in 1934 and was a secretary of Leon Trotsky (1937-40) and editor of the *Militant* and *International Socialist Review.* He edited Cannon's *Notebook of an Agitator* and is now editor of *Intercontinental Press.* This speech was given on August 23, 1974, two days after Cannon's death, at a Socialist Educational Conference in Oberlin, Ohio, attended by 1,250 persons.

popularity. A father holding socialist views was an enormous advantage to a boy growing up in the backward Middle West.

A direct result was that at the age of eighteen, Jim joined the Socialist Party. Three years later he joined the Industrial Workers of the World, dual membership being quite common and an accepted practice.

In those years, the United States was experiencing a great radical upsurge. It was a time of bitter strike struggles and violent confrontations with strikebreakers and the police. Under the leadership of Eugene V. Debs, the Socialist Party grew by leaps and bounds, striking deep roots in the labor movement.

Jim was formed as a class-conscious battler in this period, coming to the attention of such superlative fighters and organizers as Vincent St. John, from whom Jim learned invaluable lessons.

In high school, Jim starred in debating, a campus sport of much higher standing than it is today. Participation on the debating team gave Jim a good start in achieving one of his ambitions, which was to become a skilled public speaker.

He made a study of public speaking, observing the celebrities who came to town on lecture tours, reading books on technique, and doing his best to eliminate the speech defects that come natural in the Middle West. This was coupled with practical experience in soapboxing, which is a very hard school. One of the results was that he became renowned by the early twenties in the Communist movement as a highly gifted speaker.

He followed a similar course of study in writing, training himself in this field by seeing how others did it, and reading what he could find on the subject. At one time he began a novel.

In both writing and speaking he tended to be a perfectionist, continually working over his drafts and seeking to bring them to a high polish.

Thus as an organizer, a speaker, and a writer he already had solid skills when he became editor of the *Workers' World* in Kansas City in 1919 at the age of twenty-nine and of *The Toiler,* a Communist Party publication, the following year.

In his ability to present the fundamental concepts and goals of revolutionary socialism in popular terms, Jim had few equals. He was an artist in this field. Many of the short articles he wrote over the years in his column *The Notebook of an Agitator* can be taken as models of revolutionary journalism.

The IWW and the left wing of the Socialist Party in the years leading up to World War I constituted a good training ground for an activist. The lessons remained with Jim throughout the rest of his life.

But the greatest single influence in his political education was the Russian revolution, particularly the October 1917 overturn in which the Bolsheviks under Lenin and Trotsky won power.

That great event, which caught the imagination of class-conscious workers throughout the world as a living example of how to topple capitalism, inspired a whole new generation of revolutionists. For Jim, as for many of his comrades, it became an advanced school in which they were reeducated in some respects and in others received graduate training in theory and in politics.

And they learned in a very practical school. That was the assemblage which came together to found the Communist Party of the United States, in which Jim participated. It included the left wing of the Socialist Party, all the rebels in the IWW who could be convinced, and others. Jim was elected to the new party's Central Committee at the Bridgman, Michigan, convention in 1920.

It was in this school that Jim completed his basic education as a revolutionist. It was under the direct tutelage of the Russians, in conjunction with living experience in the American class struggle in the twenties, that Jim's main talent flowered and he emerged as a political organizer of the highest caliber.

The capitalist class nearly always has talented political organizers at its disposal, some of them coming from wealthy families that specialize in offering political leadership. They are rather rare in the working class, one reason being that many with the talent for it are drawn into serving the capitalist parties. A person with talent in this field must be capable of great dedication and capacity for self-sacrifice to take up the cause of the working class and to remain devoted to it for decades and even a lifetime.

Jim was such a person. It came natural to him to size up a situation correctly, to take into account the main forces, to judge accurately what ought to be done next, and to win others to these insights. Jim became a skilled technician in working out the best ways of responding to attacks on the revolutionary movement and of mounting effective counteroffensives.

In the twenties in the Communist movement, Jim was justly famed for this. It was the development of this talent in particular that won him a place as one of the key leaders of the Communist Party.

In those days, the Communist Party was something of a jungle—that is, as far as the internal struggles were concerned. At first, the Communist International under Lenin and Trotsky could play a role in ameliorating the situation and helping the comrades to learn the correct lessons from their mistakes.

But later on the Comintern degenerated and itself became a real jungle, in which Jim was one of the best of the jungle fighters. He made errors which he later learned from and never forgot.

The main difference between Jim and some of the others who also had talents along this line was that Jim operated within the framework of principles, the principles of revolutionary socialism. He sought to win, naturally. But his perspective was the long-range one of winning the final battle; that is, the final battle in the struggle to topple capitalism and to replace it with socialism on a world scale.

In his opinion this was a great perspective, the only one really worth a lifetime of effort. He saw it, too, as a realistic perspective, one that would inevitably be realized even if it required the combined efforts of several successive generations of revolutionists.

Jim was an internationalist to the marrow of his bones. He absorbed the internationalist view in his youth as a member of the Socialist Party and of the IWW. The Russian revolution offered living confirmation of the correctness of this outlook.

On top of this, Jim began gaining direct experience in international problems. In addition to the incessant discussions, debates, and factional struggles in the Communist Party of the twenties, Jim served as a delegate to the important Fourth Congress of the Communist International and later to the Sixth, where Stalin sought to smash Trotsky's defense of the program of Leninism.

The Sixth Congress of the Communist International in 1928 marked an important step in the development of James P. Cannon as a political figure of international stature. It was at that congress that he decided to take up the cause represented by Leon Trotsky.

In the previous period he had become deeply disturbed by pernicious moves made by the Comintern in the internal affairs of the American Communist Party. But he did not connect these with the struggle over "Trotskyism" in the Russian party. In fact, from the available information, he was inclined to disregard that struggle and even give the benefit of the doubt to Stalin.

At the Sixth Congress, he and Maurice Spector of the Canadian Communist Party accidentally received copies of an English translation of part of Trotsky's criticism of the draft program that was proposed for adoption at the congress. The rest is history.

The document completely convinced Cannon. He decided to battle for Trotsky's criticisms—not because of any hope of immediate success, but because he saw that Trotsky was *right.*

It was not an easy decision. Cannon realized, perhaps better than anyone outside of the Russian Trotskyists, that it would mean ostracism, the breakup of old friendships, and the end of personal relations with many comrades he had known in common battles for years.

However, it was politically necessary to make the turn. For Jim this consideration was paramount. Nothing personal could be permitted to stand in the way of moving ahead in defense of Trotsky's position and against Stalin's bureaucratic gang.

Cannon's decision offers a striking example of the importance of achieving political clarity in a factional struggle. Stalin understood that too. That was why he tried to gag Trotsky and why he eventually used assassination to silence Trotsky's powerful voice.

Thus at a crucial moment, when Trotsky was exiled in far-off Alma-Ata, blocked by force from defending his positions and from answering the most poisonous lies and slanders, one of the main leaders of the American Communist Party joined Trotsky in defense of the program of Leninism, determined to do everything he could to organize a principled faction to struggle for that program on an international scale in the Communist movement.

That decision marked the real beginning of our movement in the United States, although some anticipatory moves in that direction had been taken previously by figures like Antoinette Konikow in Boston. And that decision also marked a banner day for the worldwide movement that eventually became the Fourth International.

James P. Cannon came in on the ground floor in 1928 in the international struggle against Stalinism. He lived to see the Stalinist monolith shattered.

The collaboration between Cannon and Trotsky was particularly fruitful. Some of the detractors of our movement have pictured Cannon as a "yes man," wholly dependent on the ideas furnished by Trotsky, serving only to execute them. I can think of worse relationships; but this picture happens to be inaccurate. It actually maligns Trotsky as much as it does Cannon.

In his relations with Cannon, as in his relations with his secretaries and all members of the staff that worked with him, Trotsky's status was that of an equal. Give-and-take was easy. Trotsky elicited ideas from others and their tendency was to respond, and sometimes to rise above themselves.

This collaboration was, of course, on the political level. The team was not a group of compatible souls drawn together out of common personal predilections, tastes, and habits. Trotsky and Cannon, for instance, were quite different in personality.

In Coyoacán, I saw how Trotsky and Cannon collaborated, and I know what value Trotsky placed on Cannon's opinions as a political strategist and practitioner of Leninism in party building.

As for Cannon, he regarded Trotsky to be a genius, one of the rare individuals like Karl Marx that are born, sometimes generations apart. He accepted Trotsky's genius as a fact, a fact of enormous importance to the revolutionary movement, and he had no thought of placing himself on the same level.

But Cannon never accepted anything on faith from Trotsky, nor would Trotsky have expected it. If Cannon disagreed, he argued for his own views, and on certain questions he convinced Trotsky. Cannon was not unique in this. It was an experience shared by others on Trotsky's staff.

In founding the Fourth International in 1938, Trotsky and Cannon made a powerful combination, beginning with the conversations concerning the program to be presented at the first congress, and ending with the actual launching of the new international party.

There were a number of persons, it should be recalled, even in the Trotskyist movement, who opposed forming the Fourth International, holding it to be inopportune. Both Trotsky and Cannon favored the step, the imminence of World War II making it all the more necessary because of the turbulent new stage in world affairs that would be opened up.

When Trotsky was assassinated in 1940, it was the opinion of many, above all the Stalinists and the reactionaries in general, that this meant the end of the Fourth International and of Trotskyism.

Cannon, at the age of fifty, was considered to be the most prominent leader of the world Trotskyist movement. In his opinion it was unrealistic to believe that any single individual could fill the void left by the death of Trotsky. Most certainly no one should look to him to attempt it. He was no genius, he said, and he considered it pretentious and a mockery to play the role of being one.

However, he did have a plan for carrying on the struggle in the absence of Trotsky. The plan was not an elaborate one. It consisted of closing ranks, of trying to keep the team together, of strengthening it, of expanding it, and of renewing it.

In this way the continuity of leadership could be maintained. If another Trotsky appeared, that would be extraordinary good luck. It would help shorten the struggle for socialism. But if another Trotsky did not appear, we would continue to struggle on the basis of Trotsky's program and teachings, and eventually teamwork would win.

In this proposed course, Cannon considered the Fourth International to be of central importance. Everything possible had to be done to maintain the Fourth International and to expand it on all continents as a means of upholding the program of Trotskyism and of helping to form national leaderships capable of building mass parties and of guiding revolutionary struggles to success.

Cannon's interest in the development and welfare of the Fourth International had nothing in common with a federalist concept that viewed the international as being a good thing so long as it stayed out of the bailiwick of the Socialist Workers Party, as some have claimed.

Cannon was deeply committed to building the Fourth International along the lines laid down at its foundation. He considered the Socialist Workers Party to be only a section of the Fourth International—an important section in his opinion. He never changed in this, even though the passage of reactionary legislation in the United States compelled the Socialist Workers Party to disaffiliate from the Fourth International.

Comrade Cannon's most remarkable achievement, nonetheless, was on American soil. Sharing in this achievement were the other pioneer Trotskyists in the United States—among them Vincent R. Dunne, Carl Skoglund, Arne Swabeck, and above all Rose Karsner, Jim's companion who died in March 1968. These pioneer Trotskyists, however, would all give the main credit to Jim.

This achievement was to build a viable nucleus of a revolutionary party inside the United States, the main bastion of world capitalism. Not only did Jim build this nucleus, he maintained it and continued to build it for an unprecedented number of decades in face of enormous pressures. There has been nothing like it in the history of the revolutionary socialist movement.

Jim held this nucleus together against the lure of posts in the trade union bureaucracy, none of which are without considerable emoluments.

He held this nucleus together against the merciless blows and venomous slanders of American Stalinism, once a powerful force in the radical movement and in many trade unions in the United States.

He held this nucleus together in face of the hysteria of World War II, marching to prison at the head of the Trotskyists convicted as the first victims of the Smith Act for their political opposition to imperialist war.

He held this nucleus together during the infamous decade of McCarthyism in the United States, when the Trotskyists were hounded from their jobs by the American political police, the FBI, and when our movement was almost completely isolated politically and virtually paralyzed for lack of funds.

He held this nucleus together against the deadly combination of McCarthyite repression and economic prosperity that led to years of passivity in the labor movement.

There were casualties, of course. Valuable comrades grew discouraged and dropped out of activity. Cadres with years of experience could not endure the strain and developed political differences that gave them seeming justification for finding a road to the sidelines.

But new recruits replaced them. And some of these recruits proved to be of exceptional worth precisely because they swam against the stream in joining the movement in such a period.

Jim's stamina and stubbornness won out in the end. He succeeded in maintaining the continuity of leadership. This continuity went back directly to the founders of American socialism in the past century, and back in a direct line to the Bolsheviks, and through them to the founders of scientific socialism.

The nucleus of revolutionary socialists assembled, maintained, and renewed under the leadership of James P. Cannon is doing quite well today and we know of the satisfaction he found in this success.

During his years as the main leader of American Trotskyism, Jim became the teacher of three, if not four, generations of revolutionists. He taught us not so much through formal lectures—he did not give many in reality—or even through his writings, although here he left us a considerable legacy.

He taught us most powerfully through participating with us in struggles. Over the years he stood at our side in many situations and battles in the class struggle, where one of his chief concerns was the development of cadres, particularly the capacity of comrades to think for themselves.

But I would say that the primary arena in which Jim taught us the most important lessons was in the development of the Socialist Workers Party itself. Here I think not only of party administration, the organization of branch work, the production of our press, and the development of leadership abilities in these areas, but of the many internal struggles, including those in the early years of the Communist Party in which most of us here did not participate except vicariously through the accounts that have been handed down.

Our party owes its very existence to the way Jim handled these struggles. Through them he imparted his political know-how so that it became an acquisition of the cadres as a whole, something our party can use as a foundation in the mighty struggles lying ahead that will determine the fate of America and along with America the fate of the world.

In the aftermath of World War II, it was Jim's firm opinion that the victory of the Soviet Union, the toppling of capitalism in Eastern Europe, and the revolutionary victory in China would ultimately weaken Stalinism on a world scale, making possible new revolutionary advances. The victory of the Cuban revolution in 1959 was one of the confirmations, in his view.

His eyes were set, of course, on the American workers. In the long run, the upheavals elsewhere would have a cumulative effect in the political arena in the United States. Coupled with the ever-deepening economic and social contradictions of capitalism, the American workers, the mightiest power on earth, would be propelled into action and the American revolution would begin.

In the last years of his life, Jim was convinced that the American revolution is not far off. It has drawn perceptibly nearer. He saw the signs in the appearance of the Black liberation movement in the sixties and the women's liberation movement in the early seventies. He saw it in the incapacity of American imperialism to win outright victories, first in Korea and then in Vietnam. He saw it in the radicalization of the youth on a scale never before seen in America. He saw it in the antiwar movement that swept this country from coast to coast, shaking the capitalist political system so that one president decided not to run for a second term, and his successor—a less astute crook—had to hand in his resignation, the first time that has happened in American history.

All these signs led Cannon to believe that the time of Trotskyism is close at hand.

In his personal life, Jim preferred a simple existence, in the company of congenial comrades and friends. He was an omnivorous reader, but he also enjoyed conversation. His conversation, of course, centered on politics, or drifted there, sometimes with a little ribbing and joking woven in.

Jim smoked cigars and a pipe and was not at all demanding as to the grade of tobacco, smoking with equal relish the cheap brands he bought and the Havanas or mixtures that came as gifts in recent years. So long as the tobacco smoldered, he was satisfied.

He considered a celebration from time to time to be a necessity, and he made sure that the usual source of conviviality was not missing. For long periods, his drink was tea or at the most beer, a limitation he did not approve of; but alcohol gave him a problem he was compelled to take into account.

In his working pattern, Jim was not an easygoing type; in fact, he could be very demanding. Some comrades found this to be trying and it led to friction in some instances.

Jim had the capacity to recognize his own faults and weaknesses. To close friends, he even overemphasized them, thinking he had more than the usual share.

Jim's objectivity extended to others. It can be seen in the most striking way in his comments on figures he once knew in the Communist Party who had become Stalinists and betrayed the revolutionary socialist movement. He gave them full credit for what they once were and had sought to be, and explained how forces they did not understand had overwhelmed them.

A psychoanalytical study of Jim might be of interest, for he was very complex, but it would not tell us much about what made him tick politically. He lived as a political person and he must be judged on that level. In this he functioned as a team man, completely conscious of the power of a leadership team, and a master at constructing one; that is, a well-balanced group composed of contrasting types whether one-sided or many-sided, including some always inclined to be critical and some certain to reflect the opinion of this or that layer.

As an integral part of the team, Jim subordinated himself completely to party discipline, to "duty" as he liked to think of it, or to a call to "pitch for the party."

Jim described himself as at bottom an "anarchist," and no doubt there was some truth to this. It did not come natural to him to be a team man. He had to learn it and to apply it quite consciously to himself, harnessing himself to the call for duty. Consequently, it was observable that he indulged in his anarchistic inclinations, if that's what they were, only in small things, doing his utmost to exclude them from anything of importance to the party.

Fundamentally, Jim was an angry person. He was angry at injustice, at inequities, at special privileges, at exploitation. He was angry at poverty, lack of opportunity, oppression, racism, and sexism.

He seethed over the crimes of capitalism, its wars, its reactionary ideologies. He hated its police, its courts, its prisons, its fascism, its tendency to drop back to barbarism.

He burned with fury over Truman's dropping the atomic bomb on Hiroshima and Nagasaki and at the chance that the human race might be obliterated in an atomic holocaust.

This deep-seated and perpetual anger at capitalism, aroused every day by what he read in the papers and saw on all sides, was one of the driving forces in Jim's makeup.

He was utterly dedicated to overthrowing this monstrous system in which we happen to have been born.

Jim had a clear vision of socialism and the perspectives it could open up. He gained this vision as a youth and the vision never left him. He sought throughout his conscious life to impart this vision to others, to inspire them, and to win them to the cause.

He repeated this appeal with all the eloquence at his command in the recent speech he made on tape for the celebration of the tenth anniversary of *Intercontinental Press.*

That speech could be said to be Jim Cannon's last message to the party and to the new generation of rebels, expressing his deepest convictions.

I will not say farewell to Jim. He remains with us. He remains with us through his writings. He remains with us through the party that he did so much to establish. He remains with us through the continuity of that party's leadership and through the personal example he set of lifelong dedication to the cause of the emancipation of humanity.

Through these achievements, Jim will remain a participant, a comrade-in-arms, in the international struggle for socialism until the final victory is won.

Cannon addressing New York meeting protesting convictions in Minneapolis trial (1941). Farrell Dobbs at right.

George Novack

James P. Cannon, founder of American Trotskyism and its foremost leader for forty-six years, was born in Rosedale, Kansas, a small town near Kansas City, ten years before the end of the nineteenth century. During three-quarters of this century he saw the United States engage in four imperialist wars, experience two prolonged booms, suffer the shocks of the Great Depression, and become the supreme power of world capitalism with enough nuclear overkill to extinguish all life on this planet. He also lived through the triumph of the October revolution and witnessed the Stalinist degeneration of the first workers' state, the rise and fall of fascism in Europe, the construction of the CIO and its bureaucratization, the abolition of capitalist property relations in Eastern Europe, the Yugoslav, Chinese, Vietnamese, and Cuban revolutions, and the spread of the colonial independence struggles after the Second World War.

These cataclysmic events shaped his political personality and determined the course of his career. When he died in Los Angeles on August 21 at the age of eighty-four, he was the outstanding survivor of the pre-First World War generation of working class warriors. During his sixty-six years as a conscious revolutionist he encountered almost every celebrated figure on the left in this

GEORGE NOVACK was born in 1905. He joined the Communist League of America in 1933 and was national secretary of the Civil Rights Defense Committee that mobilized support for Cannon and the other Minneapolis trial defendants. He has written many books on philosophy and history, the latest of which is *Pragmatism versus Marxism: An Appraisal of John Dewey's Philosophy*. This article is reprinted from the October 1974 *International Socialist Review*.

country. He organized with the IWW leaders Vincent St. John, Big Bill Haywood, and Frank Little; knew Eugene V. Debs, James Connolly, Jim Larkin, Carlo Tresca, and Elizabeth Gurley Flynn; brought Earl Browder into the Communist Party. As a leader of that party, Cannon associated with William Z. Foster and clashed with Jay Lovestone. He founded the American Trotskyist movement with Max Shachtman and Martin Abern; launched the Workers Party with A. J. Muste; and led the Trotskyists into the Socialist Party of Norman Thomas for a short while before forming the Socialist Workers Party in January 1938. All this before his fiftieth year—and he gave thirty-four more years of service to his party!

He participated in and attentively studied every significant development in the life of the American working class and national politics from the frame-up trial of the leaders of the Western Federation of Miners—Moyer, Haywood, and Pettibone—in 1907 to Nixon's enforced resignation. He distilled from these experiences an unrivaled store of expert knowledge about revolutionary politics that he did his best to pass on to four generations of Trotskyists.

Cannon represented the crossbreeding of two desirable traits: a passionate plebeian hatred of the crimes and injustices of capitalist society combined with an indomitable adherence to the ideas and traditions of the original Bolshevik leaders. The fusion of these elements in his makeup accounted for the strength of his convictions, the stamina of his revolutionary will, and the persistence of his fight for the truth.

The Russian revolution that ushered in the socialist era was also a crucial turning point in his political education. The scientific insight into the motive forces of history accompanied by the organization in action of vast masses of insurgent workers and peasants that characterized this epochal event made an immediate and enduring impact on his mind. It transformed the footloose "Wobbly" organizer who had joined the Socialist Party's left wing from a provincial Midwest rebel into a Communist schooled by Lenin and Trotsky.

Unlike most of his contemporaries, he remained what he became in the first wave of wars and revolutions in our turbulent century—a pupil of the Bolsheviks. He looked to Lenin and Trotsky as his mentors and aspired to follow in their footsteps. The proletarian internationalists who headed the October revolution, established and defended the Soviet Union, and founded the Third International, pointed out to him the way to win a socialist society rid of war, poverty, misery, racism, and inequality. He was guided by their ideas for the rest of his career.

He became one of the founders of the American Communist Party, was elected to its Central Committee in 1920, and edited its first national organ. He sharply disagreed with those ex-radicals and academic historians who disparaged the pioneer days of American Communism. He regarded its formative period as a salutary step in the development of the movement toward a socialist revolution in the United States. The early CP regrouped the honest militants from various quarters and, despite its subsequent Stalinization, set their feet on a revolutionary road after the defaults of the Social Democracy and the disorientation and disintegration of the IWW.

"Allowing for all its mistakes and the inadequacies of its leadership, the party that responded to the Russian revolution was the first genuinely revolutionary political party in this country," he wrote in his account of *The First Ten Years of American Communism*. What Cannon learned in the CP, both as national secretary of the International Labor Defense and through its fierce factional battles, was decisive in his maturing as a revolutionary leader.

This is the age of internationalism, he insisted. He went as a delegate from the American CP to the 1922 and 1928 congresses of the Third International and lived for a while in Moscow with his companion Rose Karsner. The Sixth Congress of the Comintern proved to be the second major turning point in his political itinerary. As a member of the program commission, he inadvertently secured a copy of Trotsky's criticism of the program that had been prepared by Bukharin and Stalin for adoption by the congress. The arguments in this suppressed document from the exile in Alma-Ata immediately persuaded him and Maurice Spector, the Canadian CP leader, that Stalin had broken with Lenin's course and was heading in an opposite direction in working class politics.

He returned to the United States resolved to do battle for Trotsky's positions and was expelled from the CP in 1928 for advocating them. He later wrote: "I never deceived myself for a moment about the most probable consequences of my decision to support Trotsky in the summer of 1928. I knew it was going to cost me my head and also my swivel chair, but I thought: What the hell—better men than I have risked their heads and their swivel chairs for truth and justice. Trotsky and his associates were doing it at that very moment in the exile camps and prisons of the Soviet Union. It was no more than right that one man, however limited his qualifications, should remember what he started out in his youth to fight for, and speak out for their cause and try to make the world hear, or at least to let the exiled and imprisoned Russian Oppositionists know that they had found a new friend and supporter" (*The First Ten Years of American Communism,* pp. 225-26).

Not only Trotsky and his Russian cothinkers but others around the world were encouraged by Cannon's bold initiative. The *Militant,* the weekly paper he edited, had a wide circulation, and it helped spread knowledge of the Trotskyist criticism of the Stalinist gangrene to individuals and groups in England, Australia, Japan, and elsewhere.

As the central figure among his American followers, Cannon collaborated closely and constantly with Leon Trotsky through the eleven years of Trotsky's third and last exile, visiting him in France and Mexico. Together they launched the Fourth International on the eve of the Second World War. Cannon's death on August 21 of this year coincided within two hours of the day and time of Trotsky's death thirty-four years before.

Cannon deliberately rejected the notion that he was delegated to assume the place of the "Old Man," as Trotsky was called, in the life of the Fourth International. He maintained that, because of Trotsky's rare genius and exceptional experience, he played a unique and irreplaceable role. His vacant spot would have to be filled by a combination of qualified leaders from the various national sections of the world movement whose collective efforts would make up for the loss of Trotsky's guidance. The creation of such a leadership team was his constant preoccupation from 1940 until his death. This far-from-completed task will have to be carried forward by Cannon's successors.

This rugged son of the working class might have been a prosperous lawyer and even a U.S. senator; he was eyed for a career of this sort by the local Democratic politicos. He spurned this path, having been imbued at an early age with the vision of another America by a father who held socialist views, by reading the left-wing press, and becoming active in the ranks of labor. Once he grasped the necessity for a revolutionary party as the indispensable instrument for promoting the struggles of the oppressed and leading them to victory, he turned his full energies to assembling the cadres for such a party, first in the Communist Party, thereafter through the Trotskyist movement. That was the essential meaning of his lifework.

He had shouldered a herculean job. The immediate conditions in which he had to operate were hardly favorable for the quick and easy fulfillment of that objective. He had no illusions about that. All his life he had to swim against the stream, confronting one adversary and obstacle after another and coping with many of them all at once. These included the official and unofficial upholders of the capitalist order, union piecards, Stalinist and Socialist reformists, vain pretenders to the heritage of Lenin and Trotsky, and assorted phonies and crackpots. Decade after decade he dealt with all these opponents firmly, unflinchingly, and objectively.

Trotsky once wrote an article addressed to the beleaguered Soviet Oppositionists headed: "Tenacity! Tenacity! Tenacity!" So Cannon by precept and example inspired us to stick to our socialist ideas and perspectives against isolation and persecution.

Because of their opposition to imperialism and defense of union democracy, Cannon and seventeen other party members were railroaded to federal prison by the Roosevelt administration during the Second World War, just as Wilson jailed Eugene V. Debs in the First World War. Conditions were even harder throughout the deep-freeze and witch-hunting of the cold war. Through it all Cannon retained the assurance that a new wave of radicalism would arise and the American workers would again rouse themselves and take the offensive against the monopolists, as they had done during the 1930s. However imposing its might and dreadful its crimes, capitalism would have to go. Sure as ice would melt in spring, the workers would be its undertakers.

Coming from a poor Irish-Catholic immigrant family, Cannon himself gave proof of the capacities inherent in the working class. He did not have more than a high school education, although he became very well-read. He graduated from the college of hard knocks. He was trained to counter shady practices in the political arena, he said, thanks to the crooks and eye-gougers he had previously met in the rough and tumble of the capitalist jungle.

He was largely self-taught as a speaker, writer, union and party organizer. He assiduously studied the art of public speaking and had few equals as a popularizer of socialist ideas and aims on the platform. He was a working journalist for the radical press from the time he edited the left-wing Kansas City newspaper the *Workers' World* in 1919. He acquired a writing style that was as direct and crisply idiomatic as the agitation of a "Wobbly" soapboxer. His articles and speeches were carefully wrought. After he had critically considered and clarified the matter at hand in his own mind he could convey its fundamental elements and shadings to others with remarkable simplicity and freshness.

I was first impressed with his faculty for acute and forceful exposition when I listened to a series of talks he gave on revolutionary policy in the trade unions. That was early in 1934, before the emergence of the CIO. He analyzed the errors being committed by the Stalinists on the one hand during their ultraleft sectarian course of that period, and by the Lovestoneites on the other in adapting opportunistically to the union officialdom. He then formulated a correct class-struggle line under the given circumstances. He seemed more intelligent than most of the professors and philosophers I knew and I wondered how he could make so complex a situation so clear and understandable to a neophyte like myself. Of course, he was applying the Marxist method to the problems confronting working class militants, as he was to do with similar skill over the next forty years.

It took time for Cannon to dig down to the roots of the science of socialism and grasp the underlying importance of its logical method. The practical sides of Marxism and Leninism came easier to him than its theoretical premises. He finally realized the relevance of dialectical materialism to revolutionary politics in the battle he conducted alongside Trotsky against the petty-bourgeois oppositionists, headed by James Burnham and Max Shachtman, in the Socialist Workers Party at the outbreak of the Second World War.

While we had been on good terms since my entry into the Trotskyist ranks in 1933, our association was cemented through common participation in that factional struggle in defense of Marxist principles and the program of the Fourth International. At the climactic internal meeting in New York City that was the showdown between the contending sides, he presented the political positions of the majority and I spoke on the philosophical issues at stake.

The Burnham-Shachtman split left only a few intellectuals in the thinned SWP ranks. Cannon had high esteem for all those who came over with undivided allegiance to the cause of the working class and dedicated their lives and talents to the cause of socialism. But he was distrustful of the halfhearted ones, dabblers and dilettantes, like James Burnham and Dwight Macdonald, who spent some time as tourists in the proletarian movement and then when the going got rough moved back into the bourgeois world.

The opinion he gave in connection with Burnham's renegacy on what the relations between the intellectuals and workers could and should be is worth recalling:

"Our movement, the movement of scientific socialism, judges things and people from a class point of view. Our aim is the organization of a vanguard party to lead the proletarian struggle for power and the reconstitution of society on socialist foundations. That is our 'science.' We judge all people coming to us by the extent of their real identification with our class, and the contributions they can make which aid the proletariat in its struggle against the capitalist class. That is the framework within which we objectively consider the problem of the intellectuals in the movement. If at least 99 out of every 100 intellectuals—to speak with the utmost 'conservatism'—who approach the revolutionary labor movement turn out to be more of a problem than an asset it is not at all because of our prejudices against them, or because we do not treat them with the proper consideration, but because they do not comply with the requirements which alone can make them useful to us in our struggle. . . .

"The conflict between the proletarian revolutionists and the petty-bourgeois intellectuals in our party, as in the labor movement generally in the whole world for generation after generation, does not at all arise from ignorant prejudices of the workers against them. It arises from the fact that they neither 'cut themselves adrift' from the alien classes, as the Communist Manifesto specified, nor do they 'join the revolutionary class,' in the full sense of the word. Unlike the great leaders mentioned above, who came over to the proletariat unconditionally and all the way, they hesitate half-way between the class alternatives. Their intelligence, and to a certain extent also their knowledge, impels them to revolt against the intellectual and spiritual stagnation of the parasitic ruling class whose system reeks with decay. On the other hand, their petty-bourgeois spirit holds them back from completely identifying themselves with the proletarian class and its vanguard party, and reshaping their entire lives in a new proletarian environment. Herein is the source of the 'problem' of the intellectuals" (*The Struggle for a Proletarian Party,* pp. 19-20).

He was to see virtually an entire legion of intellectuals who had swung leftward after 1929 retreat and make a separate peace with the status quo once the radicalism of the 1930s subsided. He valued all the more those who did not join that retrogression, like his cherished friend, the learned John G. Wright. It was the basis of our own friendship.

Jim detested hypocrites and was no Pecksniff who held up his conduct as a pattern for others. He was cognizant of his own failings and asked only that they be weighed in proper proportion to his merits. To the dismay of his comrades he, like Jack London, had some losing bouts with John Barleycorn until he broke the habit late in life. He was somewhat self-indulgent and not as industrious as he might have been. It was as though he conserved his energies for crucial occasions when he would go into action with the sense of command of a seasoned general and see the struggle through to the end.

Although he was a first-rate politician in matters of strategy and tactics, he was not so able an administrator. The everyday affairs of the Trotskyist movement were as haphazardly managed as those of most other radical groups until Farrell Dobbs left the Teamsters and came to New York as labor secretary in 1940 to reorganize the party headquarters. The operations of the SWP attained their present efficiency under the Dobbs-Kerry "regime" that took over when Cannon retired to Los Angeles in 1952.

His most valuable and enduring contributions to the revolutionary movement were in the sphere of party organization. He sought to apply and extend the conceptions worked out by Lenin in the construction and direction of a democratically centralist combat party in the citadel of world imperialism. His writings on the principles and procedures of Leninist party building were commended by Trotsky and have served as a manual for revolutionists here and abroad. His book on *The Struggle for a Proletarian Party* stands as a worthy companion to Trotsky's classic *In Defense of Marxism.*

Cannon's final years were gladdened by the emergence of the new radicalization in the United States and the demonstrated capacity of the cadres he had trained to win the allegiance of growing numbers of Black and Chicano liberation fighters, antiwar activists, student youth, women's liberationists, worker-militants, and gays.

The key to all our work, he wrote in his *Letters from Prison,* is the appeal to the young. "The young relate the word to the deed. They are moved and inspired by *example.* That is why they demand *heroes;* nobody can talk them out of it. The young have better eyes, they see farther. Youth is not petty, timid or calculating. Far goals and grandiose ideals seem attainable to the young as in fact they are. They see the truth beckoning in the distance and run to meet her."

Jim Cannon never lost the zest and idealism of his youth, however much it became tempered by experience. I believe he was of greater stature as a revolutionary leader than De Leon, Debs, Haywood, or any American contemporary. He had more mastery of the essentials of Marxism, a broader vision of the requirements of the world revolution, and keener foresight, and left behind him a more cohesive and effective body of disciples.

He can stand comparison with Sam Adams, the premier organizer of the first American revolution two hundred years ago. Unlike Adams, he was not lucky enough to engage in the actual revolution and see it through to victory. However, he was not the least disgruntled that he could only serve as an advance agent, preparing the nucleus of the vanguard of the coming American socialist revolution. He received adequate satisfaction, as an authentic Marxist should, in and through participation in the ongoing movement itself. The interviews he gave at his home in the last week of his life evinced his irrepressible revolutionary optimism about the socialist future. He kept looking forward to the time when, in the words of the spiritual he loved: "There's going to be a great gettin' up morning" for the wretched of the earth.

New York meeting to protest Smith-Connally antilabor law, 1948.
Grace Carlson at right.

Farrell Dobbs

James Patrick Cannon was a historic political figure. In the course of his career he developed many abilities; he played many roles; he made many contributions. All I can undertake is to recount to you some of the highlights of his long and fruitful revolutionary career, and give you a few examples that help throw light on the character of the man as a revolutionary leader as I experienced them from my association with him in the leadership of the American Trotskyist movement over a period of about four decades.

Jim Cannon was born in 1890 in Rosedale, Kansas. He came out of Rosedale as a young man searching for the truth. In the many years that followed, he proved in spades that he was capable of living by the truth once he found it.

You often hear people say that revolutionists are oddballs who can't make out in society as it is; so, since everybody's got a racket of some kind or another, they take up a revolutionary racket.

Well, that doesn't apply to revolutionists, and it didn't apply to Jim. Jim was a very talented man in many ways. If he had been concerned just with taking care of number one, he could have made out real well in this society.

FARRELL DOBBS was born in 1907. He was a leader of the 1934 Minneapolis truck drivers' strikes and became the Socialist Workers Party's national labor secretary in 1940. Together with Cannon and sixteen others he was convicted in the 1941 Minneapolis trial and was imprisoned with him at Sandstone penitentiary in Minnesota. He was four times the SWP's presidential candidate and is the author of a four-volume history of the Teamsters union in Minneapolis. This speech was given at a meeting in San Francisco on September 14, 1974.

That kind of success didn't interest Jim Cannon. One day in the latter part of the 1940s Jim and Ray Dunne and I happened to be in St. Louis, where we were on a party assignment. We were sitting in a hotel room one evening, a convivial evening, and Jim got to reminiscing about his youth. One of the first jobs he had as a teen-ager was on the Katy Railroad—that's the Missouri, Kansas, and Texas Railroad. It operates out of Kansas City and to the Southwest. Jim said:

"You know, I went to work on the Katy. I was young, I was new, I was green. I had a night job. It was all you could get on the Katy when you were starting, and if you worked real hard and pleased the boss, and didn't ask for a raise too often, one day you'd get a day job."

And he said to Ray and me, "Come to think of it, comrades"— this was in 1947—"if I'd have stayed with the Katy, today I'd have had a day job!"

That summed up his whole attitude about personal success and advancement.

Jim believed in the working class movement; he lived for the movement; and he was determined one way or another to keep body and soul together and work full-time—insofar as it was humanly possible—serving the movement.

Jim became a revolutionary at an early age. At eighteen he joined the Socialist Party. By this time he was already becoming influenced by one of the great figures in American revolutionary history, Eugene V. Debs.

Debs was an incorruptible man. He was an honest man. He was a fighter. He was a man who knew how to feel human compassion. He was one to always identify with the exploited and to detest the exploiter. Jim began to derive some of the qualities that he later showed in the movement as a result of his admiration for Debs. He tried to learn from Debs and to shape himself as a revolutionary after Debs.

He recognized at an early stage the importance of being able to communicate. Here again he was inspired in part by Debs, who was a great orator. Jim concentrated on learning to speak. Starting as a soapboxer, he became a top-notch orator.

He also learned the importance of being able to write. He knew that to be an organizer, one must be able to communicate through both the spoken word and the written word.

While still quite young he joined the Industrial Workers of the World, before long becoming part of the organization staff. He worked under Vincent St. John, whom the young militants of that day fondly called the "Saint." In his own way St. John was a man much like Debs. Not the versatile man Debs was, but a solid organizer with revolutionary spirit and know-how in building a movement and in building a team out of dedicated people who want to serve a common cause.

Jim began to learn something about organization, particularly from the Saint. Many times as we talked in later years he spoke about how he hoped one day to write an appreciation of St. John. You remember he wrote one rather extensive pamphlet about Debs—a very valuable work. He wrote another very extensive pamphlet about the IWW that is a valuable contribution. And he wanted also to write one about St. John.

He didn't get around to doing it, except for a short article in the *Militant* when St. John died in 1929, and we have to take note of the fact that it was a loss to the movement that it wasn't done because now I'm afraid there is going to remain a missing link for future generations about the part played by St. John in the movement. But he contributed a lot to Jim, which Jim later, as he absorbed know-how, particularly in organizing workers, was able to impart to the revolutionary socialist movement later on.

There's a story that Jim was fond of telling about his experience as an organizer in the IWW. He was assigned by St. John to a team of organizers and sent up to the ore docks in Duluth, Minnesota. They were working under the charge of Frank Little. Little was a famous IWW leader who was lynched by vigilantes in Montana during the witch-hunt that grew out of the American involvement in the First World War. This was prior to the war.

The IWW was having a convention in Chicago, and the organizers up in Duluth wanted to get there to attend. The way they worked in the IWW was that the organizers had to get around on their own steam, grab onto a boxcar, or whatever.

So all the younger organizers were to get to Chicago as best they could. But Frank Little was getting on in years and he'd become badly stove-up with arthritis. So the organization made a special dispensation to buy Frank a ticket to ride from Duluth down to Chicago on the cushions.

Well, Jim was young, full of zip, and there was nothing he wanted more than to be respected by Frank. So he made up his mind that on the rods he was going to beat Frank Little to Chicago.

He got down to Minneapolis and got on a night express, which was the real hotshot passenger train between Minneapolis and Chicago at that time. But he had a problem of getting through Milwaukee. Milwaukee had the notoriously meanest railroad bulls that prowled the yards of any railroad terminal out there in the Midwest.

So he tried what was recognized in the knighthood of the road as one of the most dangerous ways to ride. That was to get on the express car right behind the locomotive and on top of it. You lock your arm around the little vent pipe there, and you try not to freeze to death, not to go to sleep, and not to get blinded by the cinders coming out of the locomotive.

He managed to get through Milwaukee. What got him through was that the railroad bulls generally don't bother to look up behind the locomotive. They figured nobody was fool enough to ride there. Jim was. They underestimated him.

He got into Chicago, got all cleaned up, dashed over to the convention headquarters, and sat down. He'd been there about fifteen minutes when in came Frank Little.

Frank walked over to him, grinned, put his hand on Jim's shoulder, and said, "You damned hobo."

Jim said it was one of the greatest accolades that he ever got in his life.

That was one incident in Jim's IWW experience that tells you something about the aggressiveness, the resourcefulness, the courage, the daring of the man. He had the capacity to set a goal and to have the guts to reach for that goal and to take chances to attain that goal.

Another example of an experience he learned from came later, in Ohio.

He was assigned with another member of the IWW staff by the name of Spike—I forget his last name—to help some workers who had gone on strike in one of the little industrial towns in Ohio. Spike got arrested by the cops on the picket line. And Jim volunteered to be Spike's mouthpiece when he got into court.

Jim was a good soapboxer, and he got up to plead Spike's case like he was on a soapbox on a street corner in Kansas City. He told the judge how rotten the system is, and how phony capitalist laws are. He told the judge he was a faker and that they didn't expect to get any justice out of him, but he ought to give it to them anyway.

Jim no more than got through and sat down than the judge

found Spike guilty and gave him a jail term. Spike turned to Jim and said, "Fellow worker, that was a fine agitational speech you made, but it struck me that you were mighty generous with my time."

Jim said he learned something important from that: You always have to remember where you are, what the task is, what the ground rules are. And when you're fighting the class enemy on the class enemy's ground, proceed accordingly.

Jim once wrote a pamphlet called *Defense Policy in the Minneapolis Trial,* which you should read if you have not already done so. This was in answer to a general by the name of Munis, who was very good at solving all problems from afar. He never seemed to be able to get anything done right around where he was, but in any situation a thousand miles away he knew all the answers.

He accused us after the Minneapolis trial in 1941 of not having shown proud revolutionary valor. Jim had already begun to learn in that Ohio courtroom before World War I that you've got to know how to handle yourself. You have to learn how to stand up for working class rights without giving an edge to the capitalist prosecutor.

These accumulated experiences stood Jim in very good stead when he later became one of the founders of the Communist Party. Like many other rebels of that day, Jim was inspired by the Russian revolution in 1917 and was right in on the ground floor in founding the Communist Party. He quickly rose to the status of a national leader.

Here he made a major contribution to the Communist movement in a fight over how the Communist Party should proceed to build itself in this country.

One view was that since the Bolsheviks in Russia had had to function underground virtually up to the revolutionary explosion in February 1917, the Communist Party in this country had to be underground as well.

Jim and others like him who had a rich background of experience in the American working class movement saw instantly that this was a false road. They led an internal struggle for the Communist Party to fight for the right to function as a legal party.

Here Jim added to his own knowledge, and to the knowledge of our movement, about the importance of fighting for legality. You never cut and run, you never give away one iota of any opportunity under a capitalist regime to function legally, because that's the way you reach people.

A second great contribution Jim made was the key role he played in founding the International Labor Defense in the 1920s. Two of the outstanding cases that were handled by the International Labor Defense under the leadership of Jim Cannon were the Mooney-Billings case and the case of Sacco and Vanzetti.

In the ILD there were certain ground rules established. For example, the rule that there be no factionalism in defense. Because what you're defending—in addition to the individual defendant or defendants—is the democratic rights of the working class and its allies. From this derives that famous labor slogan, "An injury to one is an injury to all."

The principles of the ILD were, first, to defend all victims of capitalist oppression on our side of the class line. Second, not to take factional advantage of a defense case. That is, not to try to use it to push your own line and thereby alienate others who might otherwise join in the defense. Because the cardinal need is to defeat the capitalist frame-up.

Jim set these ground rules very well. After 1928, when those who went with Stalin took over in the CP, the ILD was turned into its opposite and violated every one of these rules. But the ground rules were set there. And they were picked up and improved and applied by the Trotskyist movement after Jim and his co-workers were expelled from the CP in 1928.

Now, coming to the break in 1928, I want to touch on one point: what did it mean for Jim Cannon to become the founding leader of the Trotskyist movement in this country?

Jim was one of the top leaders of the Communist Party. He had a big following. He was the head of the ILD. He was a member of the Political Committee of the party. And the CP was a big movement that had great promise, affiliated with the Third International and identified with the Russian revolution in the popular mind.

What did it cost to walk away from that? How dear was the truth at that point?

Jim was a delegate to the Sixth Congress of the Comintern in Moscow in 1928. By pure accident he got on the commission that handled the distribution of documents that had been translated.

Trotsky's criticism of the draft program that the Stalinists were submitting to the Sixth Congress came into this commission and was routinely translated. The Stalinist bureaucrats hadn't quite tightened up all the holes yet. They had no intention of Trotsky's document getting before the congress, but Jim got a copy of it.

He read it, and in essence two things came through to him. First, here were the answers to things that were beginning to puzzle him. As Jim described it to me—we had quite a conversation about this once—he said, "I make no pretense that I knew all the verities of the situation. I just had an instinct that not everything was the way it ought to be. But at the same time, who was I to challenge these guys who made a revolution? For all I, here in the United States, knew, Stalin was still completely a Leninist. Who was I to challenge that?"

And he read the document and it began to give him some answers about some of the things that had made him uneasy. Having attained that, the second thing that came through to him was that he had better keep this in his pocket until he got out of Russia.

He knew instinctively that this was the way he had to go, because this was the direction in which the truth went—that is, the analysis and the programmatic projections set forth in Trotsky's criticism of the draft program at the Sixth Congress.

That meant he had to turn his back on his chance to play a bigger and bigger role in the large and thriving Communist movement. And he was experienced enough to know doing that meant going into isolation.

And he made the break.

Now that's what you call serving the truth at all hazards. That's an expression in military parlance and it's a grim order. The last three words, "at all hazards," mean you've got to keep going some way no matter what happens until you can't go any farther.

That was the criterion that Jim Cannon set for himself when he came back from Moscow in 1928. He had found the truth about the profound developments taking place in the Soviet Union and hence in the Third International. And he had to serve that truth at all hazards.

I won't say he didn't hesitate; he would have been less than human if he hadn't. But the decisive thing is he came to the right decision and he went forward to serve truth, now in the role of the central founding leader of the Trotskyist movement in this country.

Then there was the period of isolation that Jim called the "dog days" and that he described so eloquently in *The History of American Trotskyism.*

He was always on the alert, however, to build. Jim was always trying to draw into the revolutionary team every individual who was willing to serve. He also had a quality of watching tendencies and trends inside a movement, and of thinking always in the largest possible terms with respect to the recruitment of cadres. He recognized, as all serious revolutionaries must, the importance of cadres, the value of cadres, and the indispensability of cadres, and what a crime it is when people cavalierly destroy cadres, or ignore cadres, or let them wither on the vine, or wander down a bypass without really trying to help them find the revolutionary main road.

Jim had a sense for this. And with the help of Trotsky, he played a major role in orienting the initial Trotskyist cadres in this country toward concentrating first on trying to win every possible member of the Communist Party who might begin to see the truth and develop toward support of the Trotskyist movement.

Then, in 1934, there was the Toledo Auto-Lite strike, led by a group of militants affiliated with the American Workers Party. Jim was among the foremost to sense the opportunity here and to take the initiative in developing negotiations leading to fusion with the American Workers Party. As a result we were again able to enrich our cadre.

Then there was the development in the Socialist Party about a year and a half later. And again, Jim took the lead.

I'll just give you one little example of the way Jim handled this. I was by then an officer of the Teamsters union in Minneapolis, as well as a party member. Several of us were in New York and Jim had a negotiation session scheduled with that young hotshot Gus Tyler, from the "Militant" caucus in the SP.

So Jim said to me, "I want you to come along and just do two things: every time this guy makes a proposition, you scowl; and every so often shake your head like you don't like the way everything is going."

He said, "I want that little son of a bitch to think he's going to have to give away a lot before he gets the Teamster comrades to go along with his propositions."

The upshot of it was we managed to enter the Socialist Party and after a little more than a year we got thrown out by the Norman Thomas right wing. But we took with us practically every revolutionary cadre in the SP, and the American Trotskyist movement was approximately twice as strong when it was expelled in the summer of 1937 as when it had entered the SP in the spring of 1936.

In addition to these aspects of cadre building, I for one can testify that Jim was very good at helping workers who were leading struggles in the trade union movement.

I'll never forget his role in 1934 when we were having a small civil war there in the Twin Cities. What value there was in his know-how, in his capacity as a soapboxer, as a writer, in his grasp of government mediators and all the other little snares and diverse forms of entrapment that are conceived and connived by the capitalist class in order to bilk workers and cheat them out of the fruits of their struggles as well as out of the fruits of their toil.

There was another aspect of Jim's stature as a leader. He knew how to conduct himself with respect to worker militants who were engaged in struggle. I'll give you an example.

Teamster President Daniel Tobin had expelled Local 574 of the Teamsters in Minneapolis from the international, and we had fought him on this for about a year and a half. He threw everything he could throw at us and he couldn't win. So, being an Irishman, he finally went back to the old Irish political slogan, "When you can't whip 'em, join 'em," and he offered to let us come back into the international. But he laid down some stiff conditions.

We were going to have to accept a situation in which we would technically be in a minority on the executive board of seven. We would have three, the rival local that Tobin set up on paper would have three, and then there would be another Tobinite who would be the so-called impartial chairman. But we had the cadres. We had the ranks of the union.

Jim and other comrades were understandably dubious about accepting Tobin's terms. They were afraid that either we'd quickly get our throats cut, or we'd get ourselves compromised— not intentionally, but there were many possibilities for entrapment.

Jim saw that we were all solidly for accepting the terms—those of us who had the everyday task of leading the union and who were closer to the work than he was. So he said to us, "I don't wholly agree, but I'll go along with it."

And then he made the remark that showed the real sign of a leader. He said, "And if it goes bad, I'll take the blame with you."

Now that's a very, very important thing. One is not quite a leader when one looks for an escape clause. A leader always has to make one of two decisions. Either you've got to stand against an action that is proposed, and try to stop it. Or, if you agree that it's going to be carried out, then you've got to help carry it out. And you're not a leader if, when things go a little bad here and there, you go around with an I-told-you-so story, or try to find somebody you can attach the blame to. There were none of these qualities whatever in Jim.

One of the most outstanding examples of Jim's capacities came during the fight of 1941, when Tobin had not only the goon squads he brought in from all over the country but also the Minneapolis city police, the county sheriff and his deputies, the courts, the mayor's office, the city council, the governor of the state, and Franklin Delano Roosevelt on his side. They threw everything at us, including a couple of federal indictments.

Under one indictment we were charged with conspiring to overthrow the government by force and violence right then and there. It was based on an old statute enacted during the Civil War, aimed at the slaveholders.

The second indictment was under the Smith Act—conspiring to *advocate* the overthrow of the government by force and violence and to foment insubordination in the armed forces.

They brought us to trial. Jim gave the main testimony for us in that trial. You'll find the full text of it in his pamphlet *Socialism on Trial.*

When we came into that courtroom—and here I must say he'd learned a lot since he defended Spike down in Ohio—he used the witness stand in the federal court as a tribune. He handled himself in such a way that he told the class truth on every point. He gave nothing to the capitalists. And he tried also to influence the working class to support us against this frame-up.

There's much to be learned from this pamphlet, because by this time Jim was very well versed in the literature of the movement as well as having long experience. He was equipped by this combination of factors to do an excellent job that not only served our needs there in the courtroom but became a textbook for young revolutionists.

Well, we were convicted anyway, and three years later—it was New Year's Eve, 1944—fifteen of us celebrated the oncoming year by entering the county jail in Minneapolis. The next morning fourteen of us were driven by U.S. marshals up to the federal prison at Sandstone, Minnesota. (Grace Carlson served her sentence at a women's prison in West Virginia, and the other three of the eighteen defendants served their time in Danbury, Connecticut.)

We got in there and the first thing they do in the joint—as those of you who have been there know—is to put you in quarantine and vaccinate you and so forth.

You know, it's not a happy moment when you first enter a prison. Along about three in the afternoon they got through with us and let us out of our cells for an hour to sit together in a day room.

We were sitting there, not talking much, just kind of thinking things over and wondering, Jesus Christ, how did I get in here, and all of a sudden Harry DeBoer looked at Jim Cannon and said, "You and your big mouth!"

It was just what the doctor ordered. We all broke out in a laugh, Jim along with the rest of us.

I want to make one final basic point about the importance of Jim's role in the movement, and that was his relationship with Leon Trotsky.

There were many leaders of revolutionary groupings around the world in the late 1920s and the 1930s who weren't smart enough to take advantage of working with Trotsky.

I've learned in my experience that there's a certain category of people who pride themselves on being "independent thinkers." They're hung up in some kind of ego trip—I think that's the phrase you use these days.

And instead of realizing they could learn from Trotsky, they were more concerned about making absolutely certain nobody got the slightest idea that Trotsky was ever telling them what to do.

Jim looked like a giant in comparison with these types. He recognized some fundamental things. One, Trotsky was not only a genius, he was smart. I've seen a lot of geniuses in my time, but not every one of them has been smart. A lot of them are just self-proclaimed.

Trotsky was a smart genius. And he was a man rich in experience, who had led, together with Lenin, a socialist revolution; who had organized and commanded a revolutionary army; and who had been a leader of the Bolshevik party and a leading member of the Soviet government; and who knew his Marxism from A to Z.

You can learn something from an individual like that, and Jim was smart enough to recognize that.

Jim told me how he had heard that Trotsky was imperious. He

didn't know whether that was just part of the Stalinist slander or whether there was some truth in it.

Jim described an incident back in 1932 where a party member named B. J. Field got himself expelled for violating discipline and tried to inveigle Trotsky into getting him reinstated over the heads of the elected party leadership. Field went over to Turkey and visited Trotsky, who gave him a couple of assignments. Word of this came back, and the party took this up with Trotsky. And here Trotsky showed his bigness. He assured the comrades in this country right away that he had no intention whatever of cutting across party discipline. He thought we should give Field another chance, but under no circumstance would he try to override the decisions of the party on a question of discipline and he would not continue his collaboration with Field without the agreement of the American party.

(We decided to take Field back in after a period of probationary testing. In the end we had to throw him out for good and all in 1934 when he refused to carry out the party's decisions in the big New York hotel workers' strike that year.)

And Jim told me that once he recognized that Trotsky intended to collaborate on terms of equality, that was all it took. Here was a man who knew a lot about Marxism and had a lot of revolutionary experience, *and* knew how to deal with parties in the movement on equitable terms. This kind of relationship is necessary for building a disciplined organization. And discipline is a prerequisite for a revolutionary combat party.

If you don't have a combat party, you haven't got a goddamned thing. Anything else, no matter how big it is, is just like a big clod of dried dirt—it looks formidable, but you throw it against the wall and it just crumbles and splatters. It's got to be a steel fist—perhaps a steel fist with a silk glove on it, from the point of view of strategy and tactics, but a steel fist.

No matter how much genius people have, or how much experience, if they don't know how to contribute to building a disciplined combat party, they can't be much help in the last analysis.

But Trotsky passed with flying colors on that count as well as on every other count. From then on Jim became a full and unqualified collaborator with Trotsky in all spheres. The Socialist Workers Party, under Jim's central leadership, played a key role in backing Trotsky in the work of building the Fourth International.

For example, there was Jim's trip to Europe in 1939. This was on the eve of World War II, when we had a big antiwar campaign going on. We were just getting ready to put the party's paper out twice a week, and we were preparing to set up new party branches in Flint and Detroit.

Trotsky asked Jim to make a trip to France to help try to straighten out a few people—some of these "independent thinker" types that I mentioned earlier. He asked Jim to go because of his role as a central leader of the SWP, which had great standing in the world movement.

Despite all the things that were going on here, despite all the party-building opportunities facing us, Jim went to France, with the agreement of all of us.

This was the pattern that he set. The Socialist Workers Party is a thoroughgoing internationalist party—internationalist in its outlook; internationalist in the sense that we realize the necessity to collaborate in the closest possible way with revolutionaries throughout the world; and internationalist in the sense that we also realize that one of the prime criteria of internationalism is to build a revolutionary combat party in your own country.

He worked at that really from the time that he joined the Socialist Party back in 1908. He stayed at it until the day he drew his last breath in 1974 at the age of eighty-four.

He remained true to himself, true to the movement, true to the working class with which he identified throughout his whole life. And in that he set a powerful example for today's young revolutionaries. He put down indelibly for you an impelling message: Go thou and do likewise.

Carl Cannon

Jim had a wonderful way with the young. At first meeting they seemed to sense that here was a friend and they opened their hearts to him. From toddlers to teen-agers, he treated them as equals and never talked to them as though there was any difference in age. Another quality that added to his appeal was a reluctance to lecture or give unsolicited advice.

Although a half-century has passed, I still recall vividly the games he played with me, the stories he told me, and the songs he sang to me when I was very young.

The games I passed on to my own children and they seemed to enjoy them as much as I had.

None of Jim's stories came from books. Hans Christian Andersen and the Brothers Grimm were not for him. His tales came right out of Rosedale, Kansas, and were about things he had seen and done while a boy there. Because they were true, they were all the more fascinating. I'm sure they were fact and not fiction because the details never varied, no matter how often repeated.

I was about to write Jim about these stories of his Rosedale boyhood when I got the word that he had died. I was going to tell him that, while I remembered many of them, I could only recall the name of one of his companions, Baldy Keegan. The idea of a boy without hair must have caught and held my imagination.

Some of his stories may have been of a cautionary nature. I remember one about hooking rides on the backs of streetcars, or horsecars, as they must have been.

CARL CANNON was born in 1914. He is the son of James P. Cannon and Lista Makimson. He related this reminiscence from his childhood at a New York meeting on September 18, 1974.

One of the cars that went through Rosedale had a short-tempered conductor and the boys loved to bait him. One day Jim and a couple of his cronies spotted the short-fused conductor's car going by. They took off in pursuit, caught up with it, and climbed onto the rear, crouching low to avoid detection. After a while, one of them cautiously raised his head, took a look into the car, lowered it and reported that the conductor was in the center of the car collecting fares. Jim decided to see for himself. He popped his head up and caught a spurt of tobacco juice right in the eye. The conductor was a tobacco chewer and a marksman, too.

Jim never pointed out a moral in the story, but I took it to be that it wasn't a good idea to hitch rides on the backs of streetcars, and I never did.

What a marvelous camp counsellor Jim would have made! He was a natural, even though he'd never been near a school of physical education and, as far as I know, he had never read a book on child psychology. Again, for games, he drew upon his own boyhood experiences.

I remember a summer spent on a Pennsylvania farm when I was around five or six. Jim was away much of the time, but when he was there, what fun we had! There were five or six of us, boys and girls, all about the same age.

A small brook ran through a wooded part of the farm. Jim showed us how to make a dam, creating a swimming hole. Today we have forgotten how important a swimming hole was in the summer before the coming of swimming pools and public beaches and lakes.

Jim also showed us how to make bean shooters from the forks of young trees and strips cut from old tire inner tubes, and whistles from willow shoots. Also, we had fishing poles with safety-pin hooks, but I don't recall that any of us caught any fish.

But that didn't make any difference because we all enjoyed ourselves so. And, looking back, I think Jim had the most fun.

Roger Baldwin

Friends of Jim Cannon and the SWP: With these sons and grandsons on the platform I have to play the role of grandfather tonight. For Jim and I both were grandfathers. And I think that perhaps I'm the only one here who knew Jim in his younger days, when he first came into New York at least.

Jim and I were frequently in contact and cooperation, certainly in friendship, until he left New York for the West Coast. I haven't seen him since, but those were the years of his greatest activity, and the years in which I had the privilege of knowing him.

In the early 1920s we were in New York, the two of us, he in the International Labor Defense, the legal defense arm of the Communist Party, and I in the early years of the American Civil Liberties Union.

I think we had the same indignation about the same wrongs, and we had the same remedies—the good old remedies of the American tradition of the Bill of Rights.

The International Labor Defense and the ACLU parted company some years later—I think after Jim left it—on the issue of the misuse and abuse of the International Labor Defense for political purposes.

I found Jim a man of most unusual combinations—of strengths and humor and wit, and of friendship, and of understanding of all kinds of people with whom he had to deal. For the

ROGER BALDWIN was born in 1884. He was a founder of the American Civil Liberties Union and served as its executive director until his retirement in 1950. These are excerpts from his talk at a New York meeting on September 18, 1974, at which Cannon's son and grandson also spoke.

International Labor Defense, like the Civil Liberties Union, didn't confine itself to defending any one group of people. And so we both of us had to in our own ways and through our organizations operate on a rather broad scale.

Jim and I had other interests in common. In the first place, we started with the presumption that the human race has to be improved and we were going to help do it. We had to improve it—I thought—by methods of reform; he thought by methods of revolution. We had no difficulty in finding a common ground in discussing the practical measures ahead of us.

Both of us welcomed the Russian revolution. He went there; I went there. I thought it was the road; he thought it was the road to the future. When I was there, which was in 1927, there was an atmosphere that has not marked the Soviet Union since the expulsion of Trotsky and the consolidation of the dictatorship.

I wrote a treatise after I was there, trying to discover the extent of what you'd call liberty under the Soviet dictatorship. For there were some forms of liberty. But it didn't last long.

And after the expulsion of Trotsky I assisted his friends in trying to get him—and succeeding in finally getting him—into Mexico.

I tried to get back to the Soviet Union afterwards. I was invited to head a party, and I got a refusal on the part of the local people. So I went to see the Soviet ambassador. The Soviet ambassador said to me, "We know you. You tried to help Trotsky get to Mexico, our worst internal enemy. Do you expect a visa?"

And I said, Well, perhaps you're very reasonable about it. I said I don't expect a visa after that.

He said, "We don't give visas to Trotsky's friends."

Jim and I had some other contacts and interests in common. Both of us went to jail. I was in jail during the First World War as a conscientious objector. Jim was in jail later, as you all know.

We also had a common experience in an American revolutionary organization of many years ago, the IWW. He was a member of it before he came to New York. I was a member of it for a very brief period in which I tried to earn an honest living with my hands. I was experimenting with manual labor, as a preparation, I thought, for a possible role in the labor movement.

I lasted about four months. I came to the conclusion that I was better suited for something else. Clarence Darrow once said that it's a lot easier to be a friend of the working man than a working man. I found that out.

What we're celebrating here tonight is really the life not only of a comrade of yours, not only of a leader in the American radical movement, not only a man who was faithful to the principles for which I too stand—the principles of freedom and equality and justice in American life—but a man who was faithful also to a belief in the future.

The one thing that characterizes all of us here tonight is that we all have faith and hope for a world in which some of the ideals, some of the goals for which we stand, will at last be realized.

This is not a discouraging age. It is an age in which a great future will open up with the ending of all world wars, with the end of empires, and with the emergence as we have begun to see it today all over the world, of those who have been suppressed and those who have been denied the equality of race, religion, and sex, and those who have been denied their national freedom and their civil rights.

We see just the beginnings of the order for which so many have fought, so many have yearned for ages. And I'm sure that what Jim Cannon stood for, what you here tonight stand for, in this party and in this assembly, represents the beginning of the kind of hope, the kind of faith, to which so many have given their lives.

Sam Gordon

This is not a rounded account of the Jim Cannon I knew. It is rather a series of random recollections of episodes in his life at which I was present. Most of these stories date back some twenty-five to forty-five years. I did not keep a diary and have had to rely entirely on my memory. Time has dimmed impressions, and I trust I will be forgiven for an incidental error of fact. In some places I have given a story in the form of quoted dialogue. Obviously the words cannot be exact. I use this form merely as a literary device to facilitate telling what happened. I do believe that on the whole I have given a correct, even if not unified picture of the Jim Cannon I knew, one that shows him "warts and all," as English historians, paraphrasing the Great Protector, said of a work on Cromwell.

Early American Trotskyism

What characterized the early days of American Trotskyism most from a simply human point of view was the ostracism imposed by the Communist Party. If you joined the Communist League of America (Opposition), you could be sure to lose pretty nearly all your friends in the party or the Young Communist League. That held for everyone. Even relatives would shun you.

I had an older cousin, Max, who was an organizer in the Furriers union, led by the then-popular Communist Ben Gold.

SAM GORDON was born in 1910. He joined the Communist League of America in 1929 and was for many years a close collaborator of Cannon in the leadership of the American Trotskyist movement. He has lived in England since 1952.

When I first moved toward communism he became very warm and friendly. But when I decided to join the Left Opposition he changed abruptly. He used to walk over to the other side of the street whenever he saw me coming around Union Square.

Jim and Rose were as affected as any of us by this type of isolation. I remember hearing them talk wistfully about old friends, people like Elizabeth Gurley Flynn, Bill Dunne, and others who had remained behind in the CP and were no longer accessible.

Jim used to regard this situation as part of the sinister contribution of Stalinism to relations within the labor movement. Stalinism had introduced this vicious destruction of personal friendships into the movement. Hitherto there had been many political separations or partings of the way, but they did not result in the destruction of personal friendships, and the denunciation of friends in the most abject terms.

This ostracism was accompanied by an active campaign on the part of the Stalinist command to destroy the Trotskyist nucleus by any means possible. Included were defamation of the characters of the leaders, in the press and by word of mouth, crude burglaries of their homes to find "incriminating" documents, and above all, physical assaults on meetings and on sellers of the *Militant*.

Particularly the assaults on *Militant* sellers became ominous, for they were often carried out with blackjacks and with garment-cutters' knives—the latter more for the purposes of intimidation. Most concentrated were well-organized attacks by Stalinist gangs on both outdoor and indoor meetings. As a result, the early Trotskyists were to a certain extent ingrown as a group. Or, looked at more positively, they were a closely knit group.

People said it was a miracle that the frail roots struck in those early days of the Trotskyist movement were not crushed. But it was not at all a miracle. It was organized self-defense that thwarted the Stalinist goons and their directors. The key to this defense was the rallying of many IWW militants or anarchists and other strains of the libertarian wing of the working class movement. In this the reputation and renown of Jim Cannon played a big part.

Both at his home and at our headquarters there were frequent visits of old Wobbly friends of Jim's, some freshly out of prison. I remember particularly one such fellow worker, Charlie Cline, who had been involved in the Mexican revolution with Pancho Villa and had to pay for it with a prison sentence after General Pershing's military expedition across the Rio Bravo in Woodrow Wilson's time. He and Jim had been close buddies.

The Wobblies could always be relied on to defend free speech and deserve to be remembered for what they did to help us and others.

Another means of defense was the biting satire in the *Militant* ridiculing the CP leaders and all their works. Many CPers and YCLers used to buy the *Militant* surreptitiously and spread particularly biting characterizations by word of mouth. Max Shachtman was the actual author of most of these pieces, but they were thought out and shaped by collective effort. Jim was a regular and substantial contributor to this devastating humor.

Joining the Communist League at that time was not exactly like joining a sports club. You had to be very deliberate. But you could look forward to plenty of exercise. On the other hand, the participants were continually inspired by Trotsky's writings on the international events of the day and by the eye-opening analysis of the causes behind them. And they were armed with similar analyses of the American scene and fortified by the effective regular ration of razzing directed at the CP leadership.

Nevertheless, Stalinist physical attacks, although more isolated, were to remain with us for some time to come. They allowed us to take the full measure of Stalinism early on, and not to be surprised by later excesses, nationally or internationally, which left others incredulous. It was in those days that we became steeled against the later "amalgams" mounted by the Kremlin against the Old Man, and against the frame-ups of the Moscow trials.

Joining the Communist League

I first made contact in 1927-28 with Trotskyist ideas in the Social Problems Club at the College of the City of New York (CCNY), or City College as it was known. The Social Problems Club was an authorized organization on the campus. The club was more or less, but not entirely, a sort of transmission belt for the YCL. The Brooklyn branch, which I attended at first, had a club whose faculty sponsor was Dr. Jesse Clarkson, an authority on Russian history, translator of the works of the Bolshevik historian M. Pokrovsky, and a promoter of skepticism when it came to official Kremlin policy. He pricked many a Stalinist bubble in discussions in his classes as well as in occasional appearances at the club.

Clarkson's amusing and effective forays tended to put an armor of awareness on some of us moving toward communism. We searched for and got hold of Max Eastman's book *Since Lenin Died*, which first broke the full story of the Russian Left Opposition and what it stood for. Together with some who were already in the YCL, I was discussing the import of this work when we heard from Clarkson that James P. Cannon was about to be expelled from the CP for Trotskyism.

From the YCLers we had received a distorted picture of the maneuverings of the three factions in the CP—the Lovestone majority, and the Foster and Cannon minorities. It was mostly a matter of petty gossip, favorable in the main to Lovestone and derogatory of the other personalities. Thus, if Cannon had adopted Trotskyism, it was merely as a step away from the Communist movement, because he was a slick personal opportunist, etc.

It was in this atmosphere that several of us from the club went down to the Fourteenth Street Labor Temple, to one of the first public meetings of the Communist League, to see for ourselves.

As we came in and took our seats there were several commotions in the hall. A rush for the platform (where Cannon and Shachtman were seated and the chairman, Martin Abern, was trying to get some order) had been repulsed by a guard strung out in front. There were further disturbances at two entrances to the hall as Shachtman resumed a speech he had begun before we came in. Hecklers, and one particular heckler who seemed to be the leader of the CP "commando" assigned to break up the meeting, were being handled by Max with his usual verve. Shachtman eventually won the crowd around after rallies of laughter that reduced the Stalinists to silence. Cannon was the next and last speaker. He spoke quietly, in lecture style, in a ringing tenor voice, and his topic was internationalism and communism, how the two were inseparable, how the task that the Left Opposition had set itself was to reestablish this fact here and in the world movement.

What struck me at the time was the Kansas-Missouri twang in which this lesson in internationalism was delivered. It seemed to make the point all the more effectively.

Later on we saw the same line of argumentation against Stalin's "socialism in one country" in Trotsky's *Criticism of the*

Draft Program of the Communist International. And we realized that Jim's speech was really a deft translation of this thesis into American, into more popular language.

Jim's speech left a powerful impression on me, and I believe I was won over to Trotskyism then and there. But the YCLers in the club were still working hard on us outsiders, and a few of us decided we should have a look at Europe, Germany in particular, and after seeing advanced class struggle in action, we would finally make up our minds. The way to do that was to catch a ship on a pierhead-jump for Germany, work our passage, and jump ship at the other end. For all this, contact with the CP was regarded as indispensable. It was not easy with growing maritime unemployment.

We did just that, each in his own way. I got to Berlin and eventually found a job that allowed me to do a lot of reading and studying and to participate in demonstrations, etc. It was there I made up my mind to join the Left Opposition. I contacted the *Militant*, and wrote several letters to Martin Abern (the acting secretary) that were treated as articles.

Naturally I was thrilled to see these published in the *Militant*, which had in a short time gained an unequaled reputation for journalistic excellence in radical circles.

How Trotsky's Attack on "Socialism in One Country" Was Brought Out of the USSR

Jim often told how he got hold of Trotsky's *Criticism of the Draft Program of the Communist International* when he was in Moscow in 1928 for the Sixth Congress of the Comintern as part of the American CP delegation. A copy was given to him as one of the members of the Program Commission. He went to his hotel to study it, became convinced, and decided to get it out of the country.

Jim always held that it was a slipup on the part of the Stalin apparatus that allowed its distribution. Theodore Draper, in his *American Communism and Soviet Russia,* contends the distribution was a conscious act of the Stalin leadership. Of course, one cannot be certain. But if one gets to know exactly how this document left the country, one can get some indirect evidence.

Cannon never revealed how the "hot" pages actually got over the Soviet border, insofar as I know. In recent years in England I met several comrades who were in Moscow at the same time as Jim. They were Harry Wicks and Mary Morris, the widow of a comrade Jim came to know as George Weston, who had also been in Moscow in 1928. Mary Morris told how George, a favorite collaborator of Helena Stassova, the head of the International Red Aid, the worldwide labor defense organization run from Moscow, had apparently been given a danger signal. The copies were numbered and returns checked.

Weston got in touch with Jim, whom he knew very well from ILD days, and offered to help. Weston had apparently known and agreed with Trotsky's criticism beforehand. In fact he was known in Moscow as "The Mad Irishman" for talking Trotskyism freely.

Before they were about to leave the country, George somehow got hold of another, unmarked, copy and Jim was able to return his. Mary Morris (Weston) took the sawdust and shavings out of her little son's teddy bear, placed the document safely at the bottom of it, and then stuffed it again.

They went their separate ways. The customs search was quite thorough. But the teddy and all the comrades got through.

They met again at a prearranged rendezvous in Berlin. There Jim picked up the precious pamphlet and returned to the U.S.

None of those present in Moscow at that time whom I have since spoken to would believe that this document was distributed normally at the congress. Like Jim, they were of the opinion that even the Stalinist apparatus could have cracks, and this was one.

Jim at Home

I remember the first time I was invited by Rose and Jim to come to dinner. On arrival I was introduced to the children, Ruth and Carl Cannon and Walta Karsner, all teen-agers. They seemed to have a free and easy relationship among themselves and with Rose and Jim. And at the table I soon found myself completely relaxed, taking part in the conversation as if I had known them all for ages.

Talk was mostly of nonpolitical matters, of things the youngsters were interested in. It was a parental regime on the part of Rose and Jim that I, not so far removed from my own teens, heartily approved.

At that time Jim had gone out to work, in the circulation department of the *Herald Tribune.* I believe Walta's father, Dave Karsner, who was a newspaper man, was helpful in getting Jim this job. He sorely needed it, for his first wife, Lista, the mother of Ruth and Carl, had died a year or so before then, and he had taken the children, who had been with her.

His job with a newspaper caused some comic misunderstandings. The Stalinists heard a rumor about it and a *Daily Worker* hack was assigned to write it up. The hack got Jim confused with Jimmy Cannon, a popular sports columnist of the time, and did a piece denouncing him for selling out to the capitalist press, complete with excerpts from Jimmy's baseball or football column.

In those early days Rose and Jim moved house fairly frequently, but always in the perimeter of downtown New York, not too far from wherever our office was located. The reason for the frequency was obvious. It had to do with the "instability" of their income. On a couple of occasions—once when I had a job and quite a good wage for those days—I pitched in with them to pay the rent and joined the household.

Around the middle of 1931 Jim and Rose were living in a relatively spacious apartment off Second Avenue. They had obtained it through some friends from the "old days." It had been vacated by a prominent CP intellectual leader named Jerome, after a death in his family. The rent was not too high. Even so, Jim could not raise it after a few months and they were about to be evicted.

I came around to help them pack. Rose had already rented a cold-water flat on First Avenue. Finally Jim went out to get a horse and rig—a moving truck would have been too expensive— in order to make the transfer. I hopped on the seat beside him after we finished loading. Pipe in mouth, and whip firmly in hand, Jim started out on the trip swapping wisecracks with the Second Avenue kibitzers.

A cold-water flat on First Avenue was about as low as you could go in accommodation then, with the bathtub in the kitchen and other such not too convenient arrangements. It was a measure of the state of our material fortunes then.

It was about that time that I remember hearing the only serious argument between Jim and Rose. Jim had had a bout with the bottle; I had run into him somewhere and brought him home. It is easy to guess what the argument was about. It was one of the rare occasions that I didn't see him get the best of it. He slept it off for what seemed like a very long time, then got up and proceeded to get himself ready. "Tell Rose," he asked me, "that I am going to speak after all."

These were terribly trying times for Jim. In addition to the poverty symbolized by the move to First Avenue this was a period of sharp internal frictions, heading for a seemingly inevitable split with Shachtman and Abern. And despite all the heat generated in the internal fight the differences were not clearly developed enough on basic political lines to make the dispute comprehensible to the party ranks or the radical public, so that if it should come to a split the results would be disastrous for the new movement.

Jim told me then that when he drank, it was to get away from some insurmountable problem he didn't want to think about for a while.

Rose Karsner

Rose was so closely linked to Jim Cannon that it is impossible to write of him without writing something about her part in the partnership. Of course, there were many contributions she made on her own to the movement. In sizing up new recruits, or new opponents, Rose's eye was often more critical than Jim's and she was much more outspoken. It was easy to see what an indispensable aid she was to him, and to our group in this respect. For a movement is, after all, made up of people above all.

She was a small, frail-looking woman, with a mobile, very expressive, very handsome thin face. In it, set deeply, were mischievous dark eyes that most often sparkled, sometimes with good humor, sometimes teasingly, and on rarer occasions with blazing fury. She was always interesting to watch. She was forty when I first met her in 1930, but her hair was still jet black. Her figure was what is called petite. She had been ill and only slowly returned to activity.

Her household was always clean and orderly whenever I chanced to visit, particularly later on when they lived in the Village. It is hard to conceive how this could be so unless Jim gave a substantial hand at that time. I did actually see Jim push a broom once or twice—but only at headquarters. Of course, I can remember Jim preparing an occasional meal. I cannot recall seeing Rose harassed by housework ever.

Occasionally, when Jim was away on some trip I used to invite her out for dinner at one of the little Italian or Russian restaurants in the East Side. Many a time I sat there, admiring her, listening to her low-keyed pleasant voice which every once in a while broke out into an infectious gurgly laugh.

Inevitably the conversation would turn to our organizational affairs, to internal jostles, sometimes to policy and the presentation of policy.

If one said to Rose: That was a terrible speech I made last night, it must have lost us a good few votes, she was not at all reticent to agree. It certainly was, she would most likely say with a barb; you'd better learn to think on your feet before you speak. But she would soon turn the conversation to smooth the rough edge with a little pleasantry or some friendly advice.

I for one liked her style of critical conversation. When we became more intimately acquainted she used to ask me questions about my personal life. I never minded, because there was always some particle of wisdom she had to contribute in return.

Rose was, like all of us, concerned about party finances. She was always pushing for some project that would solve that constant worry. For some reason she kept pressing a pet scheme for a solution just on me, particularly in the "dog days": why didn't I try my hand at script writing, I surely must have a flair for that. It could take me to Hollywood and then our troubles would be over.

I didn't know what to make of this promotion of Rose's. Was she pulling my leg? Was she trying to hint that my *Militant* articles were so long I ought to give them up and leave town? Or did she really have all that faith in me? She was, after all, at one time secretary for the *Masses,* the outstanding socialist literary magazine of the World War I period, and knew something about good writing.

I resisted stubbornly. I did try my hand translating a fantastic German novel (whose title and author I have forgotten) about a fight to a finish between rats and men on a ship in the far North. But I never finished it and left my collaborator and friend Herman Eichnar stranded with a half-finished manuscript. *Militant* duties interfered.

The height of our joint domiciliary efforts came toward the late thirties with other comrades. We moved into a house on Washington Square owned by Dr. Paul Luttinger. Doc used to write a column of medical advice that was very popular for the *Daily Worker,* and had only recently, after the Moscow trials, broken with Stalinism and joined us. We paid him a more or less nominal rent, and several comrades luxuriated in that marvelous location until he died not long afterward.

We all lived our separate lives without interference from the others. It was after the 1938 founding convention of the SWP in Chicago.

One memorable event at Washington Square in the fall of 1938 was a reception, organized by Rose, I believe, for the Black revolutionist C. L. R. James, author of *The Black Jacobins*. At that time James was one of the leaders of the British section of the Fourth International, although he was originally from Trinidad. Jim had just returned, with James, from the founding conference of the Fourth International.

All sorts of prominent intellectuals were there, people like James T. Farrell and Mary McCarthy. It was shortly before the "flight of the intellectuals." Rose looked very elegant that night and her distinctive laugh rang out to every corner of the house, for guests were standing on stairs and balustrades as well as in the main downstairs drawing room of Dr. Luttinger's apartment.

Jim was in a circle with Max Shachtman and James Burnham engaged in earnest discussion with some of the literary fraternity, of whom there was a fair representation. Some of them figure in that famous article "Intellectuals in Retreat" written by Shachtman and Burnham for the January 1939 *New International.* It was at the height of our prewar influence, and of our prewar party unity. For soon Shachtman and Burnham were to join their quarry in the retreat from Marxism.

(This was the first time I had met C. L. R. James, and he was full of praise for Jim's recent settlement of the British disputes during his visit to Europe. Jim had succeeded in cementing the unification of several groups into a single section of the Fourth International.)

There were occasional discussions of the "woman question" in our organization from the beginning. I remember Rose and Sylvia Bleeker as among the most fiery reporters or contributors. They minced no words. Rose especially had, I believe, early on been a supporter of the suffragists. It was sad that she died just a few years too soon to see the rise of the women's liberation movement in the United States.

Young People and Internal Difficulties

In the early days of the Trotskyist movement we were so few in number that there wasn't any possibility for a separate youth organization. Youth who joined tended soon to take an active, even a leading part in the Communist League.

While the other leaders were inclined to patronize young comrades, Jim treated them as grown-ups and expected them to live up to it. When I joined the League I was at once recruited by Shachtman to work on the *Militant*.

Working on the *Militant* then meant not only writing articles, editing copy, reading proof, etc. It also meant learning to set type, to make up pages, to get forms ready for the press, and to wheel them to a flatbed press set for a run.

Max had great dexterity in all printing processes and a unique flair for typography. But he was not a very good teacher. I did the best I could to learn from him nevertheless, and in a short time became sufficiently proficient to occasionally see a whole issue through the press myself. Some of the benefits of that early experience remained with me for the rest of my life. At that time it meant that I was thrown a good deal into Shachtman's company, and became a close companion of his. After we had put the paper to bed we would usually repair to an Italian restaurant off Second Avenue, where we found friends from the broad labor movement like Carlo Tresca or Vanni Montana, and we would relax with a meal and wine and amusing talk. On a few occasions I found it necessary to spend a night in the printshop.

I only rarely saw Jim in those days. But I could detect an undercurrent of dissension between the two leaders. Max did not make anything explicit himself. Nor did his close co-worker Martin Abern, who was also often at the office as business manager of the paper. But associates of theirs from among the newer recruits were less reticent. One such was Joe Carter, who had come to us from the Young People's Socialist League after a short stay in the Young Communist League. Joe was an incurable gossip and, after I had done a day's work at the *Militant* office, he would corner me on one pretext or another and talk to me about internal problems.

Most of the internal problems he talked about seemed to have Jim as the centerpiece. Jim dealt wrongly with the youth; Jim wanted to "retire" but at the same time would not relax his hold on the organization; Jim was not a "theoretician." And so on and so on. And added to that there were the aspersions that I was familiar with from my early contacts in the YCL during the factional struggle in the CP—Jim was an opportunist, he was really a right-winger for whom Trotskyism was a pretext, he was lazy, etc.

After a while, I mentioned some of these charges to Shachtman. He either laughed them off or denied them outright. Not too, convincingly, I thought.

It was not until the internal dissension between the leaders had reached a high point of tension that I had occasion to talk to Cannon about the whole matter at a social in our headquarters. Jim explained the situation as mainly due to our isolation, to the poor social composition of the New York branch, and to some of the leaders yielding to petty-bourgeois pressure. He saw the main political reason in the "left" turn of the Comintern and the CP, which revived the flagging confidence of many workers in these organizations and cut off that source of recruitment. He explained his own situation which had given rise to rumors of withdrawal, etc., as having to do with family problems. For the rest, he was content to be judged by what he had written or spoken publicly. He outlined a series of steps he wanted to see taken to repair the situation in the New York branch. I was favorably impressed by this explanation and thought over this conversation after we had parted. On the next occasion I told Jim that I agreed with him. I had already decided to support him. (The charge of laziness had not registered with me, because I witnessed his regular collaboration on the paper after a full-time job on the outside.)

For some time Shachtman had not put in an appearance at the office. It must have been at the peak of this early dissension with Jim in October 1931. One day Jim came into the office and invited me out for a talk. He told me that Shachtman had walked out of his job as editor of the *Militant*. Then he put it to me directly: Could I take over? Would I take over? Otherwise we were heading for a bad crisis. I was, I must admit, somewhat startled and confused by the proposal, and it took me some time to regain my composure. I had told Jim I would support him. This occasion was a test. After a brief "soul-searching" (I cherished Max as a personal friend) I agreed, but explained just how much help I would need. Jim assured me of increased editorial contributions, and of any other help he could give. He was working full-time on an outside job, but within those limits he would spare no effort.

Others will perhaps judge the quality of the *Militant* in those days, what was good and what was bad. But in any case there was no hiatus. The paper carried on. In about five or six months the situation had eased, and Max came back to resume his editorial work.

I had not yet turned twenty-one when I assumed my editorial duties on the *Militant*. No young man of that age could have undertaken such a responsibility on mere self-confidence. I was not particularly ambitious. If anything, the contrary. But it was the self-confidence inspired by the feeling that I was doing what was politically correct and necessary that kept me going. And it was really Jim who infused that feeling in me. This was Jim's way of acting toward young comrades generally, when he concluded that they were serious about our movement and ready to "pitch."

That was the case at that time with comrades like George Clarke, Tom Stamm, Murry Weiss, and others then still in their teens or barely out of them.

When we had grown a bit, two or three years after the founding of the League, there was a certain amount of recruitment of youth, the first small groups from colleges, mainly in New York. A Spartacus Youth League was formed. I recall Jim being very proud of his daughter Ruth, who quite on her own had become one of the leading lights in Spartacus. He greeted the founding of the SYL in the *Militant* and lent his encouragement to it. But the time was not yet ripe for a Trotskyist youth organization on a broad basis.

In later years Jim indicated that his approach to youth was really something he owed to his teacher Vincent St. John of the IWW. The "Saint" used to size up a young "feller," give him an assignment in a strike or similar situation, ask him if he could handle it, and then observe him if he said he could. If he did, that was it, he was a Wobbly organizer.

Insofar as Jim was concerned there was no distinction between revolutionary youth and adults, no discrimination whatever. They were on an equal footing. A youth organization was merely a specialized organization with a specific task: the task of preparing the future of the revolutionary movement.

Cannon's Minneapolis "Handraisers"

In the internal struggle during the early days of the Communist League, when political issues were only embryonic and Cannon's problem was to ward off a loosening of our principled Marxist program, the organizational need was for the group of National Committee members in New York, who functioned as the day-to-day leadership of the League, to reflect the majority of the National Committee in the country at large.

There were three delegates from Minnesota who came to the NC plenum in June 1932 as part of that majority, which included other prominent members such as Arne Swabeck and Hugo Oehler. The Minnesotans were Carl Skoglund and V.R. Dunne, who were full members of the NC, and Oscar Coover, who was then a candidate member. At that plenum Cannon proposed to co-opt Louis Basky and myself to full membership in the committee and to make George Clarke a candidate member. This would give the NC majority a working majority among the New York NC members.

Shachtman, Abern, Spector, and Glotzer did not at first oppose co-optation on principle, but they were strongly opposed to the specific nominees. Suddenly, and not altogether honestly, Shachtman decided that co-optation was not constitutional after all. On our side only Jim and Arne spoke. The rest kept quiet. When it came to the vote, the Cannon resolutions and proposals carried by a comfortable majority. The decisive votes were those of the quiet men from Minneapolis. They were soundly denounced as Cannon's puppets—the "handraisers"—both inside and outside the plenum.

The PC motion had included a provision for a membership referendum on the co-optations, and Shachtman raised such a hue and cry in the ranks that in the national vote the co-optations were narrowly defeated.

I had an opportunity for the first time to get together with Ray, Skogie, and Oscar after the plenum at a Fourteenth Street cafeteria. We discussed at great length what had happened at the plenum, on which they made shrewd remarks. They explained why they thought it was unnecessary for them to take the floor when it could only be superfluous after Jim and Arne's speeches. But, more important, they told me a lot of what they were preparing in the coal yards at home and what their perspective was. I remember that on parting I glowed with confidence at the prospect for their trade union work and for our League as a class-struggle organization.

Less than two years later Cannon's "handraisers" were universally recognized as among the most important Trotskyist militants in America. They had helped make Minneapolis a union town. They had forged a cadre that was to prove impregnable in the struggles to come. Their fame reached out to wherever there were Trotskyists in the world.

In the United States not only the national press made them a byword—a popular book, *American City,* by a sympathetic writer, Charles Rumford Walker, acquainted many thousands of young people with their real story, which newspapers most often distorted. Their voices, too, so silent at that plenum, could be heard over radio networks on occasion. In nearly all their big advances—and occasional setbacks—Jim Cannon's name was linked with theirs up to and including the trial of the eighteen rigged by Roosevelt with an assist from Dan Tobin.

Jim and the Needle Trades

In the early days practically all of our trade union work in New York was in the needle trades, where Jewish workers predominated. We had early gained the adherence of a prominent leader in the field, Sylvia Bleeker of the millinery trade, a long-time Communist whose considerable abilities were universally recognized by both the rank and file and the bureaucrats. Sylvia brought workers from other sections of the trade for discussion of strategy and tactics.

It was the "third period" and the Stalinist line of the CP called for dual unions. Our line was to disentangle from these sterile "trade union" bodies and to get into the main swim of the AFL unions. But the hitch was to do this without giving the reformist labor skates like David Dubinsky, Sidney Hillman, and Company, an opportunity to use the transfer of our comrades for their anticommunist campaigns.

This was, of course, a very touchy problem: to combine a correct trade union line with our generally correct political line and orientation as a faction of the CP. There were many gruelling sessions, most of them with Jim taking the most active part in suggesting and devising moves that would not violate union rules and at the same time present an unexceptionable front to the CP militants. Finally, at one such session a course was adopted.

As they filed out of the meeting one of the comrades, or perhaps a sympathizer, convinced that effective countermeasures had been devised against those of the wily and devious bureaucrats in their unions, said to another: "That Cannon's got a *Yiddischer kopp.*" Although it was meant as a compliment Cannon, who heard it and probably understood it, said nothing. Its chauvinist tinge could hardly have left him indifferent. And yet, as with other workers carrying over tinges of bias from their past, it was an indication in their own way of their high appreciation of Jim as a fighter against the bureaucracy.

Jim and Minorities

Jim was, of course, an early defender of American minorities—Blacks, women, homosexuals, etc. I remember one case vividly. A young leader of the organization, with a good record going back to the YCL, not only in the States but abroad, had fallen afoul of the New York homosexual laws, and was clapped into jail one day early in the thirties. Some of the other leaders were inclined to joke about the whole thing. Not Cannon. He earnestly set in motion the machinery to get the young comrade out and cleared, enlisting the help of the comrade's uncle, who was a linotype operator on a Brooklyn daily. The case was finally quashed. Our comrade continued to be a leading member and later even became one of the leaders of the Oehler group that left the organization in 1935.

To me this case was particularly interesting because only a short time before I had witnessed in Berlin the battle put up under the leadership of the left-wing academician Dr. Magnus Hirschfeld for repeal of the notorious Paragraph 102 (Homosexuals) of the Weimar Constitution. It was, if I am right, a successful struggle in which he eventually enlisted the support of both the Communist and Socialist parties against the Nazis and their conservative allies—a struggle that took on class proportions.

The Lovestone Debate

Jim had a terrible reputation with the Stalinists and even their rank-and-file sympathizers as a trickster, a purveyor of "slick" maneuvers, a man to watch like a hawk. Others repeated this.

In reality no one in all the years that I spent in the American movement could point to a single unsavory action that Jim had ever committed, to a single deception, to a single case of unfair advantage he had taken of anyone.

He was, to be sure, made in the cast of Huck Finn and one often wondered what he must have been like as a boy. He was not above borrowing quips or oratorical tricks from someone like Mark Twain. Certainly he was apt in making up stratagems of his own.

One such that I remember was on the occasion of a debate with

Jay Lovestone, once the general secretary of the CP, then the leader of an expelled right-wing Communist group, and a long-time political opponent. It was sometime in 1934 and was in essence on the subject "Third International or a new Fourth International?" The debate drew the largest radical crowd outside the CP up to that time, over a thousand if my memory serves me.

Lovestone trotted up briskly to take his place on the platform. Then Cannon followed, more slowly, carrying a stack of books and, I believe, with someone to help him carry another stack, all the books being deposited on a table at Cannon's side of the platform. Jim then sat down with an angelic look on his face and lit his pipe. There was a hubbub in the audience and even Lovestone raised an eyebrow after directing a glance in the opposite corner.

I don't remember what made Jim get up, whether it was a question directed to him by the chairman or someone in the crowd. But soon Jim was on his feet explaining to the audience that he had no intention of using that heap of books—he had just brought them along to check up on any misquotations that Lovestone might attempt.

A wave of laughter greeted this explanation. Even Lovestone had to join in with a sporty grin.

Probably this stratagem did disarm Jim's opponent to some extent. But then Lovestone's case, defending the Comintern, which had let the Nazis into power in Germany, was one Cannon was bound to demolish anyhow.

Farrell Dobbs

It is hard to think of the period associated with the SWP and its immediate predecessors without relating Cannon to Farrell Dobbs.

I believe it was after the very first Minneapolis strike, the coal-yard strike, that Jim met the young Dobbs. When he came back to New York and told some of us of the extraordinary young rebel, Jim had an expression in his eyes like that of a man hinting he had struck gold. He was sparing in his praises. He said just enough to make you want to meet the comrade yourself. Dobbs had "decision," a word Cannon used out of the vocabulary of Vincent St. John in his IWW days.

As the years passed and Farrell proved himself in the great struggles of the Minneapolis labor movement, it became clear from Jim's references to him that in his own mind he had picked him as his successor, that is, as the comrade to propose as national secretary when the time came. Jim was then often in Minneapolis, and certainly at all crucial moments. So his judgment was based on a close view.

There were some who were skeptical. Would Dobbs accept party work at the center? After all, he soon became steeped in the Teamsters' over-the-road drive. He was getting a comfortable wage; he had three young teen-age daughters to raise. Jim had no doubts. We knew from some contact with Teamster organizers themselves, people close to types like Jimmy Hoffa, that they regarded Farrell as an unusual, a remarkable character. Not only because of his fertile organizing mind. As one of them said then, "He is the kind of guy who would work for the union just for 'coffee and.' " They didn't know any other like that.

So no one was greatly surprised when one day early in 1940 Farrell chucked his job with Tobin and, with Marvel, came to work as labor secretary of the SWP. He began to introduce the slide rule in the working of the party, later served for a spell as editor of the *Militant,* and eventually as national secretary.

Insofar as Jim had anything to do with Farrell's progress in the SWP it was certainly one of his most important contributions to the party's advance and continuity.

Successes and Failures

Our first "failure" was the cessation of recruitment with the "left turn" of the CP in 1929-30, which many sympathizers in the CP took for good coin. It was an international phenomenon and brought about the capitulation of Karl Radek and other well-known figures in the International Left Opposition. Each of these capitulations was a blow we felt in America. Our access to the CP rank and file was almost sealed off.

After a year or so the "left turn" of the Comintern began to be recognized for what it was—an ultraleft, sectarian line with dangerous slogans like "social fascists (Social Democrats) are worse than fascists," etc., etc.

Toward the end of 1932 the tide began to turn. To have survived the period up to then, to have survived the "dog days," was in itself a kind of success. Now, however, came another day more positively successful.

Jim and Max started a series of public meetings in greater New York and other East Coast cities on the peril of fascism in Germany. The meetings were well attended and some individual recruitment began again.

Then in January 1933 Hitler was called to power. The *Militant* appeared three times a week sounding the tocsin. The meetings were transformed into a campaign up and down the country for a united front of Communists and Socialists against fascism. Stalinist goon squads made their appearance again, but were usually repelled. CP militants often used to take the floor against ranting Stalinist spokesmen and recruitment stepped up. A notable acquisition for us then was Albert Goldman, one of the CP leaders in Chicago.

I remember that in Cleveland, where I was organizer then and an active leader in the CP-controlled Unemployed Council, this situation was also reflected. I had made a speech calling attention to the Nazi threat and advocating the united front of Communists and Socialists at a mass meeting of about 5,000 in the Public Square. This earned me a merciless punch-up at my next council meeting which was packed with Stalinist strong-arm men. Ordinary workers, mostly Slavonic immigrants, were also there, and were completely bemused by the CP organizer's harangue and charge that I, with whom they worked daily, was a "fascist agent." I took the floor to defend myself and the fists flew. After I went to the hospital to have my broken nose dressed, the cops drove me to the scene of the fracas trying to get me to name my attackers. Workers were milling around. The cops finally gave up and nothing further happened over the incident. But at a campaign meeting on the united front against fascism a few days later, when Hugo Oehler, then on tour, was the main speaker, we had a packed hall at the Painters' headquarters on Euclid Avenue. We were prepared for roughhouse, but none came. Instead the CP sent a speaker, who avoided the usual vitupera-tion in taking the floor. He was answered by Hugo in like fashion. There were some there who had been at the Council punch-up. Several joined the League shortly after.

The success of the united-front campaign, the growth in membership, for the first time gave us wind in our sails. Trotsky's "French turn" policy followed shortly thereafter. Jim and Max both immediately supported it and the Oehler opposition arose against it. Relations between Cannon and Shachtman had been on the mend for some time, and Oehler's sectarian challenge cemented the Cannon and Shachtman forces into one group. Abern and his personal clique remained alienated. Although more or less in agreement with Cannon and Shachtman politically, he often combined forces in unprincipled fashion with the sectarians.

It was at that time that we put on enough flesh to be able to tackle the American Workers Party led by A. J. Muste in a drive for fusion. The campaign for unity opposed by *our* sectarians, and by a motley group of CP sympathizers as well as union officials in their ranks, coincided with two great trade union developments. Our comrades were leading the Minneapolis Teamsters' strikes that were hitting the headlines everywhere. Young AWP leaders like Ted Selander, Sam Pollock, and Art Preis were leading the similarly important and publicized Auto-Lite strike in Toledo. When they met people like Farrell Dobbs, Harry DeBoer, and the Dunne brothers, they found they spoke the same language. These objective facts plus skillful maneuvering with the central leaders of the AWP, in which Jim played the central part—the story is told more fully in his *History of American Trotskyism*—finally resulted at the turn of the year 1934-35 in complete success. No similar feat has been registered by any other Trotskyist organization anywhere before or since. It meant in reality the equivalent of an incipient mass recruitment, amalgamation with a whole cadre of young workers' leaders who almost all became convinced Trotskyists in due course.

A whole wave of important intellectuals, previously held in tow by the CP, around that time began to veer in our direction. George Novack, Felix Morrow, Herbert Solow, and John McDonald actually joined the party, as did Dwight Macdonald a little later. Others like James T. Farrell were sympathetic.

Max Eastman more or less represented this whole intellectual fringe at a New York mass meeting to greet the new, fused party, speaking along with Jim and Muste and other leaders of the new Workers Party of the U.S. It was probably Eastman's last act as a revolutionist, for he was soon to be a precursor in the flight of the intellectuals from support of the degenerated Soviet Union against imperialism, and that meant from us.

Of all the intellectuals of that time, after the Stalin-Hitler pact and the Soviet-Finnish war, only Morrow remained for a time with us, until 1946, and only George Novack proved to be able to absorb the party principles and purpose and to become integrated into the central leadership.

I suppose in a way this wholesale departure of the intellectuals could be considered a failure for the party. Intellectuals are certainly necessary to a revolutionary party. Perhaps a greater effort should have been made to keep some of them. But it was in any case a struggle against the stream for us as far as they were concerned. With the oncoming war the intellectuals were turning away from revolution—toward which they had turned en masse in the days of the depression—almost like a mob stampeding in panic. During one party meeting a young intellectual said heatedly, "I would give up five Soviet Unions for one Sibelius symphony."

The loss of nearly 40 percent of the party, particularly most of the Young People's Socialist League—won from the Norman Thomas socialists, which we had joined in 1936—was certainly one of the heaviest blows we suffered in the fight against the petty-bourgeois opposition in 1940. It was a loss not only in members. Many talented and devoted young leaders left, who later made their mark in various other fields of endeavor. In large part, they were influenced by that stampede.

Again, the survival of the SWP, while practically all those who split from it and its predecessors disappeared from the scene organizationally, can in itself be considered the greatest success of all, especially considering the times.

In all these divagations of American Trotskyism it was Jim Cannon above all who, of any single individual, assured the survival and progress of the SWP, that is, of the party of the workers' revolution against capitalism.

Cannon and Trotsky

One of the interesting features in the relationship between Cannon and Trotsky was the occasional reversal of roles between them. For instance, in the 1940 struggle, it was Trotsky who dubbed the Shachtman-Burnham faction "a petty-bourgeois opposition in the SWP"—a clearly organizational rallying cry.

On the other hand Cannon was the first to use the trade union analogy—the USSR as a union come to power—in elucidating the defense of the Soviet Union against imperialism which this opposition was contesting.

Both contributions became part of the struggle and the original authorship mostly forgotten, and were used interchangeably by the authors themselves.

If I refer to Cannon's contribution in the way I do it is because I recall that in a speech of his entitled "The Fifth Year of the Russian Revolution" (delivered in 1923, originally published as a pamphlet, and printed in his *Speeches for Socialism*) he expanded on just this theme long before it became an issue among Trotskyists.

Yet Cannon never faltered in his allegiance to Trotsky as the political leader, that is as an initiator and at times innovator of revolutionary policy and theory, including, of course, Trotsky's criticism of "socialism in one country" and his theory of the permanent revolution. This was true also for strategic policies and turns, as on the promotion of a labor party in America, and the so-called "French turn" toward entry into the mass Social Democratic parties after Hitler's coming to power, as a prelude to the proclamation and founding of the Fourth International.

It was different when it came to the whole problem of the organization of the party and its attitude toward other organizations and even individuals. Cannon felt quite confident that he had absorbed fully the Leninist tenet here, and that he could illustrate it and apply it on American soil on the basis of his own rich experiences in the labor movement.

Trotsky could certainly teach him on this question too, and he was ready to listen. But here he frankly regarded himself as an equal, as a peer. He was also prepared to differ and, if necessary, to dispute.

There was, for example, the case of the notorious B. J. Field, a man of some talent in the field of economics, whom L. D. befriended, but who was inclined to flout the rules of the Communist League. A grave disagreement arose over this case in 1932. Although the League was divided into tendencies at the time, headed by Cannon and Shachtman, those of us in the Cannon grouping in New York, after hearing Jim and reading a letter he wrote to Prinkipo at the time, agreed to support him should a firm stand have to be taken in the top committee and the organization. It turned out not to be necessary because the Old Man proved conciliatory on this issue, as is known. But it was not the only instance of such a character.

In the 1940 fight against the petty-bourgeois opposition the organizational—as well as initially the political—lead was undoubtedly taken by Jim, and it was after that was over that

Trotsky wrote without flattery that if nothing had come out of it but Cannon's *Struggle for a Proletarian Party,* it would have been justified.

A flicker of a dispute arose on the last visit an SWP delegation paid to Trotsky in June 1940. From the moment we arrived there, both formal and informal discussions took place in larger or smaller groups. Jim and L. D. were on a familiar footing, obviously very fond of each other. It was shortly after the May 24 assault and the atmosphere was still tense, still full of a sense of shock. The Old Man showed us the bedroom where he and Natalia lay on the floor while the Stalinist machine guns pumped bullets all around them; the place where Seva, their grandson, had been grazed by a shot; the fortifications that were being built.

After a day or two the mood around the house had lightened quite a bit. Jim, and Farrell too, cracked a few jokes at dinner, and this stimulated a response in kind from Lev Davidovich.

It was after the split in the SWP, but the Old Man was still faintly hopeful that some of the former minorityites would return to the party. However, he recognized that the organizational measures we had taken toward the opposition were unavoidable and justified. But he considered Cannon's methods "hard," i.e., tough. One day as we were walking in the courtyard, he stopped to feed the fowl in the chicken run. I believe there was a turkey rooster among them who was giving the household some trouble. He took the rooster out and it was crowing blue murder. He gave it a short rap over the head, and the noise stopped. "Cannon's method I have tried. It works," he joked.

We went on to a report on the April convention, given by Jim. A report was also given on the conference of the Fourth International held in New York in May, and a discussion of the alignment of the sections on the disputed issues—they were overwhelmingly with Trotsky and the SWP majority. Trotsky, of course, had already received preliminary reports on these events, but this was the first opportunity he had to discuss them with a leadership delegation from the SWP.

After Cannon's report, a general discussion ensued about perspectives for the future in the U.S. L. D. was of the opinion that it would be a testing time for us. He was sharply critical of the *Northwest Organizer,* the Minneapolis Teamster paper, for being too exclusively concerned with trade union issues and ignoring national politics. He felt this was a form of adaptation to the pro-Roosevelt trade union milieu. A certain amount of adaptation was inevitable, but our comrades now had to be conditioned against it because the time was arriving for a merciless showdown with F. D. R. Elections were coming soon. What would we do?

Then the Old Man proposed—partly, I think, to orient the SWP and particularly our trade unionists in the tougher situation we would face with the approach of war—that we give critical support to the Browder ticket in the coming elections. (This was during the Stalin-Hitler pact and the CP was more critical of Roosevelt than it had been in its People's Front period and was at least on paper against U.S. intervention in the European war.)

Jim was put on the defensive, but he would not go along with Trotsky's proposal on supporting Browder and he sought to explain the actual position our trade unionists were in. Comrade Antoinette Konikow, who was present, heatedly protested against the proposal on the grounds that Stalinist hooliganism was continuing against us and that the Stalinists would not even let us in their hall in Boston much less permit us to work in support of their candidate. How could we call for a vote for them when in other parts of the world they were killing our supporters?

Trotsky replied that the issue was not the crimes of the Stalinists but their influence in the labor movement. In the United States they commanded the loyalty of thousands of workers. Their gangsterism would make it difficult for us to carry out the tactic of supporting, critically, their candidate but it was not on this subjective basis that we should decide whether such support was correct. Right now the CP was the only working class party running a candidate against Roosevelt, and moreover, for the moment, its line was close to ours on some of the major issues in the election (anti-imperialism, etc.).

I believe that it was at this point that Jim went into a description of the situation within the labor movement, the carry-over among large sections of militants of detestation of the Stalinists from their People's Front, class-collaborationist line, etc. He thought we would be too compromised among these anti-Stalinist workers if we supported Browder and that the tactic would not produce any significant gains from the ranks of the CP anyway.

The Old Man answered that of course it would be preferable, if we were unable to run our own candidate, to have someone in the field who represented the broad labor movement, even a John L.

Lewis or a Tobin. But in the absence of such candidates it was better to vote for the CP than to abstain.

I tended at the beginning to agree with L. D.'s reasoning, but Jim's argumentation was powerful and I said I supported him and was against the maneuver with Browder. In the end we did not support the Browder campaign.

Informal Discussions

Contrary to most leaders of left-wing organizations that I knew, Jim used to like discussion of some important questions to be initiated informally, over a glass of beer or a highball. He felt that the start of a discussion in formal committee was often inhibiting and tended to fix positions taken by participants so that it became difficult for them to change their views freely. It was a method of his own.

Of course no member of the leading committee was obliged to come to these, and some didn't, at least for some of the sessions. Others didn't drink. But most came. I can recall that it was at one such session that the approach to the Musteites was born and the outlines of that letter to them with an offer they couldn't refuse.

There were also faction caucuses which, at least at the top, were informal gatherings. In these, strategy and tactics of factional combat were hammered out. That certainly was so in 1939-40 during the fight against the petty-bourgeois opposition of Burnham and Shachtman.

But these were mainly meetings of NC people, that held to the informality rule. In such meetings a practical proposition like an organizing campaign would come up. In one Jim recalled Wobbly organizing drives and expanded on them. The "Footloose Rebels" campaign of the early postwar period was initiated that way.

All sorts of questions of party interest were "mulled over" at these discussions, even the assignments of individuals. I remember that an assignment abroad for me was broached at one such session in 1943 by Jim, although it didn't materialize formally till after the war.

To be sure, these were only informal initial steps. Every proposition came up for formal discussion and decision subsequently in the full committee. But by then the question had not come up "cold."

On the whole this method worked well and proved politically fruitful, in splits as well as in unifications.

Recreations and Relations to Comrades

Jim Cannon's cultural and recreational bent was simple.

I never saw him play any outdoor game except once, and that was, of all things, croquet. Some of the family and a few of us young comrades were staying a weekend at a summer cottage in New Jersey—I believe it belonged to Esther Karsner, wife of Dave Karsner. Jim organized a game with Rose, Ruth, Walta, and the rest of us. A young comrade named Shackley soon took a commanding lead. "Stop Shackley, stop Shackley," Jim called out in mock alarm. "We've got to stop Shackley." So, every one of us went all out to block Shackley. Naturally, after this diversion Jim outdistanced all of us and was the winner in the end.

Indoors, Jim used to like to play solitaire sometimes. But his favorite recreation was sitting back and listening to Fred Allen and Jack Benny or other dry comedians on the radio.

He liked film comedies, particularly if they made some satirical social comment. But he also saw the outstanding social dramas like *Grapes of Wrath*. Novels were among his regular reading matter, as he has indicated in his writing. I don't remember him going to plays, though he must have done so. He was absorbed by Sean O'Casey's autobiography. But then O'Casey wrote about mutual acquaintances, like Jim Larkin, in his memoirs.

O'Casey's account of the Easter Rebellion and the fight against the Blacks and Tans was of special interest. Jim had previously heard about these Irish struggles from comrades like Jack Carmody, who had fought in the Irish Republican Army before escaping to the U.S., and from Tom O'Flaherty, the brother of Liam, who used to do a popular column for the *Daily Worker* before his expulsion in 1929. He later made a stab at a similar column for the *Militant* in 1932 which he called "On the Spot" and signed "Ride 'Em."

Jim liked biographical works best for light reading. But he kept up with all sorts of publications. He had an eye for a new author of promise. Once, at his house in the Village in 1948 or 1949, he showed me Isaac Deutscher's first published book, a slim volume on the Soviet trade unions. He pointed out a number of acute observations made by Deutscher, which showed what the writer had yet to offer. It was my first acquaintance with that name.

He didn't much care for opera and classical music. Jim was inclined to like spirituals and even popular hit songs. I can still hear him in memory singing to himself: "I don't care if the sun don't shine, I get my lovin' in the evening time."

I should add that he knew dozens of rebel songs from Wobbly days that no one else seemed to know. He didn't often sing at socials, but I remember one time in the early days hearing him sing the old IWW songs "I've Been Working on the Railroad" and "Oh, for Overalls and Snuff," to the tune of "For the Wearing of the Green." That certainly was a favorite of his. Later on he used to like to lead us in a rendition of "There is power, there is power in a band of union men."

Jim's relations with comrades were always warm. No one felt reluctant to approach him, especially when there was personal trouble. One time a comrade "Hans" knocked on the door very late at night at the house on Washington Square, accompanied by his girl. Both looked scared. It turned out that "Hans's" wife, from whom he had been separated for years but not divorced, had sought him out and attempted to pump a few bullets into him. Jim consoled the pair and helped them regain their cool as well as to work out a plan to avoid a repetition.

When I was organizer in Boston in the early thirties, I stayed with Dr. Antoinette Konikow at her Beacon Hill home. The situation of "the hill" for snazziness was no less then than it is now. When I wrote back to New York expressing my satisfaction with my accommodations, I got a note back admonishing me against becoming a "boudoir socialist" in the tradition of Ferdinand Lassalle. . . .

People whom Jim won over to his ideas were usually long-term adherents. On one trip through the South we stopped off at Memphis. On a farm on the outskirts of the city Farrell and I were introduced by Jim to the Rust brothers, two gray-haired men who had earlier in their life invented the famous cotton picker. They talked like old buddies to him and gave us all a warm welcome. We saw several models of the machine. Before we left, after they had a talk with Jim about developments, there was a monetary contribution from them, I believe. The Rusts were former Wobblies.

There were always unpaid bills in the "dog days," gas, electricity, rent, a linotype operator to pay (after Charlie Curtiss left New York). Particularly the lino operator, who was a deaf-mute but could become very aggressive after missing three or four weeks' pay (he was luckier than the rest of us). All the "staff" went out on special expeditions to raise money—there were too many unemployed and underpaid in the membership to get the sum needed from that source. Jim, sometimes with Max and

Abern, or Arne Swabeck, would organize these forages, assigning given people to certain sympathizers.

I remember one or two such expeditions in about 1932 to visit sympathetic people in the theater who were living in the Village. On one occasion George Clarke was with me. We were submitted to close questioning about the *Militant,* particularly the antifascist united-front line, which appealed to them. We came away with a considerable contribution, considerable for that time anyway.

Later on, when the CP swung over to the Popular Front, all these people followed the big drift to Stalinism, with the rest of the well-known left-wing figures in the art, entertainment, and literary fields.

Another source of financial help, not as big but certainly reliable and steady, was the household of Usick and Edith Vanzler. Edith was the daughter of Antoinette Konikow, and Usick was then producing and marketing a contraceptive jelly invented by Antoinette. At that time, although warm and friendly personally, Usick was politically very aggressive toward us.

As an avocation Usick produced a magazine together with his friend, the artist (and later TV raconteur) Alexander King. They called their magazine *America.* Politically its line called more or less for a revival of the moribund IWW as the solution to the political problems of the left. Usick was much more militant for this line than his friend, who not long after produced the prototype of the weekly picture magazine and later sold it to Henry Luce as *Life* magazine.

While King took the road to fame and fortune in the bourgeois world, Usick Vanzler, after a few visits (in which we learned that he was an able Russian translator) was induced to translate Trotsky's articles for the *Militant* as well as pamphlets and books later on for our Pioneer Publishers. In the course of that work he became a Trotskyist and, with Edith, joined the party. He will be remembered in our movement as John G. Wright, and by many of his comrades as one of the most devoted as well as learned proletarian revolutionists. Jim's tribute in *Notebook of an Agitator* was not lightly given.

In 1948, when I returned from a couple of years in Europe, I stayed for a while with Duncan Ferguson, a comrade who had rendered the party services in many fields. Duncan was also a sculptor of high standing whose works were exhibited in museums long after he gave up his art and joined the SWP to devote himself to the revolutionary cause. I once saw a few of his sculptures unexpectedly in the Whitney Museum of American Art, then on West Eighth Street in Manhattan.

We were sitting one evening in his flat in the garment district in Manhattan, when my eye fell on a clay bust on a stand. I looked but could not see too well in the dim light. Duncan directed a bright light on the sculpture. Now I could see it was Cannon, but I gazed on for a while.

"Well, what do you think of it?" Duncan asked.

"It's Jim all right," I said. "Jim to a T. The lofty, defiant look of the rebel with a social cause. . . . But it also has a touch of the ward heeler."

I don't know what made me use the pejorative expression. But my comment certainly expressed sharply the contrasting sides of Jim's character; his unflinching devotion to revolutionary socialism and his earthy practicality in its everyday promotion.

Duncan didn't say anything but his face wrinkled into one of his inscrutable smiles.

Around about 1949 there was a newspaper story, probably an interview, in which Harry S. Truman was asked how he felt about being returned to the White House. The president explained that in a personal sense the presidential mansion felt like a prison to him. He had had no private personal life since he entered it. In there he was probably the loneliest man in America, he thought.

Cannon read or paraphrased these remarks of the president to me when I came to see him one day.

"You know," he said, "I have no use for Harry Truman. But as a human being, especially coming from ordinary folk, he must find that kind of life deadening. No one can like to be transformed into a political robot, even a high-class robot, serving the richest robber barons in history."

Jim made coffee and poured us a couple of cups.

I said I thought he was right enough, but what had brought on this sudden sympathy? I couldn't remember a similar favorable emotion for anyone across the class barrier from Jim before.

"Well, I'll tell you, Sam," he said. "Truman came from a background not much different from mine. He became part of the Pendergast machine in Kansas City when he was very young. He was loyal to the boss, and the machine in turn helped him up the ladder of the Democratic Party."

Cannon took a sip and reflected further.

"When I was in my teens, just before I joined the Wobblies, I was scooped up by the Pendergast machine for a while. I could possibly have been in his place if the radical streak in my upbringing hadn't rescued me from that life."

James P. Cannon and Rose Karsner

Fannie Curran

I first met Jim Cannon in January 1929, when he was in Minneapolis on his first speaking tour for the Left Opposition on the subject "The Real Situation in Russia and the Truth About the Left Opposition." I was just nineteen years old then, but I had already spent four years in the Young Communist League.

Despite the fact that Jim warned us that we had better come to the meeting early and be prepared, that the Stalinists would try to break it up, no one took that warning seriously. We just couldn't visualize that the comrades whom we had known and worked with for years would go so far as a physical attack.

But that is precisely what happened. Oscar Coover and Carl Skoglund, who did appear somewhat early, were attacked and badly beaten. Oscar even spent some days in the hospital. An edition of the *Militant* of that period will show his picture with scars of that beating.

Comrade Cannon kept right on speaking throughout all the heckling and name-calling of "counterrevolutionist," "sniveling Trotskyite cur," "renegade," and all the others with which we are now only too familiar. Then all hell broke loose. The landlady of the hall called the cops. Four of them showed up and by that time a number of chairs were broken and a free-for-all ensued. The cops were nonplussed. Here were communists fighting communists.

At that point one of the members of the YCL pointed at Cannon

---

FANNIE CURRAN was born in 1910. She was a founding member of the Communist League of America and participated in its first national conference in 1929. She made these remarks at a meeting in Minneapolis on September 6, 1974.

and shouted to the cops: "Arrest him—he's a counter-revolutionist!" A general roar broke out and the cops cleared the hall. At that moment it became crystal clear for the first time to me and I am sure to others present that the Stalinists considered the Trotskyists (who then numbered less than a hundred members nationally) and not the capitalist class their main enemy. Jim in his speech had placed heavy emphasis on this point.

Comrade Cannon said the matter could not end there. We contacted the Wobblies, who were always ready to defend the right of free speech, and the meeting was held at their headquarters a few days later. We were well prepared with baseball bats—or as Jim said, shillelaghs, "just in case we should suddenly go lame."

Despite the fact that C. R. Hedlund went into the headquarters of the Communist Party and dared them to try to break up our meeting, not one of the Stalinists showed up. They evidently realized that their valor at this particular meeting was not the better part of wisdom.

I also attended the conference in Chicago in May 1929 where we first established ourselves formally as the Communist League of America (Left Opposition). Jim opened the meeting by declaring that this was the most historic conference in American revolutionary history. How very prophetic his words turned out to be.

Bill Kitt

Looking back over the almost forty-five years I knew Jim, one memory among many stands out above all the others. This concerns the time in June 1930 when I first met him. At that time Union Square on Fourteenth Street in New York City was a hotbed of political activity, with members of the Communist Party, Lovestoneites, Trotskyists, IWW, and various shades of anarchists holding forth.

I had arrived in New York some time earlier, after several years in the IWW in the western part of the country, and was immediately caught up in a hectic round of discussions, attending meetings and reading the literature of the different contending groups.

While trying to sort out the positions of the various organizations and how I related to them, I met a young Trotskyist, Sam Gordon, a student at City College of New York, which was then a center of radical activity. Under Sam's guidance, the fundamental differences between Stalinism and Trotskyism were made clear to me and I found myself in agreement with the Trotskyist position.

When I had reached that conclusion Sam took me to the headquarters of the Communist League of America (as the organization was then called). It was in an old loft building on East Tenth Street. We walked in the entrance and entered a tiny

---

BILL KITT (1904-1975) joined the Communist League of America in 1931. He remained an active member of the Socialist Workers Party from its founding in 1938 until his death, participating in party branches in New York City, Buffalo, Toledo, Minneapolis, Detroit, Los Angeles, San Diego, and San Francisco.

office on the left. It was furnished with an old desk and chair and there, in those bare surroundings, I was introduced to Jim Cannon.

He evidently knew I was coming (in those days the recruitment of one person to the movement was a big event) and asked me a few questions about myself. He then spoke about the significance of the Russian revolution, the dispute between Stalin and Trotsky, and the revolutionary potential of the American working class.

He strode up and down the narrow room stating his firm belief in the ultimate victory of socialism. It was not only his words that moved me, it was also the overwhelming feeling that he gave me—that here was a man who had the determination and the iron will to fight against all odds for his convictions. When he finished I was speechless.

The courage, determination, and conviction that marked all of Jim's life flamed just as brightly at the end as it did on that day more than four decades ago. These qualities which are the mark of the true revolutionary are no small part of the tremendous legacy that Jim left us.

Art Sharon

My first meeting with Jim was an unfortunate one. It was at a national conference of the Communist League of America (Opposition) in 1934. I had broken with the Stalinist movement the year before under the impact of the tragic events in Germany. I came to this conference in New York City from California eager to meet and know the cadres of the American Trotskyist movement. After several days of animated and heated debate I looked forward to a social evening to be held at a private apartment. This would be an opportunity to personally meet and talk with some of the conference participants. Jim was there and I wanted to talk with him, but I considered it presumptuous to approach him so I sat on a piano stool, drink in hand, relaxing and observing as well as sorting out my impressions of the past week. I had a special interest in Jim not only because he was one of the leaders at that time but his name was the only familiar one to me. I had heard about him in a peripheral way as a teen-ager listening to the stories of my seniors about the internal warfare of the CP—most of it, I must say, quite deprecating of Jim. Detaching himself from one of the groups at the social Jim caught my eye and sauntered over to the piano. He inquired about my trip East and after some further small talk he turned to questioning me about the movement in Los Angeles and my reaction to the debates at the conference.

ART SHARON was born in 1914. He became a political associate of Cannon in 1934 and was his collaborator during the next thirty years. He is a former member of the National Committee of the Socialist Workers Party. These remarks are based on a talk he gave in San Francisco, September 14, 1974.

Somewhat flattered by his interest, I was at the same time very much on my guard that he might divine a pocket of doubt that I had about the prospects of this very small group of people who seemed to be past masters of argumentation with amazing endurance. I thought then—and now for that matter—that any political debate that couldn't be wound up by 10:00 p.m. went beyond politics into the realm of punishment.

I responded to his questions very quickly with what I considered the correct replies one gives to an important leader. Such was my training in the CP. One only talked frankly and openly with close friends. Jim stood there listening and then without comment or even change of expression he abruptly turned away and shortly after he left the apartment. I was surprised and disturbed by this and realized with regret that I had made a mistake. Obviously this leader was unlike any other I had met in the past. I had a lot to learn.

This small episode didn't go unnoticed by others in the room and particularly by those who had arranged my personal accommodation. That night my hostess steered our discussion to a somewhat guarded but obviously pointed commentary on the then leaders of the Communist League. Here I learned of the merits and demerits of Jim Cannon, Shachtman, and Marty Abern, the three principal figures at that time. The last, I learned, had all the merits that Jim lacked and more besides. Considering the strange experience of my first encounter with Jim her explanations seemed to make sense.

This later led to my becoming the recipient of lengthy onionskin letters which contained all the inside information on what was going on in New York and elsewhere. That these were in part sheer gossip made me uneasy but my scruples were overcome by the feeling that this was probably an organic part of party political life, especially since I later learned these letters were widely circulated. Those who received them enjoyed the feeling of being privy to the most important internal political information.

Changing objective developments began almost immediately to have their reflection in important political discussions and shifts inside the movement. First there was the unity with the Musteites at the beginning of the great upsurge of the new labor movement. Following that came the turn toward entry into the Socialist Party which should better be characterized as intervention into a favorable political arena.

These objective developments put all forms of sectarianism on the defensive and eventually to rout and incidentally freed me from the closed circle of Abernism. And here Jim's great talent of principled political intervention led the movement onto a higher stage. His carping critics dragged at his heels and it turned out that the man they characterized as a has-been from old factional wars in the CP and too old and therefore rude and moody was the man who knew how to answer correctly the question—what to do next?

Later when I had occasion to talk with Jim about those years and their lessons he would draw on his pipe thoughtfully, smile almost benignly, and comment, "If you live right you get the breaks." Usually this would be followed by a chuckle as he would recall one or another episode in his experience and follow up with—"I could never understand why those people who had better things to do always wanted to go after me." As I write this down I find myself smiling again. He didn't feel it necessary to use some classical analogy when in truth he could have without the slightest hesitation cited the motto of Dante, said by the elder Liebknecht to be Marx's favorite: "Go your own way and let the tongues wag!" I can't think of one more appropriate to Jim.

Jim felt very strongly about the continuity of revolutionary tradition of which we were a contemporary link. This was a very deep source of strength for him and of course for ourselves too. I recall with what emotion he would reminisce about his early teachers in the IWW—particularly Vincent St. John. On one occasion in a room at the old Hotel Albert talking about the "Saint" he suddenly asked rhetorically, "Am I worthy of the great tasks to which he first directed me?" This impressed me as a demonstration of how powerfully he felt about this continuity of revolutionaries from one generation to another. This will appear to some as an overly sentimental feeling not suited to revolutionary politics. I can only answer from my own conviction and experience—more the pity to them. This strong sense of debt to his forebears that he felt is common to the spiritual life of all the outstanding revolutionists from Marx's time to the present.

This conviction of his had its expression in what appeared to me at times as an overly generous appreciation extended to much lesser figures who played a role at one time or another in the revolutionary movement. When I would protest my objections to what appeared to me as an exaggeration of the role played by some of the early leaders of the CP in this country, for example, he would remind me that we stood to a certain extent on their shoulders. I wrote to him once upon reading a manuscript for a forthcoming article or book of his that I considered it a mistake to give some of these figures as much credit as he did. He answered me that I knew them only after they became renegades to revolutionary Marxism. They had indeed served at one time as dedicated fighters for communism in America but had become victims of Stalin. Their early work remained part of our tradition.

As so many have testified, Jim took a direct hand in initiating many practical projects for building the movement. One of his favorite ideas over a long period of time was the concept of "footloose rebels." This came directly from Jim's experience in the early Wobbly movement. The "footloose rebels" of that time would get the word that they were needed in any one of a dozen hot spots and usually within a matter of hours were on their way. The footloose rebel was also the Wobbly organizer who carried along the "rigging" (application blanks, red cards, literature).

I recall how in early 1936 I attended the last convention of the Workers Party where we decided to join the SP. On the last day of the convention as I prepared to leave for the Coast, Jim asked me to stay over for a day and he invited me to his apartment. When I appeared there the next day he told me of his fears about how the Chicago organization would carry out the entry into the SP. This branch was a stronghold of the Abernites, who were less than enthusiastic about the entire project. With a $10 stake advanced by Rose I was on my way the next morning, a "footloose rebel," to begin a very fruitful two-year stint in Chicago.

Ironically the SP entry that made the Abern clique so unhappy turned out in the long run to be a boon to its fortunes. It was inside the SP youth movement that they recruited so many of the forces which gave them the strength to throw the party into the greatest crisis of its history on the eve of the war. In 1939 they formed their unprincipled coalition with Burnham and Shachtman and declared war on what they called "bureaucratic conservatism." As it turned out, they were already in flight from our basic program under the pressure of the then growing tide of democratic liberal social patriotism. This internal struggle gave us two priceless documents, Trotsky's *In Defense of Marxism* and Jim's *Struggle for a Proletarian Party*.

In the latter book Jim settled accounts with the Abern clique once and for all. Their subsequent history was an ignominious one, too pathetic to relate here. All that Jim had discerned in that clique formation many years before came to full flower in a relatively short time following that historic debate. That was Jim as our teacher at his best.

Following the war years I had the opportunity of observing and working with Jim at first hand in New York City. Living in the Village when I first got there, I remember meeting him in the street and accompanying him to his stepdaughter's apartment where, as he explained, he had an important assignment that night as babysitter. That was Jim as a loving grandfather taking great pleasure in playing with a young child. My companion at the time was astonished at this sight which seemed so utterly out of character. He loved children and took great pleasure in their company, as we were able to see so often at the camp we had in the Pocono mountains.

The children who grew up in the movement and came into contact with Jim all had some special kind of affection and love for him that is manifest even to this day when as young adults they tell their stories about the Jim they knew. His love for children was coupled with his uncompromising hatred of capitalism and the menace it posed for the entire future of humankind.

Jim's implacable hatred of capitalism grew stronger, if that was possible, as he grew older. Here one is reminded of Hyndman's story of Marx in his last year of life. Hyndman, who was the founder of the British Social Democratic Party, remarked to Marx that as he (Hyndman) grew older he became more tolerant. Marx turned to him in surprise and in great heat exclaimed: "Do you?—Do you?" Hyndman of course made his peace with British capitalism not too many years later.

Harry DeBoer

I'm proud to stand here before you tonight to tell you that I had the opportunity to work with one of the greatest revolutionists this country has produced.

I first met Jim Cannon at a staff meeting of the Minneapolis strikes in 1934. I can remember that now as if it was yesterday. We were in a meeting and Cannon walked in. Skogie was sitting on the side of the hall. And Jim said, "What the hell kind of trouble are you gettin' us into now?"

When he made this remark, Skogie put the same smile on his face that he's got there in the picture on the wall and didn't say a word.

To me, that meant that Jim was our kind of people, and he really proved that to me as we worked together.

I tell you this just to give you an idea of what Jim was like, working and living with him. When Jim was here in Minneapolis speaking or giving lectures, he always spoke differently than he did when he, should I say, "let his hair down" and spoke with us truck drivers after these strike meetings.

That is what Jim liked to do. He liked to take a drink. He had a sense of humor. He was witty, and some of the truck drivers were too. So that is where he felt at home.

He always made a point of getting a room at the West Hotel that was practically half as big as this hall, so that he would

---

HARRY DeBOER was born in 1907. He was a leader of the Minneapolis Teamsters union from 1934 until the Smith Act trial in 1941. He was one of the eighteen defendants convicted in the case and served time with Cannon at Sandstone penitentiary. These remarks were made at a meeting in Minneapolis on September 6, 1974.

have a place for gatherings of his kind of people.

One word Jim would often use at these gatherings was "savvy," and another was "moxie." He used to say, "Give me a worker that has savvy and moxie, and we'll take over this world."

Well, history will show that truck drivers in 1934 under the leadership of the Trotskyists built one of the best unions the Northwest has ever seen.

When Roosevelt was preparing for war, he knew the leadership of this union would not support a war, and they had to try to get rid of the union leadership. But it took the local government, the state government, the federal government, all of the finks and bureaucrats in the trade union movement—it took that whole shebang in order to get us out of the union, and before they could do it they had to put us in jail.

I want to cite a little experience from prison that, again, shows the kind of man Jim was. The first thirty days in jail we were in quarantine. We weren't even allowed to have a newspaper. But we *were* able to play checkers.

So we started playing checkers. And everybody claimed to be the champion checker player. Jim, I admit, was an exceptionally good player. And I think he could probably be considered the champ. But after arguing over who was the champ, we finally decided on a tournament. And in the elimination it so happened that Jim got beat. I don't know how; he probably turned his head to spit or something. But nevertheless, Jake Cooper and I turned out to be the two to play for the championship.

Jim comes to me and he says, "Harry, I'm going to make you the champion." So he was my coach. And the result was, I beat Jake. Jake and his followers immediately claimed foul play.

So Jim comes to me and says, "Harry, you just dummy up and keep your mouth shut. I'll be your mouthpiece."

He says, "Jake's a pretty tough boy, so we won't play him again. But I'm going to propose to him that we have a hearing and a trial, so to speak, to decide this. I'll go and talk to Jake and I'll propose that Skogie be the judge, because," he says, "I got something on Skogie—he hasn't got papers."

So we went to trial. Jim set me on the stand, and he said to Skogie, "Your honor, I'm DeBoer's mouthpiece. I've told him to dummy up. The reason I'm telling him to dummy up is because he wants to prove that he's the champion. He's a fighter, and he wants to play checkers and play it over the board and prove that he's the champion.

"But that isn't the point here. There is the charge of foul play. And I don't want that young man's name to have a black mark on it. He could play checkers and win every game till doomsday but that mark would still be there. That's why, your honor, I am asking you to decide this issue, and after you hear our opponents, I'm sure you will agree that DeBoer can take that black mark from his name and agree that he is the true champion."

Well, after the trial, Skogie agreed that I was the champion.

Now, at this gathering and farewell to Jim, I can proudly say to Jim that I'm speaking to a group of workers that have savvy and moxie, and I can assure you that they're not going to let you down.

1922

Ted Grant

Everyone who had the good fortune to hear Comrade Cannon knows that he was an inspiring public speaker with great wit and eloquence. To me he excelled as a Marxist educator in inner-party struggles. Although some forty years have elapsed, the speeches he gave at the June 1935 plenum of the Workers Party are still outstanding in my memory. It was a critical period in the history of the American Trotskyist movement. The Workers Party, only six months after the fusion of the Communist League of America (CLA) and the American Workers Party (AWP), was paralyzed with the first of two internal struggles over whether we should devote major attention to the newly radicalized left wing of the Socialist Party. Cannon and Max Shachtman proposed this priority in a resolution but they were in a minority. A. J. Muste, Hugo Oehler, and Martin Abern, in an unprincipled combination, were opposed and had the big majority in the leadership and membership. (The question of entry into the SP could not be posed until December 1935 after the SP Old Guard split away.)

Intertwined with this main struggle was a fight-to-the-finish battle with the sectarian Oehlerites over what they referred to as "principles." In March 1935, a Plenum and Active Workers' Conference in Pittsburgh had been completely disrupted by the Oehlerites. They were hell-bent to expose the "opportunism" of

TED GRANT was born in 1903. He joined the American Workers Party, led by A. J. Muste, in 1933 and became a National Committee member of the Workers Party of the United States after the AWP's fusion with the Communist League of America in December 1934. He was active in the trade unions in Ohio in the 1930s and in the work of the SWP in New York in the 1940s. He withdrew from political activity in the mid-1950s.

the leadership and at the same time give the centrist Musteites a crash course in Bolshevism. They filibustered every point on the agenda, demanding that "principled" questions be discussed, e.g., the "French turn," Ethiopia, China, etc. Every one of these was important, of course, but inappropriate at an Active Workers' Conference. Muste joined with Cannon and Shachtman in their efforts to stem the factional hysteria of the Oehlerites, but Jim said Muste was too much of a gentleman to handle these bare-knuckle fighters. The conference was literally a shambles. Jim told the Oehlerites that the leadership was going to take off their coats and give them a discussion they wouldn't forget: "We'll take every issue to the membership and educate the whole party against this sectarian sickness."

I was one of the field workers from Ohio, Pennsylvania, and West Virginia. After the Pittsburgh fiasco, the June 1935 plenum was our first experience in an organized faction fight. As members of the former AWP we supported Muste's position that our highest priority should continue to be recruitment to the WP. Since our bloc had a numerical majority, we expected the three-day plenum would adjourn on time and we could get right back to our mass work (unemployed demonstrations, eviction fights, and strike struggles). We underestimated by a country mile the power of a Marxist minority led by Jim Cannon and got the shock of our lives when we realized that this would be a "knockdown drag-out fight" as Jim described it in *The History of American Trotsky-ism*. He was so right, because it went hammer and tongs for seven days and into the early hours of the eighth!

We had been warned that Cannon was a "dirty, roughhouse factional fighter." All kinds of tales were circulating about the "Cannon regime," "bureaucratic rule," "bad administration," and in addition there were charges that Cannon had met secretly with the right-wing SP leaders, the topper being that Cannon had already made a deal with the SP: if he brought the WP into the SP he could have the vice-president's slot on the 1936 SP ticket with Socialist Mayor Hoan of Milwaukee as the presidential ticket! So many members from all tendencies talked to us at length about Jim Cannon, pro and con, that we came to the conclusion that he was the most admired, hated, and feared man at the plenum. On the second day, a control commission was elected to examine all the fantastic charges and rumors. Replying to the charges Jim assured the commission that they were totally false because "I never met the right-wing SP leaders to talk to in my life." The New York membership, aroused to a fever pitch, clamored to be allowed in and when they were admitted, there was standing room only in the hall. It was the longest and most tumultuous plenum I ever attended.

When the plenum finally returned to the agenda I could see Jim with sleeves rolled up, a carton of milk for his ulcer in front of him, his face icy calm as he concentrated on his notes. He looked like a fighter waiting for the bell. When he rose to speak an unusual thing happened—the hubbub subsided and the stormy hall became silent. We fully expected him to shout brutal insults, loud denunciations, etc., but to our complete surprise Jim spoke quietly, calmly, and convincingly in language that any ordinary worker could understand. He began with a rich, all-sided examination of the rapid changes that were taking place in the SP, painstakingly explaining why it was important for us to give our major attention to its emerging left wing. Because the SP was much larger than we were, the ferment in its ranks was attracting and recruiting worker activists and rebel youth while the WP was stymied. There wasn't much time to take advantage of this opportunity because the Stalinists and Lovestoneites were ready to move in and grab off these militants. He reminded us that the WP was not yet a party, simply the propaganda nucleus with which we could build a mass workers' party. He spelled out the methods we would use, e.g., more articles about them in our press, personal contacts, establishment of Trotskyist fractions. Exactly how we would unify our forces organizationally with their best elements would have to await further developments. Finally, he said, this question will not be settled here; we will launch a full-scale democratic discussion of the political differences with the aim of educating the whole party. Then the rank and file of the party will make the final decision at a convention—that's the Marxist method.

This Bolshevik method of a free, democratic, organized factional struggle to settle serious differences over program and policy was brand new to us. In the Conference for Progressive Labor Action and the AWP, when a difference arose, all sides were given equal time to present their views, with A. J. (as we always called Muste) in the chair. He would speak last, skillfully reconciling the different viewpoints into an "all-inclusive" motion which was generally accepted. His prestige and influence were so great that almost everyone would defer to him. In 1933-34, when I was a member of the CPLA and AWP, Muste was steering a leftward course which fused with our anticapitalist militancy.

(In a letter to Nat Hentoff, July 9, 1960, writing about Muste, Jim said, "Innumerable people from various professional circles dabbled with the radical labor movement in that time, but Muste was one who went all the way, or at least tried to. It was characteristic of him, I think, that he didn't merely sympathize and comment; he took his place on the firing line where personal hazards and hardships outweighed possible personal rewards. . . . In that rough and rowdy world of militant strikers, impatient unemployed demonstrators and godless revolutionaries, he was accepted and respected on all sides.")

Jim's speeches gave us our first lesson in the ABCs of principled Marxist politics as he fairly but mercilessly dissected the political position of each group in our bloc. We noticed at once that Jim didn't stoop to petty debater's points or misrepresent an opponent's position. He stated each position fully and fairly and answered them squarely in such a way as to obtain the maximum educational value for the membership. Oehler, the die-hard sectarian, was opposed in principle to turning our attention to the SP now or ever. We had seen how disruptive the Oehlerites were at the Pittsburgh Active Workers' Conference in March. Their arguments were completely sterile and unrealistic. Muste was opposed on the grounds that we should be exerting all our efforts to recruit to the WP, a policy that could lead us into stagnation and decay. Abern, the perennial cliquist who substituted personal relations for party discipline, had no interest in political questions, only used them to serve his organizational ends.

Jim's critical analysis was a revelation. For the first time it became apparent to us that each member of our bloc had different principles and motives for joining the bloc. Jim put the right name on it—an unprincipled bloc. He stressed that rigid ultraleftism and organizational fetishism could seriously restrict the party's freedom to make the tactical moves necessary to consolidate all potentially revolutionary militants on a Marxist program, and build a workers' combat party. We could easily understand this last point because we were leading mass organizations and were going through similar experiences in the field; in fact, this point illuminated the very essence of the different positions at the plenum.

During a break, Jim came over to our table and made a few humorous remarks about the wild statements of some of the speakers. "It was enough to make a grown man cry," I seemed to hear him say with a grin and a helpless shrug of his shoulders—a typical gesture. We were genuinely surprised that he would come over to "our side," so to speak, and be friendly and comradely despite the vitriolic attacks. When he sat down to discuss the situation in our branches and mass work it was obvious that he had a great deal of experience in the mass movement. He was a man of revolutionary action—a fighter—no doubt about that. We felt an immediate kinship with him and we communicated easily. Later, we all agreed that he was a serious working class leader and a man not to be trifled with in his drive to build a proletarian party.

When the plenum finally came to a conclusion, Jim was still going strong but the rest of us were near exhaustion. As soon as we adjourned some of us urged Muste to join with Cannon and Shachtman in their fight to isolate and defeat the Oehlerite disrupters because they were the immediate danger to the unity of the party. As a result of the thoroughgoing discussion in the membership, Muste did join with them against Oehler at the October 1935 plenum and shortly thereafter the Oehlerites were expelled for violations of party discipline and preparing a split.

In January 1936, a month after the SP Old Guard split away, Cannon and Shachtman submitted their resolution to enter the SP. A. J. Muste fought a hard but losing battle for his position in the preconvention discussion. At the February-March 1936 convention the decision to enter the SP was approved by an overwhelming majority including a number of Muste's leading supporters. This defeat—plus the disgrace of three of Muste's key leaders joining the Stalinist Communist Party the day the convention opened—were catastrophic blows that shattered the Muste group. Shortly thereafter Muste left to attend an international meeting in Europe and also visit Trotsky in Norway. While there, the Moscow show trials and the bloody violence of the Spanish civil war were the final events which we believed caused him to break with Trotskyism and return to religion and pacifism. Years later, Isaac Deutscher told Muste after he had read all of Trotsky's correspondence, "You're one of the very few people to whom Trotsky always referred with respect and affection" (quoted in Nat Hentoff's *Peace Agitator*).

Under Cannon's leadership, in less than a year the Trotskyists had achieved a unification and a split and both were progressive. At the June 1935 plenum Cannon was in a minority but at the February-March 1936 convention the overwhelming majority was convinced not only that Cannon's political line was correct, but in addition, he stood head and shoulders above all the others as *the* American Trotskyist leader. I'm sure the important accomplishment in Jim's mind was that the Workers Party was solidly unified and politically prepared for its next step in the building of a proletarian revolutionary party—the entry into the Socialist Party.

Photo by Joseph Hansen

Cannon and Wong in Pennsylvania, August 1942

Morris Chertov

The old adage regarding the value of first impressions, if applied to James P. Cannon, could be most misleading, as I learned from experience. The first time I saw him was during the summer of 1934, in the New York City headquarters of the American Workers Party, which I had joined a few months before, propelled into it, at age twenty-six, by the forces one experiences on the final assembly line of an auto plant. Though I was a very green newcomer to the revolutionary movement, I was rich in the experiences of the time.

A group from the Communist League of America had come in to meet with AWP leaders. Comrades informed me that the meetings were for the purpose of sounding out the possibilities of uniting the two parties. This was the first I had heard of the Trotskyists, or of the fact that unity was even being contemplated. They pointed out Jim Cannon as one of the leaders of the Trotskyists. While he was greeting some of the comrades he knew, I took another look at him.

I saw a middle-aged, stocky man, of medium height, whose expression I read as suggesting an inner bitterness; who seemed unable to manage more than a wintry smile; who suggested, even while engaged in greetings, a heavy preoccupation. And he didn't particularly stand out from his group.

MORRIS CHERTOV was born in 1907. He was a member of the American Workers Party, led by A. J. Muste, and first worked with Cannon after the fusion with the Communist League of America in December 1934. He has been a trade unionist and active member of the Socialist Workers Party, most recently in Philadelphia, Chicago, and New Orleans.

There was nothing to suggest what I then somewhat romantically pictured as a revolutionary leader. He did not seem to have the appearance of a tribune of the people, or to be possessed of a revolutionary elan that breathed defiance of all the powers. Yet there was a sense of hardness, of toughness.

That this individual was to have the influence on my life that he did, and on so many others of us—that he would win us to a conviction that the cause of the world proletarian revolution should occupy the first place in our lives; that this grumpy-looking man was, in a year's time, to be the principal force in opening the door for us to so unexpected a view of the realities of the world—would have seemed simply incongruous. But, as I've said, first impressions regarding Jim Cannon could be misleading, and I suspect were to many.

Through the years that followed, I never reached an intimate personal relationship with Jim Cannon. I was regarded as one of Cannon's constant supporters in the proletarian cadre of the party. And so my recollections of him stem from party experiences, in which his knowledge, his theoretical powers, his abilities as a strategist and tactician became revealed. Since Cannon's personal life and party life were so closely intermeshed, observing him in his political role provided sufficient opportunity for insight into, and assessment of, his personality.

In the months that led up to the fusion, we met and heard a number of the CLA leaders. I heard Arne Swabeck speak at a CLA public meeting on Hitler's conquest of Germany. The speech and the discussion period left me profoundly astounded. And for a reason. Prior to Hitler's victory, one heard everywhere in New York City the conviction that Germany's fate would be decided by a death-struggle between the forces of the huge German Communist Party and Hitler's legions. After Hitler's victory over a nonresisting Communist Party, the ensuing fear and confusion led to meetings of all sorts, addressed by renowned speakers; prestigious publications carried analyses by the most authoritative figures—but their audiences and readers were left uneasy, dissatisfied, and still beset by unanswered questions.

Yet, here, an obscure speaker for an obscure organization, in a meeting of 300, cut through the whole fog of confusion with an easy assurance, laying bare what had been really at work in Germany, revealing the world forces focusing on it. He told how Trotsky had sounded a warning, long before the catastrophe, that Stalin was disorienting the German CP to the point of impotency.

He cited Trotsky's final urgent calls for the only course that offered any real hope—the united front of the German CP and SP against Hitler. And he drew the conclusion that these terrible events definitively marked the death of the Third International and made it necessary to build a new, Fourth International.

No one who heard this presentation could have helped but contrast its penetrating clarity with the pretentious superficiality of other talks we had heard by the "authoritative" and "renowned" representatives of the better-known tendencies on the New York left. (Not to speak of the liberal or bourgeois publications, which were delving into the darker regions, seeking the cause of Hitler's ascendancy in his apparently irresistible "mystical powers.")

It was my first experience with the illuminating power of authentic Marxism. I raided the literature table after the meeting and began to learn of the titanic struggle waged against the degenerative forces of Stalinism by the small forces led by Trotsky, and, in America, by James P. Cannon.

I heard other CLA speakers, like Max Shachtman, who definitely offered entertainment, but still was impressive as a speaker. Though my image of Cannon was enlarged by my reading, and occasionally hearing him, by contrast, he came through as "gray," his surface appearance at odds with the picture evoked by his record.

The fusion of the CLA and the AWP in December 1934 produced the Workers Party. The activist forces set to work with enthusiasm, those from the AWP unsuspecting the tumultuous internal life we would soon experience. In April 1935 the Oehler group broke loose, declaring opposition in principle to the "French turn." Hitler's victory had not only discredited the CPs of the world; it had also cast a heavy cloud on the SPs too. But in the world Social Democratic parties, left wings formed to fight for a more revolutionary policy. Trotsky had advised the French Trotskyist group to temporarily enter the French Socialist Party, to aid the budding left-wingers in finding a principled revolutionary policy. The Oehlerite sectarians considered it a violation of principle for the Trotskyist groups to give up their independent organizations. They feared that the WP leaders had their eyes on the American Socialist Party, within which a ferment to the left had developed.

The Oehlerites won over Muste, the former AWP leader, now Workers Party national secretary, to a bloc against Cannon and

Shachtman on this question. They were joined by the clique headed by Martin Abern. These internal developments put Cannon's forces into a minority on the National Committee, and in the ranks as well.

Continuing left-wing developments in the Socialist Party kept on raising the "French turn" issue in the WP. It all came to a head at the June 1935 plenum of the National Committee, held in New York. Its sessions were declared open to the membership.

Cannon, in his *History of American Trotskyism*, claims that it lasted three days. I am willing to take oath that its duration was at least five if not six days. I had never heard of any kind of meetings that lasted as long as these did—from 10:00 a.m. to 1:00, 2:00, and 3:00 o'clock the following morning! But I don't recall missing a minute of it.

Those from the CLA had been through such debates before and stood already on a higher level than those of us from the AWP, and new WP recruits. But even they had something to learn during the remarkable experience of that open plenum. It constituted a revolutionary course in Marxism.

While the first session was waiting to be called to order, Cannon could be seen sitting on the platform, among the National Committee, in front, his jacket off, sleeves rolled up, and arms folded. In contrast to the others, who exhibited varying degrees of tenseness, he appeared relaxed, his eyes apparently vacant, scanning the audience. Every so often, he took a swallow from a quart sitting on the floor beside him—a quart of milk! Former CLAers filled us in. True, Jim had a fondness for a glass of cheer, but when battle impended, his preparations included the soothing of an ulcer.

The appearance of this bottle of milk became invested with political omens. This was going to be a fight with no holds barred.

The general issue was the sectarian infection of the Oehlerites, and their anathemas hurled at the "French turn," their demand that solemn oath be sworn that even contemplation of a course toward intervention in the SP would never profane our minds.

But in contending against the sectarians, who took any turn in strategy or tactics as an open or hidden violation of principle, it became necessary to restate the whole basis, if not the whole experience, of Marxism. And that is what was done. Cannon reviewed the history of the movement, on a world scale and in the United States. In recalling earlier conflicts over principles, he distinguished between the basic principles of Marxism, which could be violated only by placing the future of the movement in jeopardy, and their tactical application, which could be quite flexible.

He discussed dialectical thinking, which perceived real class forces in motion and development, as opposed to the rigidity of the sectarians' thought, which was guided by abstract and sterile formulas. A failure on our part to see past the discredited Socialist Party label to the hundreds of revolutionary workers being drawn to the ranks of the SP would cut us off from these workers. These potential recruits to revolutionary socialism would fall prey to reformist or Stalinist leadership and instead of strengthening the revolutionary forces in America would be used against us by our enemies.

Shachtman, Swabeck, and others contributed importantly, each in their own way, to this encyclopedic discussion; but Cannon, overshadowing all, grew in stature, to the height of a master in our eyes—now no longer "gray," undefined. Gone was the dour expression. He became avidly alive. We began to understand that the inner tensions we had sensed were better compared to the vibrations of a tightly coiled spring, ready for release at an opportunity to lead forward.

His eyes now looked straight out at us, reading us. We were, under the banner of Trotskyism, the authentic heirs to a hundred years of Marxist struggle against forces seeking its destruction, often internal forces, that sought its end through attempts at corruption of the doctrine. We were heirs to great traditions, which, if absorbed in our blood and bone, would ennoble our lives. We were heirs to great conquests in the realm of theory—our theory was the generalization of hard and bloodily bought revolutionary experience, which, properly applied, would illuminate our problems. The historic revolution of 1917 was ours, its defense from internal and external attack was our proud privilege. Our theory analyzed sectarianism, how it could destroy us, in this period of rapid, deepgoing change.

Cannon's style was distinctively in a class by itself. His speech was not bespangled with glittering phrases, or coldly aloof in the realm of the abstract. His delivery was full-voiced, never slipping into inaudibility. He taught us, over the years, that the responsibility to make oneself heard and understood rested solely with the speaker. Especially for a revolutionary spokesperson, who dealt with conceptions usually higher than the level of those addressed. Thus, practicing what he preached, Cannon could be easily heard everywhere, his diction clear, his voice rarely ascending in volume. The forms his thought took reflected his shaping in the actual workers' struggles, where he had learned the high art of distilling a complex thought into simple phrases, without losing content, depth, or flow. And an undertone beat with the living reality of the present, and of the past; not from the remoteness of a mere observer, but from that of one long a participant, of one completely involved and committed to the depths of his being. From those depths welled an optimism, mature and tested, as to our future.

His presentations were sprinkled with analogies, but unlike Shachtman, who chose obscure and barely known events, Cannon would strike home with earthy epigrams drawn from his Midwest origins. Thus, to illustrate the potential of our movement: "In Kansas, cyclone country, we learned to watch the horizon for a small, ink-black cloud, no bigger than your fist!" Or, in deriding some seriously propounded fantasy: "Where I come from, there has always been a lot of talk about a purple cow—but no one has ever yet claimed to have seen one."

Muste, obdurate, his narrow conceptions revealed, lost many of his followers, including those, like myself, who had developed a sense of personal loyalty to him. A group of us demonstrated this by approaching him during a lull in the meeting, and telling him that we were convinced he was dead wrong. Then we moved over to where Cannon was sitting, and told him that we had broken with Muste, and were now supporting him.

His reaction showed his probity as a political leader. His grouping had entered the plenum as a minority, and under a cloud of suspicion. Our statement to him reflected an important break in the ranks toward his stand. Did he respond effusively in any way? Did he shake our hands? Did he even smile? Not Cannon. Inner-party "politiking" of this kind, and that is how he would have seen it, was simply not in his makeup. He simply looked at us, deeply and penetratingly. I saw his eyes close up— and at this moment, how complexly expressive they were. I read his glance as absorbing our statement's meaning and its possible scope in the context of the situation; a trace of doubt as to whether we had really comprehended all that we had heard, knowing our limited background; possibly a trace of feeling for Muste, whom he liked, at the blow he had received—then, with just a trace of warmth, a simple affirmative nod of acknowledgment. Which was enough for us.

There had been two new members sitting with me. They had been on the National Committee of the Young Communist League, and had been sent by the YCL to the Soviet Union, by way of Germany, prior to Hitler's victory. What they saw in Germany, regarding the way CP leaders sabotaged the desperate efforts of CP and YCL units to form true united fronts with Socialist Party units against the Nazis, the circumstances of Hitler's victory, stunned them, and led to their investigation of Trotskyism. They joined about two months before the June plenum. Later, over a cup of coffee, they poured out their amazement at the command and practice of Marxism-Leninism they had just experienced. They expressed their view of what a contrast existed between the CP and the WP, and their regret at having wasted seven years in the CP and at having been taken in by anti-Trotskyism. They knew many of the national leaders of the CP, for whom they felt the deepest contempt, stating that not one of them could come within a mile of an ordinary branch leader of the WP.

I lived at 110th Street, and two or three times walked the five miles from Twelfth Street, in the quiet early morning hours, attempting to digest, to put into some order, the tremendous store of knowledge poured into my aching head.

What my layer in the movement was experiencing was Cannon's method in fitting us for the new tasks that faced Trotskyists. First, educate the whole party as to the new realities appearing, through a truly democratic discussion of conflicting views. To comprehend the evolution of the new, developing out of the old, in conflict with it, the contending class forces at work that produced them, how to think about them; to be on guard that the outward form not deceive us as to the true inner content. And finally, to know how to make up our minds as to what to do next, and at the right time with all highly conscious of the task—do it!

Cannon taught us better than anyone else how to view leadership; not first of all as an honor, but above all as a responsibility. The higher a leader stood on the rung of the ladder, the more profound a responsibility had been incurred. Jim Cannon had to win the standing he held, but in the movement he led in building, such standing was determined by the membership.

Cannon, in many ways, made clear that while he was the first leader, he was first among equals. It is impossible to picture Cannon acting the mandarin, or affecting an air of self-importance. Not that he didn't understand his importance—but it never inflamed his ego. If anything, the responsibility of his standing wracked him. I believe he examined, and reexamined himself pitilessly, seeking out weaknesses that might prove injurious to the movement, and if found, to seek ways to offset, or compensate for them.

I haven't heard all of Cannon's speeches, but in my experience the most memorable one was his address at the 1946 convention of the party, in Chicago. He spoke on the coming American revolution. His audience consisted of delegates and visitors, who at that time were mainly industrial workers, part of the historic strike wave that was sweeping the country.

No theme unleashed the depths in Cannon like that of the coming American revolution. It encompassed his whole life's experience, meaning, and purpose. It had shaped and formed his every fiber, every nerve, his dreams and passions. So, what came forth was not a cold clinical dissection. Neither was it even suggestive of demagogic bombast, or of a blind, maudlin, affirmation.

When he reached the area of how the American proletarian revolution would be the climactic event of the world revolution, auguring its speedy completion; when he drew the genesis of the American working class, its metamorphosis on the anvil under the hammer of capitalism; its shaping into the conquering power of the future—one could sense that all he knew embellished the theme with a class fervor that penetrated the beings of all there.

During the long address, the assemblage sat transfixed. Eyes glowed, bodies tense, one could, literally, have heard a pin drop.

With his concluding words—". . . to organize and lead them to storm and victory!"—a thunder of applause crashed forth that explosively testified how deeply that speech had entered the hearts as well as the consciousness of all there.

Yes, Cannon was a great orator. His speeches, though carefully, even painfully prepared, were given that effort toward most fully fashioning his best expression of that which he most deeply and honestly understood and felt. It would have been completely out of character for him to include an oratorical gimmick to artificially evoke a response.

He understood his class, its psychology, its changing moods, its varied reactions to events. There was nothing artificial, nothing forced, about his optimism, for, as one who best reflected the proletariat, he understandably reflected that quality that is so distinctive of it. But this was highly reinforced by his mastery of

Marxism-Leninism, now expressed as Trotskyism, and its scientifically demonstrated conclusions as to the working class's ultimate victory.

Viewing Cannon's six decades of service to the movement, and the sharp, jolting shifts he experienced, from triumphs to isolation, might prompt the question: did Cannon ever experience despair? This question has been asked regarding many of the great leaders, from Marx and Engels on. I feel that there have been too many instances of answers that were unreal. There have been denials that during the dedicated lifetimes of the great, they never wavered in their devotion. To present such an image is to remove those leaders from comprehension as human beings, from any possibility to identify with.

Those who compose the movement quite naturally seek in the great leaders of the past models to try to emulate. But what relevance can they find in their hour of personal crisis, when they find themselves wavering in their commitment to the movement, in figures drawn out of human context?

Yes, Cannon, like all his great predecessors, knew his moments of despair. Some of them he has publicly spoken of. Others, I for one, witnessed personally, when he spoke of them to me. But we also witnessed how his great fighting heart rebounded, overcoming the weakness. So the point, the point that permits of human comprehension, is that the despair was only for a moment.

Anne Chester

How does one of my generation view Jim Cannon? Jim was part and parcel of our political lives, and for a fortunate few a close part of personal life as well.

Jim was complex and many-sided, a very human being with a tremendous sense of humor, both subtle and broad. He had a real feel for and a sensitivity to people to an extraordinary degree. These characteristics, together with his highly developed political acumen and conviction that an enduring revolutionary party could not be built on anything less than a collective leadership based on a firm body of revolutionary principles and program, enabled him to unite people of varied abilities, strengths and weaknesses into a party that has stood the test of forty-six years.

Just consider—Jim built the initial cadres of the American Trotskyist movement with such diverse people as Max Shachtman, Marty Abern, and Albert Goldman, each of whom had some very good qualities as well as serious weaknesses. On this point Jim taught us a basic political lesson: never compromise our revolutionary principles in a political struggle with those who break with the party for whatever reason; but always give them the credit they have earned for the valuable contributions they had made to the Trotskyist movement.

ANNE CHESTER was born in 1905. She joined the Conference for Progressive Labor Action (predecessor of the American Workers Party) in 1932 and participated in the fusion with the Communist League of America in December 1934. She first met Cannon while working in the Paterson, New Jersey, silk mills in 1934 and worked with him in New York between 1940 and 1944. She has been a silkworker, a machinist, and a waitress, and in the late 1950s and early 1960s worked in Pioneer Publishers, the Trotskyist publishing house of the time. These remarks were made at a meeting in San Francisco on September 14, 1974.

The fusion between the Communist League of America and the American Workers Party took place in December 1934. We of the AWP who became part of the Workers Party of the U.S.—the new name of the fused organization and the forerunner of the SWP—carried with us a great suspicion of Cannon based on the fear that he and his comrades would make internationalists of us. But we had great faith in Muste and continued to look to him for leadership in the united organization. Six months later an internal struggle developed between Oehler and Muste on one side, and Cannon and Shachtman on the other over the question of entry into the Socialist Party. As in all struggles of deepgoing political differences, rumors and slanders ran rampant, aimed especially at Cannon. I wanted to hear Cannon's answer to the charges, but they remained unanswered. Jim patiently waited for the political differences to develop until they became clear to the entire membership, brushing aside all such secondary matters as slanders, so that decisions would be made on the issues that counted—the political issues.

In the process of this tremendously educational battle, Muste proved himself incapable of revolutionary political thinking and our attitude, which previously had been that of children looking up to our papa, began to change. We became convinced that Trotskyism—internationalism—was the correct road to the socialist revolution and that Jim Cannon understood how to use the Marxist method in daily tactical application toward the achievement of our goal.

There were many instances of sharp differences between Cannon and other comrades on important questions, but when the differences were resolved not the slightest shred of animosity remained. The best example that I know of is the relationship that existed between Jim and John G. Wright, known as Usick in the party.

In the early years of the Communist League of America these two took a different position on nearly every question that came up. But when their differences were resolved, a good working relationship was established and Jim and Usick became very close friends as well as comrades. That friendship lasted until Usick's death in 1956. Cannon wrote a beautiful tribute to Usick which appears in *Speeches for Socialism.* Jim's book *Letters from Prison* shows their relationship at work, where Usick's vast knowledge, which runs like a thread throughout the letters, helped Jim study his way through prison.

During the Second World War we had several seamen comrades

who risked their lives on ships delivering matériel to Murmansk, that northernmost port of the Soviet Union above the Arctic Circle. We lost some of them to the submarines and airplanes operating under and over those icy seas. Jim made it a point to see every seaman who returned, to listen to his experiences, bring him up to date, and to inquire about those who had not yet returned.

I remember one Saturday night at a party—Jim attended all the party's social events in those days—where who should walk in but Abe Marcus, the latest returnee from the Murmansk run. Jim threw his arms around Abe, hugging him with great joy. Another comrade had survived the horrors of the imperialist war.

There is another interesting story that points up the impish glee Jim took in certain peculiar situations. The Soviet Union had made a practice of giving a bonus to seamen who survived the run to Murmansk. One of Jim's friends, Jack Maloney, was a recipient of the bonus. When Jack got back he decided the best thing to do was to use that bonus money from the Soviet Union to outfit Jim in some badly needed new clothes. Sitting near Jim at the party that evening, I commented on how nice he looked and asked if that was a new suit. With great pride Jim replied, "Yes indeed, and it's of very high quality. You know who bought it for me? Joe Stalin. See these beautiful new Florsheim shoes? Also bought by Stalin. And the shirt, and the tie, and the sox. Stalin also bought me the underwear I have on, but I can't show that to you."

James P. Cannon, Jim to all of us, was a great man. As a human being he had faults which no one understood better than he himself. As a political being, with his Leninist organizational methods he welded together an assortment of people with a variety of backgrounds into a tight revolutionary fist, holding firm to the principles and program that will lead the socialist revolution which is surely coming—if not today, then tomorrow.

George Breitman

The first time I spoke with James P. Cannon was in January 1936, at his flat in a tenement on East Thirteenth Street in New York. It was shortly before his forty-sixth birthday and my twentieth.

On the preceding night the members of the "Cannon-Shachtman caucus" in the Newark branch of the Workers Party had held a meeting to discuss their strategy for electing branch delegates to the national Workers Party convention scheduled for the end of February. The faction headed by Cannon and Max Shachtman was proposing that the Workers Party be dissolved so that its members could enter the Socialist Party to win over its left wing to our ideas.

A letter from Cannon was read about the faction's urgent need of financial contributions from its supporters, and a collection was taken. As faction secretary I had the job of transmitting the money. Since I had no access to a checkbook and was going to New York the next day for another purpose, I decided to deliver it in person at the national faction's address on Thirteenth Street.

I didn't know this was the home of Cannon and Rose Karsner until I got there. I didn't know much about Cannon at all, although I had heard him speak a couple of times. In fact, I knew little about politics altogether, being a relatively new member.

It was well after eleven in the morning when I mounted the stairs and rang the bell. Nothing happened, so I rang several more times, and was about to leave when the door opened

---

GEORGE BREITMAN was born in 1916. He joined the Workers Party in 1935 and worked with Cannon while serving as editor of the *Militant* in the 1940s. He has edited a number of books by Trotsky and Malcolm X.

111

partway. There was Jim, clad only in slippers and a towel held around his middle, still damp from the bath or shower I had interrupted.

Jim was of medium height and without excess weight for a man of his age. His body was sturdy but starting to go soft; the shoulders had already taken on a slight stoop, and his hair was turning iron gray. His eyebrows were raised in mild surprise, but otherwise he appeared unruffled.

It seemed to me, not yet liberated from my puritanical training, that it was not fitting for a leader of the revolutionary movement to be taking a bath so late in the day. But I smothered the thought, mumbled an apology, thrust an envelope with the money into the hand that was not occupied with the towel, briefly explained its purpose, and left hastily without giving my name.

The incident reminds me, perhaps incongruously, of something about Jim that struck me later when I got to know him better: under all the circumstances in which I saw him, public and private, he always bore himself with great dignity. It was the kind of natural dignity that I associate with other leaders who must have known themselves well and were sure of what they were doing—people like Malcolm X and the George Washington of the legends. I suppose that people who knew him intimately, and saw him under the stresses and strains of everyday life and tribulation, could offer testimony to modify this impression. I should add that I never heard him say anything vulgar or petty, even about people he disliked or was fighting politically.

An important responsibility of the older and more experienced members of the revolutionary movement is to help educate the newer and younger members. The main way is to set a good example, but when mistakes are made, direct criticism is necessary.

All the mentors and teachers in my eight-year apprenticeship were considerate and restrained. But no one was more tactful than Jim in making criticisms of the younger members. Sometimes I didn't perceive until later that he had been making one.

In September 1937, shortly after our expulsion from the Socialist Party in Newark, we acquired a headquarters at Market and Mulberry Streets and announced a series of Sunday night forums, the first of which was to be a talk by Jim. Fixing up the headquarters took longer than we had counted on, and we didn't complete work on the forum area until about an hour before the forum was to begin. Everyone else went out for a bite, leaving one member to sit at the door and me to retire to the office area, strewn with lumber and debris, where I lay down on the floor to rest. No sooner had I got comfortable than Jim came in. He urged me not to get up, and sat by the window, looking down at Market Street and puffing on his pipe.

When the audience began to arrive, I told him I was too dirty and tired to go out into the hall with him and would listen to his talk from the office. He said he understood and got up from the window. "This is kind of a Bowery neighborhood, isn't it?" he said. It was more like a statement of fact than a question.

Not knowing anything about the Bowery in New York, I didn't know what he was driving at, and didn't have the sense to ask. Instead, I explained that it was a very good location because we were only one block south of Broad and Market Streets, which was the main center of the city, where almost all the buses passed, etc. He didn't answer that and went out into the forum hall.

Later I realized that he had been questioning our choice of neighborhood for the headquarters. He had come to Newark by the Hudson Tubes, getting off at Penn Station, three or so blocks south of our headquarters. Walking north on Market Street he had passed a plentiful number of bars, honkytonks, drunks, panhandlers, and at least one burlesque house. He didn't want the party associated in any way with bohemianism, lumpenpro-letarianism, or anything else that might prejudice workers against us, not even geographically.

I didn't begin to see Jim regularly until after the SWP's national convention in July 1939, when I became a member of the National Committee and started attending meetings of the Political Committee, where I could hear Jim and the other central leaders discuss the most important issues facing the movement. The more I learned politically, the higher he rose in my opinion.

Then World War II began in Europe, setting off the bitter factional struggle in the SWP that resulted in the serious split by Shachtman, Burnham, and their followers in 1940. Everything I had learned in the preceding years—from Shachtman as well as Cannon—combined to make me a member of the Cannon faction that saved the SWP from the degeneration that overcame the Shachtmanites.

In June 1941, the FBI raided our headquarters in Minneapolis and St. Paul in obvious preparation for the prosecution of the SWP and its leaders. Partly as a result of this I was transferred from the post of Newark organizer to member of the *Militant's* editorial staff, which had been badly depleted by the departure of the Shachtmanites. My credentials as a journalist were rather meager outside of some local writing I had done, but it was thought that I might learn the ropes under the tutelage of the *Militant's* editor, Felix Morrow. Anyhow, Jim's small office adjoined the editorial room on the third floor of the SWP headquarters at 116 University Place in New York, so I now saw him more frequently, almost daily.

Working on the *Militant* staff was a great educational experience, but before I could catch my breath the government handed down its indictments charging the SWP leaders with sedition and violation of the recently adopted Smith Act, and two months later the central leaders of the party took off for Minneapolis to prepare for trial. Since Morrow was one of the people indicted, I ended up, somehow, as acting editor of the paper. As basic training periods go, it was on the short side.

In November, around a week before the Minneapolis trial ended, I committed a bad blunder in the paper. As readers can see in *Socialism on Trial,* the book containing Jim's testimony at the trial, the government prosecutors had combed through the writings of Marx, Lenin, and Trotsky for selected quotations designed to show that they favored force and violence to overthrow capitalism, and they kept firing these quotations at Jim to support their claim that as avowed supporters of Marx, Lenin, and Trotsky the SWP defendants must also be advocates of violence.

Then, in the midst of the trial, the *Militant* appeared with an article entitled "Trotsky Showed How to Defend the Soviet Union." It consisted of a long selection from a 1934 Trotsky pamphlet stating that in wartime "The policy of a proletarian party . . . should therefore be directed towards the revolutionary overthrow of the bourgeoisie and the seizure of power," whether or not that bourgeoisie was allied to the Soviet Union. To avoid ambiguity, the selection was preceded by an unsigned introduction explaining that Trotsky's remarks "retain their full force and pertinacity to this day."

My excuse was that we were very shorthanded on the *Militant* staff at that time. When the head of the SWP education department, one of my seniors, gave me the article I read it rapidly, grateful that I had something to fill a hole. Besides, it was by Trotsky, something we had all read many times, so what objection could there be to reprinting it? (That was the last time I ever gave a perfunctory reading to any article for the paper, no matter who submitted or wrote it.)

Fortunately, the prosecutors didn't see my blunder in time, or maybe by then they were too discouraged by the way Jim on the witness stand had handled all their other carefully chosen quotations.

But I did hear about it as soon as the paper reached Minneapolis. Charlie Curtiss, who was holding down the national office while I was holding down the *Militant,* gave me what was probably a watered-down, expletive-deleted version of the message from the defendants. I asked if Jim in particular had said anything, and Charlie said Jim had told him the article was fine but the timing was poor.

Still blushing, I started to discuss this incident several weeks later, in January 1942, when Jim, Farrell Dobbs, and Felix Morrow asked me in to the national office to propose that I become editor of the *Militant.* They and fifteen of the other Minneapolis defendants had been convicted under the Smith Act charge and sentenced to federal prison the day after the bombing of Pearl Harbor, but were out on bail while the verdict was being appealed. The U.S. had entered the war formally as a belligerent, and we were beginning to brace ourselves for prosecution under the antisubversive laws that automatically went into effect with the declaration of war. In an attempt to make it harder for the government to go after the SWP, our basic manifesto on U.S. entry into the war was issued in the form of a statement signed by Jim rather than by the SWP.

When I tried to bring up my blunder over the Trotsky selection, Jim brushed it aside. On the other hand, he didn't engage in any flattery about my great editorial potential. In World War I, he said, the government had always gone after the editors of antiwar papers, and there was a good chance they would do the same now. Felix, who was still listed as editor of the *Militant,* had just received a prison sentence—it didn't seem fair or equitable that he should get another merely because he was editor. Besides, the national office wanted him to concentrate on writing for our magazine. They were confident that as a good party member I would do a creditable job, whatever happened.

Pleased by this expression of confidence, and even more pleased by the straight talk, I went no further with my doubts and reservations about my ability to handle the job. When I said I would need a lot of help, Jim promised that I could count on that.

Jim and the other Minneapolis trial defendants went off to serve their prison sentences at the beginning of 1944, a few weeks after I was drafted into the army. When I returned in 1946 and became acting editor of the *Militant*, I used to see him again frequently in New York until he moved permanently to Los Angeles in the 1950s.

Our relations in these years were always friendly (except in 1953, when I refused to join the majority faction until long after he thought I should have). By "friendly" I mean that they were cordial, that we worked together easily, but not that we were friends. Our age differential and the teacher-pupil relationship militated against that. He never invited me to his home, nor I him to mine. But we often went out to lunch together, usually with other comrades like John G. Wright or George Clarke, and infrequently alone, and the conversation sometimes would range beyond the purely political. Also, he would stroll into the editorial office when it was not busy and we would exchange information about things we had read that we thought might interest the other.

He followed the *Militant* closely, down to the most insignificant details. Once he asked why, in the datelines at the beginning of news articles, I was spelling March and April as "Mar." and "Apr." I told him that the prevailing newspaper practice was to abbreviate the month in datelines, as he could verify by checking any of the New York dailies. But when he suggested that I check it too, I discovered that the abbreviating practice applied only to the seven months that contained more than five letters.

Most of his criticisms were, of course, political. In January 1942 the first United Nations declaration was signed in Washington, and I wrote an article pointing out the worthlessness of promises in all such declarations and pacts. Jim called me aside to complain that I had put the Soviet Union, one of the signers, on the same plane as the imperialist powers, or at least had not sufficiently differentiated the workers' state from them. Feeling that the criticism was unwarranted (I saw a clear distinction between the workers' state and *Stalin's* diplomacy), I said

nothing but was somewhat offended. Sensing this, he changed
the subject a little by asking if I knew why it was that I wrote less
formalistically, more popularly, and with greater feeling about
the Negro struggle than I did on other subjects. It was probably
an attempt to soften his rebuke by indicating that he did not
dislike all my articles.

The only time I saw Jim lose control of himself over something
in our paper occurred when we printed in a "Notes from the
News" column a sentence about an announcement by a Detroit
United Auto Workers leader that he and his wife were going to be
divorced. Shortly after the new issue arrived from the printshop,
Jim came marching out of his office into ours, waving the paper
and so incensed that his face was red. By God, he exclaimed to no
one in particular, such a thing was impermissible in the *Militant*!
It was not a scandal sheet, and who was divorcing whom was
none of its damned business! And so on, before he turned and left.
He was always very strong on what was proper and improper,
and absolute respect for personal privacy was high on his proper
list.

In some ways Jim's ideas about the paper were old-fashioned.
About the size of its pages, for example. When he was growing
up, a large format was considered the mark of a serious paper
while a tabloid format was associated with sensational or
scandal-mongering sheets, and he retained this prejudice most of
his life. By the end of World War II most union and radical
papers had switched over to tabloid size, and so had many
metropolitan dailies following the success of the New York *Daily
News*. But when a number of people on the editorial staff and in
the national office proposed going over to a tabloid *Militant*, Jim
resisted it with all kinds of arguments. And even after he was
voted down in the Political Committee he was able, thanks to the
higher price that the printshop said a tabloid would cost, to
postpone the change until several years after he left New York.

In addition to being a close reader of the *Militant* Jim was also,
in the years I am writing about, its best writer. Trotsky's articles
had been the chief political attraction of the paper up to his death
in 1940; thereafter Jim's were the most eagerly read and
appreciated. It was also during this period, I think, that his style
flowered and matured and took on the characteristics that were
so distinctively his own. Many of the best have been reprinted in
Notebook of an Agitator (Pathfinder Press, 1973), which was also

the title of his occasional column in the paper. Rereading them now, I note with some surprise that many consist of what today might be called "cultural criticism."

The articles Jim submitted were the stuff that editors dream of—clean, carefully constructed, and complete. He worked and reworked them, rearranging and polishing them with the conscientiousness and devotion that both craftsmen and artists give to their work. In part this was possible because he usually did not write for a deadline, but it was also because in his writings as in his speeches he was guided by the maxim that anything worth doing is worth doing well. My complaint that he did not write more for publication has to be balanced against the fact that what he did publish was of the highest quality.

He himself reminded me that as editor I had the formal right to change his copy: Feel free to fix something that is wrong or unclear, he said, but please don't rewrite me. But I was a light editor anyway and knew enough not to try to improve things so good; and when I did have a suggestion I was usually able to consult him about it before acting on it. On one rare occasion, when I couldn't reach him, I decided that in a phrase he had used, "the indispensable *sine qua non*," either the "indispensable" or the "sine qua non" was redundant, and deleted one of them. He winced but said nothing when he saw it in the paper.

Unlike some other writers, who fretted about their articles after they had submitted them and had second thoughts after the articles had been set in type, there was only one time Jim asked to reexamine an article in the late stages of production. That was in July 1950, shortly after the start of the Korean War, when he wrote his memorable first "Letter to the President and Members of the Congress" denouncing Washington's imperialist intervention in the Korean civil war. As we were putting the final touches on the issue in which this open letter was spread across the top of the front page, he appeared and asked to read it again. After he had gone through it, he made a few minor changes, which we still had time to effect. He must have been especially concerned about the political nuances—the postwar witch-hunt was getting worse every day.

I pleaded with him several times to let us run his Notebook column on the front page, and to have it signed with his full name. But he was quite obstinate about keeping it on the second page, where it was usually signed only with his initials.

On a number of occasions Jim was charged, during factional fights, with being hostile to "the youth" (in the party or its youth affiliate) or of not appreciating their contributions or of preventing them from playing a greater role in the party leadership. These charges were usually made by factional opponents fishing for support among the younger and less experienced members, who did not hesitate to exploit the generation gap to mobilize sentiment against "Cannonite conservatism."

If there had been an iota of truth in these charges I surely would have detected it in the dozens of youth-related discussions and conversations I heard Jim participate in during the 1940s and early 1950s. There simply wasn't any truth in them. Jim felt as great an affinity for young revolutionaries and rebels as anyone could possibly feel. There was no contradiction between that feeling and his belief that flattering or courting "the youth" was neither in their interest nor in the party's or his conviction that they should be tested in the class struggle before being promoted to party leadership.

But when continuity or experience were being ridiculed, or when the old-timers of the movement were being baited as having outlived their usefulness, Jim sometimes would lose his temper and answer his critics with expressions that played into their hands. I recall one such incident at the SWP national convention held in Chicago in November 1946.

At the end of this convention Felix Morrow was expelled for persistent violations of party discipline. Before that happened the convention was subjected to a series of tirades at every point on the agenda by the two or three delegates representing Morrow's point of view. One of these was a particularly obnoxious type—a petty-bourgeois radical who knew it all and made Jim the prime target of his lectures to us backward elements. I must admit that he had a pronounced talent for getting under people's skins.

Jim answered him very effectively, dissecting his arguments and exposing their true content. But he spoiled it for me somewhat when he referred to the Morrowite as "this young whippersnapper." I told Jim about my reaction after the convention. "I've looked up the meaning of whippersnapper," I said, "and it almost could have been invented to describe that guy. But what has his age got to do with his whippersnapperism?" Jim thought about it for a moment, then said it had been a mistake. And he went on to tell how "allergic" he had become to that type ever since he first met it among the Lovestoneites in the early days of the Communist Party.

Part of the problem, I think, arose from the fact that Jim was older than virtually everyone else in the central leadership of our movement and this affected his concept of where youth began and ended. Recently I read for the first time the transcript of unpublished remarks Jim made at the close of the November 1943 plenum of the SWP National Committee. I attended most of the plenum but had to leave before the end because I was being drafted early the next morning. Jim was defending himself against charges by Morrow and Albert Goldman that he was hostile to "the youth," and among other examples he mentioned me as evidence that promising young candidates for leadership met with cooperation and not resistance from him. And Breitman, he said, was "a mere boy." Hell, I was then twenty-seven years old, that is, the same age Farrell Dobbs had been when he was leading Minneapolis truck drivers in their 1934 strikes, and older than Trotsky had been when he was leading the soviets in the 1905 revolution.

Jim's sense of humor had a wide range—sharp or savage when aimed at the class enemy; sarcastic toward opponents in the labor and radical movements; more on the wry or ironical side when it was about ourselves. At lunch he used to enjoy relating or hearing accounts taken from the day's newspapers that emphasized the ludicrousness of bourgeois politics or morality. Sipping his beer and fastidiously munching his ham or corned beef sandwich, he would lift his eyebrows and shrug his shoulders slightly as though to say, What a crazy world—you'll go crazy too if you don't learn to laugh.

Jim was not above practical jokes, and he played one on me once as a way of underlining his complaint that I did not speak often enough at committee meetings or conventions. It was at our 1942 national convention, where Jim had given the main political report. In the discussion from the floor that followed, he noticed that many of the delegates were concentrating their remarks around what we then called the Negro struggle, so he asked me to jot down some notes on the points they were raising that I thought might be useful for him in his summary. I did the best I could, and passed them to him before he began his summary. Jim spoke on other points but said nothing about the subject of my notes until the end, when he told the delegates that I was better informed about current developments in the Negro struggle than he was and that he was turning over the remainder of his summary time for me to comment on them and related questions raised during the delegate discussion. With that, he left my notes on the speaker's stand and sat down. I managed to stammer a few things. From the expression on his face I gathered that he viewed it as some kind of joke, but I didn't think it at all funny, even though the only thing I was forced to do was read my own notes.

While he felt I didn't speak often enough at meetings, he thought I spoke too much—or in the wrong way—when I was in the chair. I was a light editor but a heavy chairman, insisting not only that sessions begin on time but also that speakers should stop promptly at the end of the time allotted to them by the convention or plenum rules, ten minutes or whatever. Jim thought I was too formalistic about this in general, but especially in connection with the older leaders who, he pointed out to me, sometimes had more to say and should be allowed to finish their remarks without interruption by the chair. I retorted that if they had more to say then they should ask the body to extend their time and if the delegates wanted them to say more, they would extend it, whatever I as chairman thought. Once he hissed something at me when I told a venerable comrade that his time was up. After the meeting I asked him if he realized how ludicrous it looked for veteran leaders to be trying to chisel an extra half-minute or two more speaking time. Why didn't they organize their remarks better so that their precious final point could be stated earlier, and why didn't they ask for an extension of time instead of making spectacles of themselves? But I am afraid Jim's sense of humor deserted him in such circumstances.

In 1939, a month or two after the war began in Europe, Jim spoke at an SWP election rally in Newark where most of the people in the audience were members of the local unemployed movement, middle aged and Black. So Jim spent part of his talk discussing the conditions of the jobless as the government prepared to enter the war. All went well until he spoke of the "niggardly" allotments that relief clients were getting while billions were being appropriated for military purposes. At that point a large portion of the audience froze on him. Being a skilled speaker, he sensed it immediately, but he couldn't figure out why it had happened. When he finished, to little applause, the chairman, a young Black worker who also was unacquainted with the word Jim had used, felt it necessary to assure the audience that "Comrade Cannon didn't mean any harm when he used the word 'niggerly.'" Jim looked ready to sink through the floor. I don't think he ever used the word "niggardly" again, in speech or print.

Jim found it very difficult, often impossible, to concentrate on more than one important problem or project at a time; he himself didn't know whether to call this a curse or a blessing. It certainly was not a blessing insofar as it affected his work as the party's chief executive officer, and was responsible for his not being a good administrator. Fortunately, beginning in 1940, he received the able collaboration in the national office of people like Farrell Dobbs and Morris Stein, who took most of the administrative load onto their own shoulders and freed him for other work, both political and literary. This not only made the SWP more effective organizationally but also, I believe, facilitated the flowering of Jim's writing talent during that decade.

Administration requires attention to details, sometimes minor or dull, and to a certain amount of routine; no organization can be maintained without them. There is of course the danger that attention to routine can become transformed into routinism, which makes it hard to recognize new conditions and easy to miss opportunities for expanded political action and organizational growth. Jim was not only a critic but a violent enemy of all signs of routinism, and he was always among the first to call the party to arms against it. But lack of attention or indifference to routine questions can also lead to political and organizational mistakes. An example involving Jim occurred in the spring of 1940, shortly after the Shachtmanite split.

The SWP in New Jersey had decided to run me for U.S. senator and was about to collect the nominating petitions for a place on the ballot in November. The New Jersey ballot requirements were the most liberal in the country, and we were not only sure of a place on the ballot for senator but also could have a presidential slate on the same ballot without getting additional signatures. So I went over to New York to ask the national office to consider running the SWP's first presidential campaign that year, even if only in a few states. Jim was very firmly against my proposal, on the ground that we did not have the forces to get on the ballot in New York State, where our membership was the largest; and he persuaded me not to carry the proposal further. A little later, in June, when Jim and other SWP leaders visited Trotsky in Mexico, the SWP's failure to run a presidential candidate served Trotsky as a takeoff point for his criticisms of SWP policy (see "Discussions with Trotsky" in *Writings of Leon Trotsky (1939-40),* Pathfinder Press, 1973).

Jim may have been right in contending that we didn't have the forces to get on the presidential ballot in New York in 1940 (although we did it with substantially the same forces the first time we tried eight years later). But the way he reached his conclusion was faulty, because, as he admitted several years later when I reminded him of the incident, he reached it on the basis of reports he recalled about the difficulties of Communist Party ballot work in New York *in the 1920s,* and not by taking the routine trouble to make an examination of the problems and the forces available in 1940.

But some of the traits that hampered Jim as an administrator seemed to work the other way in his far more decisive role of revolutionary politician. If he avoided being worn down by routine, he always was able to summon up the energy needed for special occasions—to take advantage of new opportunities in the class struggle, to mobilize our maximum response to attacks from the government and our political opponents, or to challenges from inside the party to the revolutionary integrity and orientation of the organization. Then he was like a man transformed, no longer so easygoing or tolerant of our weaknesses and sins of omission, no longer like the gladiator resting and waiting before the bell sounds. In times of crisis he was always at the top of his form, giving everything he had and inspiring others to do the same. He was a master of timing in political matters, and he evidently had also learned how to pace himself so that he could contribute his maximum when it counted the most. He did not have Trotsky's almost superhuman capacity to chain himself to his desk and drive himself to do whatever needed to be done, even in the most unpromising circumstances, and he did not write all the books or complete all the projects that he had hoped to do. But his political-literary output, which together with the party he built constitutes his legacy, was considerable, as will be seen when the best of his uncollected articles, speeches, and letters are published.

In seeking to assess Jim's strengths and weaknesses, it helps to view him alongside the movement that molded and shaped him and his generation. Elsewhere (in *Towards an American Socialist Revolution,* Pathfinder Press, 1971) I have discussed the three major periods of radicalization that have occurred in this country in this century. The first was the period associated with the name of Eugene V. Debs, which began around the start of the century and came to an end during U.S. participation in World War I or soon after; the second was the Great Depression-industrial unionization period, which began in the early thirties and ended with the outbreak of the cold war after World War II; the third began around 1960 and was still alive and deepening when Jim died.

Despite their differences and disparities, there is a clear line of continuity through these three radicalizations since each represented a mass response to the changing conditions of class and social struggle under capitalism and each nourished the growth of movements to fight the capitalists. This line of continuity is personified by a small number of people who succeeded in surviving as revolutionaries from the first into the third of these radicalizations. Jim was an outstanding example, probably the outstanding example, because he not only remained a revolutionary to the end but he also managed to maintain rapport and the ability to communicate with the best elements of the third radicalization. A striking instance was his perceptive and positive reaction to the beginning of the antiwar movement in 1965, shortly before his failing health compelled him to withdraw from active political participation (see his speech on "Revolutionary Policies in the Antiwar Movement" in *Revolutionary Strategy in the Fight Against the Vietnam War* [Education for Socialists Bulletin, 1975]).

Jim was a product of the Debsian radicalization. He embodied its main virtues—its honesty, courage, activism, and revolutionary idealism. He also shared, in his youth, its worst defects—its provincialism and its ignorance of theory, strategy, and tactics. But he wasn't just a product of the Debsian radicalization. Because he was able, after the Russian revolution led by the authentic Marxists in 1917, to do what most of his political generation could not do—he recognized the shortcomings of the pre-1917 American movement, rose above them, studied and became a Marxist, and dedicated the rest of his life to the construction of the revolutionary party at home and abroad.

In the task of building the first communist party on American soil Jim was of course not alone. But by 1928 the overwhelming majority of the charter members of the Communist Party had given up the struggle, discouraged and demoralized by objective conditions and subjective difficulties. More than that: virtually all of his peers in the CP leadership, who had set out after 1917 on the same road he had chosen, had by this time become infected with the deadly disease of adaptation to Stalinism, which was to lead them a few years later to outright support of capitalist reforms and class collaboration. Jim's stand for Leninism and against Stalinism in 1928, alone if necessary and practically alone in fact, put him in the position of the tiniest possible minority of a minority, and testified how much he had learned since 1917 and how far he had gone ahead of his generation.

Jim was starting all over again when the second radicalization began. He refers to the early thirties (in his *History of American Trotskyism*) as the "dog days" of our movement. Recently I have been reading the documents of that period, and I am inclined to reject his designation as a gross understatement. In my opinion it was the bleakest, most dismal, most frustrating stage in the entire span of our movement; it must have been much more difficult to try to function as a revolutionary in our tiny, hemmed-in movement in the early 1930s than it was two decades later in the worst days of the McCarthyite witch-hunt. It could not have been anything but discouraging for Jim, with his hatred of isolation and his love of action, and he wouldn't have been human not to have been affected by it now and then.

But he stood fast, and he inspired others to do the same, and by 1933 the tide turned and the cadres of the revolutionary party were on their way up again. When I use the word "inspired" I am referring not to the effects of his oratorical powers, although they were great, but to his ability to draw for our benefit on the vast fund of political and organizational knowledge he had accumulated in his early days, which he had reflected on very carefully, and which he polished and adapted so that we could use it and be certain that we were doing the right thing at the right time. How many mistakes we avoided thanks to the line of continuity he personified! Thanks to it, we escaped the worst consequences of the ultraleftism that scourged the radical movement in the early thirties, and we emerged with a clean banner from the subsequent tidal wave of opportunism that virtually engulfed the rest of the radical movement.

In fact, Jim was still performing this service, on a smaller scale of course, in the last year of his life. He evidently had been thinking back to his earlier days and to the way things were done and conceived, especially before 1917, and he went out of his way in several talks he had with different SWP and Young Socialist Alliance members to stress his opinion that the early movement, primarily out of ignorance and inexperience, had badly handicapped itself with ultraleft theories and practice. He didn't do this to derogate the early socialists and Wobblies, whom he revered as pioneers, but because he felt that today's revolutionaries could get the full benefits of the experience of the past only if they were correctly apprised of its negative as well as its positive sides.

In his sixtieth birthday speech (1950), Jim drew a distinction between what he should or might have done and what he actually did do: "Because I know myself, I don't claim great accomplishments. I am well aware of all the negligences and all the faults. I can't, in good conscience, stand up and say that I did the best I knew; I only did the best I could. That's quite a difference. I only did the best I could, falling short of the best I knew, because I am human and therefore fallible and frail, prone to error and even to folly, like all others" (*Notebook of an Agitator*).

This passage can be read in various ways: As an apology for his shortcomings. As a plea not to be judged by ideal or impossible standards. Or—as I took it at the time, and still do—as an appeal for his comrades to recognize and not emulate his negative or weak sides. (His influence on some of the SWP cadres was so overwhelming that they unconsciously imitated the way he gestured when he spoke.) Whatever the interpretation, the distinction Jim made is useful, because he didn't always do himself what he urged others to do.

For example, Jim said in his memorial speech after Trotsky was assassinated in Mexico, "We must all write down everything we know about Trotsky. Everyone must record his recollections and impressions. . . . Millions of people, generations to come, will be hungry for every scrap of information, every word, every impression that throws light on him, his ideas, his aims and his personal life" (*Speeches for Socialism*). It was typical that Jim should be among the first to see the need for this. But he failed to write what he exhorted other co-workers of Trotsky to write.

One of Jim's most valuable contributions to Marxist organizational theory and practice was his proposal on how the leading body of the revolutionary party should be selected at national conventions. I lack the space to describe it fully here, but you can find its best formulation in his *Letters from Prison,* written in 1944 (although he first proposed it in 1939). Its essence was that the National Committee slate recommended to the convention should be the product of the delegates from the branches themselves rather than the choices of the outgoing National or Political Committees or of any of the central leaders, no matter how prestigious. Being delegates too, regular or fraternal, the leaders of the outgoing committees had the formal right to try to influence the selection of the new committee, but the implication of Jim's proposal was that the interests of the party would be best served, and the most representative and authoritative committee would be elected, if they refrained from exercising this formal right.

More than thirty years of practice have proved the excellence of this proposal; it is inconceivable that the SWP will ever return to previous ways of choosing its leadership. But it should be noted that on certain occasions Jim, when he felt that an injustice was being done, did not refrain from using his formal right to intervene and exert his considerable authority to try to get this or that person added to the slate. It should also be noted that he was not always successful in such attempts. These were cases where the delegates, representing the party as a whole, showed that they preferred the best Jim knew to the best he could. I think it speaks favorably for the party created and educated by Jim more than anyone else that sometimes it could go farther in carrying out his best ideas than he did. Indirectly, that speaks favorably for Jim too.

Perhaps Jim overstated the distinction. In any case, it seems to me that the best he could, while inferior to the best he knew, was still better than the best of his predecessors and contemporaries in the American revolutionary movement. Because I believe the United States's future is socialist and that socialism will be attained through the kind of revolutionary party Jim was building, I have no doubt that future generations will cherish his memory as one of the chief American architects of the socialist society and will want to know as much as possible about him.

Frank Lovell

Jim came to the Bay Area early in 1936 after we had entered the Socialist Party of California. Since I was one of the few comrades with a car I was occasionally assigned to give him a lift in the East Bay or from Oakland to San Francisco. He did not talk much during the short trips we made, but on one occasion Jim asked what I was reading and I told him *The Poverty of Philosophy* by Marx and also that I had read a book called *Landmarks of Scientific Socialism* by Engels. He made no comment about the Engels book, but he said *The Poverty of Philosophy* is pretty heavy stuff. He asked if I had read anything by Lenin and suggested the pamphlet *What Is to Be Done?* He must have thought that Lenin's ideas on the kind of party that is needed to lead a revolution would be of some interest to a young college student who had just entered with other Trotskyists the all-inclusive Socialist Party, but he didn't say that. It may be he also wanted to recommend Lenin as the best introduction to the writings of Marx.

Many years later he recalled that Trotsky had once remarked that those who wanted to understand Marx and Engels ought to read Lenin, the implication being that those who wanted to understand Lenin would do well to read Trotsky.

FRANK LOVELL was born in 1913. He joined the Workers Party in 1935 and worked with Cannon in the Bay Area in 1936-37 and then in New York starting in 1938. He has been trade union director of the Socialist Workers Party since the late 1960s and is a labor columnist for the *Militant*.

In the summer of 1936 three of us were assigned to get jobs as sailors and become members of the Sailors Union of the Pacific. It was not an easy matter at that time to get a permit from the union to sail and that was the only way to get out. One of our comrades, George Trainor, had an uncle who was a sailor and who had been active in the 1934 maritime strike. He had promised to recommend George for a permit in the union, but I had no one to recommend me and didn't yet know my way around the waterfront. One of our most experienced comrades, Barney Moss, had been working on the union newspaper, *Voice of the Federation,* the weekly publication of the Maritime Federation of the Pacific. Barney had promised to let me know when the union membership committee was meeting so I could go before it and ask for a permit to sail. I had already put in my application.

Of course I tried to find out what was going on at the union hiring hall and listened to all reports. When I heard that the union membership committee was meeting and that my name had not been posted to appear, it looked as if my chances of going to sea were pretty slim.

Jim heard about this and asked what I had done to get my permit. I told him and he suggested that all the comrades in the maritime industry, including myself and others who had been assigned, should meet to find out what our chances were of getting jobs. Barney Moss said he was busy on the union paper and wouldn't be able to attend our meeting, but Jim urged him to find time to come. The purpose of the meeting as it developed was to find out from Barney why he had neglected to help us all get a little better acquainted with members of the union.

It was a short meeting. Barney came late and seemed to be in a hurry, but Jim took the opportunity to say that we should all find our sea legs if we expected to accomplish anything in the maritime unions.

I went directly from that meeting to the office of the *Voice* where Barney introduced me to an old-timer in the Sailors Union who took me to the union hall and looked up my application for a permit. The membership committee interviewed me and issued me a shipping card.

At the time I didn't exactly understand Jim's remark that all of us ought to find our sea legs. Later I learned that it was intended for Moss's benefit who was not by nature equipped for the stormy weather of revolutionary politics. Jim had also suggested to

Barney that he could better serve the party and the union by taking a job aboard ship instead of seeking to become editor of the union newspaper, but there was no hint of this in our small fraction meeting. I am sure the double significance of the remark was not lost on Moss who knew Jim from the early days of the Communist League of America.

The ninety-nine-day maritime strike of 1936-37 was a time of great internal union struggles. There were sharp disputes over strike strategy and defense policy against the government, which was preparing to issue continuous discharge books for all seamen and replace union hiring halls with government employment offices.

Jim was in close touch with all the debates and wrote articles in the Socialist paper *Labor Action,* which he edited, about the strike and some of the strike issues. His column, "Notebook of an Agitator," also took up some of the disputes and some of the prominent union leaders. His writings were popular, and some of the seamen who were becoming interested in politics used to visit the big meeting hall and offices of the Socialist Party on Van Ness Avenue.

Cannon occasionally spoke at public forums of the SP. Many sailors, marine firemen, cooks, and longshoremen attended those forums. They had heard about Cannon but they knew next to nothing about Trotskyism. Some were imbued with syndicalist prejudices or infected with Stalinist poison.

Whether in small private meetings or at the public forum, Jim was always patient with the syndicalist-minded seamen who thought they were continuing in the tradition of the Industrial Workers of the World, the Wobblies.

On one occasion, several of these latter-day Wobblies were arguing the virtues of revolutionary unionism and deprecating the vanguard party. Cannon told them in his easygoing way that we Trotskyists were Wobblies who had learned something from the Russian revolution—the necessity of a revolutionary working class party.

Strike struggles in this country, Cannon explained, would benefit from the Bolsheviks' example. Strikes were weakened in some cases by a syndicalist outlook that ignored the political needs of the workers, and were endangered in other instances by the class-collaborationist policies of the Stalinists and the old-line labor bureaucrats. Both dangers stalked the 1937 maritime strike.

Jim often told the strikers about the Trotskyist leadership of the 1934 Minneapolis Teamsters strikes, and about how to avoid the mistakes of syndicalism and at the same time defeat the treachery of Stalinism.

He never missed an opportunity to teach the need for a revolutionary party as opposed to talented leaders who operated in the mass movement without benefit of such a party. Being in a revolutionary party is essential to keep them in tune with the needs of the working class, he said. It helps develop a layer of new leaders to extend the struggle against the employing class beyond the confines of a single union or one industry or even a country as large and powerful as the United States.

Some of us were sometimes invited to the house on Gough Street which Jim and Rose shared with others during the 1936-37 winter. Usually these meetings were limited to Trotskyists and the discussion was often about developments in the Spanish revolution. The Socialist Party was undertaking to organize a West Coast contingent of the Debs Brigade and send volunteers to fight the Spanish fascists. Jim was worried about the fate of our comrades in Spain at the hands of the Stalinists.

At one of these meetings during informal discussion Jim showed us a copy of *The Revolution Betrayed*. He said it was surely one of Trotsky's greatest books. He had meant to show us the depths of Stalinist treachery—even to the betrayal of the revolution in Russia. But the end of the discussion took another turn. None of us had yet seen the new book and one comrade, whom we all regarded as the best educated Trotskyist in our region, asked if he could borrow Jim's copy.

Our most educated comrade was full of quotations from the Marxist classics and sometimes threw in a few from Hegel, Clausewitz, Kant, and Aristotle to dispel any impression that his knowledge was limited to Marxist writings.

Jim disliked these traits and must have suspected an effort to impress upon us younger and less experienced comrades that we were privileged to associate with one who possessed a genuine thirst for knowledge. In outward manner, Jim seemed pleased that at least one of us was impatient to get the new book and said that he was glad to pass it along, "but on the condition that you will read it."

For a time in 1937 while we were still in the Socialist Party, Jim and Rose lived in Santa Monica. He was interested in developing and extending a circle of friends in Hollywood who had become interested in Trotskyism as a result of the Moscow frame-up trials that were in full swing then. Most of the Hollywood people he knew were screen writers and he was trying to arouse interest among them and their friends in the Dewey Commission of Inquiry into the charges made against Trotsky in the Moscow trials.

I probably did not visit Jim more than two or three times in Santa Monica, driving over from San Pedro where I was then working for the Sailors Union. These trips were made with other maritime workers—some of them union officials—who were engaged in bitter factional struggles against the Stalinists for control of the maritime unions.

Jim was a good listener and he was able to sort out the central problems and make useful suggestions. But he also tried to interest those workers in the bigger political questions, the developments in Spain—the hypocritical arms embargo imposed by Roosevelt against the Spanish government, the Stalinist treachery—and the Moscow trials. When he talked about these questions it was always in connection with the particular problems that these workers and union officials had come to talk about. He used to say that if we could offer some practical answers to problems that arise in the union movement, we might be able to convert the trade union militants to our political program and make party activists of some of them.

At that time the big problem for the maritime unions was the U.S. Maritime Commission, a government agency to regulate the industry and especially the unions in the industry. The problem within the unions was the Communist Party, which was seeking a basis of collaboration with the Maritime Commission. Jim looked for ways to explain and illustrate these problems, and relate them to the daily—sometimes routine—affairs of the unions. In the course of one of the conversations he remarked that most of the daily waterfront battles were of little consequence when the whole world was going up in flames, beginning in Spain. Still he listened to all the sea stories, the recounting of longshore disputes, problems with arbitration, even the agenda for the next union meetings, which were held weekly then in most of the maritime unions. In the end he usually made helpful suggestions that would be handy the next day.

Half jokingly Jim once remarked that the Stalinists, who were concentrating some forces in San Pedro, were not doing much good for the union when the fight against the shipowners was taking place aboard the ships. "Those Beacon Street sailors are suffering from a bad case of shore fever," he said. This remark was picked up by Joe Voltero, an ex-lightweight fighter in the U.S. navy, who soon started a one-man campaign to cure the Stalinist seamen of their shore fever and cut out some of the disruption they were causing in the meetings of the Sailors Union and the Marine Firemen's union.

One of the seamen who used to occasionally visit Jim in this period was Henry "Blackie" Vincent. He was the San Pedro patrolman of the Sailors Union and had sailed bosun on the Dollar Line. He had been a union member before the 1934 strike, sailing out of San Francisco. Because of his prestrike reputation and popularity he became prominent in the union when the sailors fought to establish their own hiring halls on the Pacific Coast in 1935. During a visit to Jim at Santa Monica, Blackie listened mostly and was not very talkative. But speaking to him afterwards I could see that he was plainly impressed. "That man," he said of Jim, "can be successful at anything he tries."

There was another sailor in San Pedro at this time who had known Jim in New York, where he had been briefly a member of the Communist League of America. His name was Count Delaney and if he had another name I never knew it. For as long as he could hold out on the beach, the Count was part of the bottle brigade stationed near the corner of Sixth and Beacon Streets. Some of this gang had been in the Wobblies, the Communist Party, or the Trotskyist movement. They all knew or claimed to know Jim Cannon from the defense of John Soderberg, a sailor who was charged with blowing up a barge in New York harbor and railroaded to Sing Sing in the early 1930s.

I don't think any of these ex-radicals and veteran booze fighters ever saw Jim during his stay in Santa Monica unless it was at a public meeting, but Count Delaney had proof that he was protected by James P. Cannon in the form of a signed document which he proudly displayed on occasion. It was a handwritten order which said:

"To the Firing Squad:

"Do not shoot Count Delaney as he gave me a pipe and some smoking tobacco at a time when I badly needed it.

"Signed,
"James P. Cannon"

Sharp differences over the editorial policy of *Labor Action* developed within the California Socialist Party soon after the paper was launched under Cannon's editorship. The "native socialists," as they sometimes called themselves, resented the intrusion of Trotskyists and other newcomers in their party. They resented even more the intrusion of the class-struggle program.

A good deal of the criticism of the paper centered upon the publication of articles by Trotsky. The critics said they wanted more local news about the big developments in the California labor movement, less polemics by Trotsky on events in Spain and elsewhere. Sometimes these criticisms spilled over into informal free-for-all discussions at the party headquarters.

Although Jim was sometimes present when these discussions started, I don't believe he ever participated in them. What he had to say was usually written in the paper. Once after a public forum when a large number of people were still around for coffee and informal talk, one of the "native socialists" whom I had never seen before and don't recall ever seeing again confronted Jim with the kind of questioning that was becoming common among these people. Their arguments were slanted to political support for the Spanish government and often developed a Stalinist twist, inferring that Trotsky's call for peasant seizure of the old landed estates, workers' control of the factories and the arms industry, and independence for Morocco were somehow counterrevolutionary. This had become a familiar litany to most of us who were on the waterfront because we conducted a running debate with the Stalinists at the Sailors Union hall and around the old Longshore hiring hall on Clay Street, and we were always interested in new arguments.

It was only natural that several of us would gather around to see how Jim would handle the questions of the "native socialist," who was quite aggressive in manner and seemed to be insisting upon answers which he had formulated to his own satisfaction in advance.

There was a rather extended tirade against Trotsky's "unreasonable" demands upon the Spanish government and the "impractical" hope that the embattled Spanish workers could organize their own government in the midst of civil war. At one point during this presentation of the problem, Jim dropped out of the discussion. He had seemed interested at the beginning, but his attitude changed and in such a way that he was very far removed before his aggressive critic had finished shouting. Jim was still standing there at the end, but his interest was elsewhere and he just turned around and walked away.

This so infuriated our "native socialist" that he left the hall and so far as I know never returned.

Later that evening Jim was talking seriously and quietly with a young sailor who was a recent recruit to the Communist Party, explaining the treacherous policy of Stalinism in Spain. The sailor had doubts about Stalinist politics, but he had been recruited to the CP by friends to whom he was personally loyal. Jim told him that there was no need to try to defend Stalinism on this account, but that he should first try to understand it. "It would be good," Jim said, "if you could help us arrange a debate with one of the CP leaders who is experienced at defending their position."

Of course, no such debate was ever arranged because the Stalinist leaders would never agree to it. But these two incidents, in which Jim was trying to win a hearing for Trotskyist ideas, were typical of the way he habitually distinguished what was frivolous and what held promise of serious gains.

Max Shachtman made a speaking tour in 1937. His subject was "The Spanish Revolution in Danger." A meeting for him was held in San Pedro at the Carpenters Hall and Jim was chairman. A dozen or so of those who came were from the Yugoslav community, tuna fleet fishermen, who sat together in the center of the hall and seemed to be a very serious group.

Shachtman had a part in his speech where he told about the treachery of the Stalinists in Spain. He said that every rifle and every bullet that was sent by the Soviet Union to the Loyalist government had a tag on it with specific instructions, "To Be Used Only for the Defense of Bourgeois Democracy."

At this point one of the fishermen stood up and said, "That's a lie. They wouldn't go to all that trouble." The others with him got up and they all left.

This demonstration stopped the meeting temporarily. Cannon, as chairman, did nothing to restore order. He just sat there smiling and looking at Shachtman.

After the disbelievers had left, Shachtman resumed speaking as if nothing much had happened. When the meeting was all over, Jim laughed about the incident. He said, "I thought that would teach Max a lesson—always keep in mind who you're talking to."

My first visit to New York was in 1938. I had shipped in San Francisco on an intercoastal freighter which docked in Brooklyn. The subway system was a new experience for me but I discovered that the BMT train I was on stopped at Union Square, which was a familiar name, so I got off there and soon found 116 University Place, national office of the Socialist Workers Party.

Lillian Roberts, whom I had met in Los Angeles, was Jim's secretary at that time. It was late in the day and she called him at home and then walked with me to 5 Washington Square where he and Rose had a small apartment.

Jim was anxious to learn about our work in the maritime industry on the West Coast and to test my feelings about the development of our work on the East Coast in the Stalinist-controlled National Maritime Union and in the newly chartered AFL Seafarers International Union. There had been some correspondence about this between me and others in New York. Jim told me right away that he had read all the correspondence and was not sure that we should urge all our comrades to make New York their base port, but he leaned in that direction.

I told him that I did not have much to add to what I had said in my letters, which was in support of maintaining and continuing our work on the West Coast.

He saw very quickly from the account I gave of my first ride on the subway that I was more interested in the wonders of New York than in trade union policy. It was a pleasant evening and he suggested that we go for a walk and get a glass of beer.

We walked through the Village across Sixth Avenue and past the women's prison on Greenwich Street. He remarked upon the cruelty and hypocrisy of capitalist society represented in those prison walls. The women prisoners were caged up in the center of the city in a building that was constructed to look more like a modern apartment house than a jail so as not to offend the sensibilities of some of the well-to-do who lived in the vicinity.

He talked about the torments of life in New York in contrast to the easier way we lived on the West Coast at that time. It was clear that he was not trying to persuade me that there would be any personal advantage in a shift of our work. Later we talked about the East Coast maritime unions.

One of the reasons I came to New York in 1938 was to learn what I could about an anti-Stalinist group that had formed in the National Maritime Union and was publishing a paper called *The*

Rank and File Pilot. This paper consisted mostly of attacks on the Stalinists for their bureaucratic control of the union. The paper was popular, but little was known of its auspices.

I found the leaders of this rank-and-file group to be rather secretive and uncommunicative. But most of the others were anxious to talk about their union and about the West Coast maritime unions. They were young seamen who did not spend much time ashore. They had some genuine grievances about the way NMU meetings were run by the Stalinist fraction.

Jim was interested in these seamen and agreed to meet with several of them. They talked mostly about their run-ins with ship's officers and union officials. They never got a chance to speak at the big NMU meetings and tell what was happening aboard ship. Little attention was paid by the Stalinist officials to conditions of work or even to overtime pay that they felt they had coming.

All this was several stages removed from such questions as the government attack on the maritime unions and a defense strategy against government control of hiring halls. But Jim suggested to these seamen that they organize their own class in public speaking. This would be a chance for them to prepare for more effective participation in NMU meetings, he said. And he volunteered to give the classes.

This was no idle suggestion. He was enthusiastic about working with even a small group of young seamen although he was busy at the time with many other matters. He collected textbooks on public speaking and parliamentary procedure. They will learn quickly, he said, and in the process they will discover what is wrong with Stalinist policy in their union as well as some new ways to handle the Stalinists.

Nothing came of this particular project, but Jim's interest in working with rank-and-file seamen and helping them find their way was an example for our party that helped us recruit steadily from the maritime industry all through the war years.

When I was ashore in New York on and off in 1938 and part of 1939, I had a room at 5 Washington Square where Jim and Rose lived, and saw them frequently. When Jim returned from Europe in 1938 after participating in the founding congress of the Fourth International, which was held at the time of the Munich crisis, he was convinced that World War II was not far away. He seemed to accept this as part of the political reality. He must have been troubled by signs of disaffection within the party leadership, as his later writings and speeches in the 1939-40 fight with Burnham and Shachtman showed, but at the time he did not betray any such feelings to me as a rank-and-file member of the party and probably not to many others who were then in the leadership.

He talked a good deal about the mobilization of troops in Europe and I asked him what the party here would do to prepare for war. He said we will probably be in for some rough times at the beginning and then he turned the conversation aside. "I think I'll find a good dentist and get my teeth fixed," he said. "They don't do very good work on your teeth in jail. If something goes wrong they pull them."

It must have been shortly after my arrival from the West Coast, because I think Jim and Rose were the only comrades I knew, when we went to a big social affair given by the New York local of the SWP. It was held in the ballroom of the Hotel Diplomat. We were in the balcony and Jim looked at the crowd and said with some satisfaction, "This begins to look like a movement." Of course, at that time our forces were small compared to the Stalinists.

There was amateur entertainment at that social. Some comrades put on an imitation burlesque and the chorus sang a song called "I'm a Dialectical Dope." This didn't go over very big with Jim. He grumbled about it, and found it unfunny. "It's good to joke and kid around and have fun," he said. "We are not pompous and we don't care very much for people who are, but we can't afford a light-minded attitude about our basic doctrine."

When C. L. R. James came to this country from Britain, where he was a leader of the Trotskyist movement, he was welcomed into the Socialist Workers Party and given leadership responsibilities.

James was an impressive speaker with his British accent and his poise. He was a tall, handsome Black man, originally from the British West Indies. He spoke without notes, standing aside from the podium in the center of the speakers' platform. It was as if he were a great actor delivering a famous oration.

At his first appearance he shared the platform with Shachtman and Cannon in the Irving Plaza meeting hall where Trotskyist meetings were often held. Shachtman was the first speaker and was not brief. James came on next and even though his talk was longer than Shachtman's, he completely captivated the audience and received a big ovation.

Cannon was the last speaker. Although he was the national secretary of the party and had been announced for a major speech, Jim had no intention of standing on his dignity or trying to hold the audience so late at night in order to have his turn. He put aside his notes, congratulated James on his speaking ability and welcomed him to the Socialist Workers Party. Dispensing with the formalities he brought the meeting to a successful conclusion with a speech that lasted no more than five minutes.

Shortly before the Minneapolis defendants were sent to prison at the end of 1943, George Clarke and I visited Jim one evening at his home. He wanted to talk about the absence of a youth movement of any kind during the war and the effect of this on our party. He worried about the loss of a whole generation in the continuity of our party. In the radical movement we count the generations by decades, he said: We attracted a youth movement in the decade of the 1930s, especially those we won over to our program while in the Socialist Party. But we were not able to assimilate these youth and most of them left with Burnham and Shachtman at the beginning of the war. In the war years the youth were drafted and shipped off to war or herded into the war industries. The political climate was hostile to independent youth activities of any kind. All the pressures of government and society were for the total mobilization of all young people either into the army or industry.

Our recruits were slow in coming and those who came were already in industry. Jim was looking for hopeful signs of a new generation still in school that would surely turn against the terrible slaughter, the regimentation of the war years, the hypocrisy of wartime propaganda.

He was uneasy about our failure to find even a few young people still on campus who could be inspired by the humanitarian goals of socialism. He didn't expect that much was possible in this direction but he thought we should be alert to any possibilities and pay some attention to what was happening to the younger brothers and sisters of all those young men and women who had been swallowed up by the war machine.

Jim was always conscious of the difference in generations and the need for the party to retain continuity, especially in the leading cadres. George and I were then a year or two past thirty, about the average age of the party at that time. Neither of us had ever thought much about this problem and we had nothing of importance to contribute to the discussion. What could we do about such a problem?

"Well," Jim said, "I don't think you comrades know what I am talking about, but this is a problem that we must be aware of and find ways to solve."

Later in speeches at National Committee plenums he would return to this theme, reminding the leading cadre that the revolutionary movement must be a young movement. Only the young can make a revolution, he said. Always in a viable working class movement, the "old men" were in their forties, never older. This was true of the IWW in its pre-World War I heyday when St. John and Haywood were looked to as the "old men," and it was true of the Bolsheviks at the moment of the Russian revolution when Lenin was forty-seven and Trotsky was thirty-eight.

At the start of the 1946 maritime strike the Seafarers' International Union and the Sailors Union of the Pacific (AFL), having negotiated a $22.50-a-month wage increase which was rejected by the Wage Stabilization Board as "inflationary," were preparing to strike against this ruling by the government agency. The National Maritime Union (CIO) had accepted a $17.50 monthly increase, but the membership was dissatisfied.

The officials of these unions were jockeying for jurisdictional advantage. The AFL unions were hoping to raid the NMU if they could establish a higher pay scale. But it was clear to us that the NMU would not allow this to develop and was ready to join the strike.

Most Trotskyist seamen were then in the NMU, and some were secondary officials. A few of us remained in the SUP. Our position in both the AFL and CIO unions was for united action, a joint strike committee, and coordinated bargaining.

When I argued for this position in a large SIU-SUP strike meeting the chairman hit me with the gavel and inflicted a scalp wound that required some stitches and a bandage for a few days.

At SWP national headquarters Farrell Dobbs, who had heard about the incident and had been in more serious fights in the Teamsters union, was inclined to make the best of the situation and prepare for another round. He advised against getting the head in the way of flying mallets. I made the lame excuse that something like this is liable to happen if you turn your back on your enemies. But Jim, who was there, was angry about the whole matter and told us it was not something to be laughed away. He thought we should prepare to defend ourselves against repetition of such attacks, and retaliate in kind at the first appropriate opportunity.

As it turned out, I gained some support in the union, partly as a result of the incident, was elected to the strike committee, and all maritime unions in New York collaborated—at least for the duration of the seventeen-day strike.

There was never anything in Jim's behavior to show that he harbored grudges, but he had a long memory and was a firm believer that Trotskyists should establish a fighting reputation that would discourage unprovoked physical attacks.

During the labor resurgence of 1946 one of our comrades who had been wounded in the war and was discharged got an airport job. He got along well wherever he was and made friends easily. Before long he had a group of workers at the airport who wanted to form a union and he had encouraged other comrades to get jobs at the same location. Meetings were called, union officials were invited to explain the benefits of organization, and the management was advised that the workers wanted more money and a signed contract. A strike seemed imminent. All this happened very quickly, and two or three of our comrades who had been hired were deeply involved.

Suddenly the comrade who started it all pulled out of the situation. We called a meeting to decide what the others should do, because he had been the most active and respected union advocate and some of the plans depended on him.

We had known this comrade for some years before the war and were aware of some of his weaknesses. But those comrades who had been working with him in this particular action felt as if they had been walked into something that was beyond their control. They thought we should get hold of our delinquent comrade and instruct him to get back in the action.

Jim believed in discipline but he also knew the folly of issuing orders that couldn't be carried out. "Maybe this comrade knows something about this that we don't," he said. "There is something inside him that drives him to do these things. The other comrades there will just have to do the best they can without him."

I don't remember what happened exactly, but not much. The

comrades who remained in the situation must have consoled themselves with the fact that if nothing had been started, they would never have had the chance to help organize the union at the airport and maybe make a few friends in the process.

Cannon's speech on "The Coming American Revolution" at the 1946 SWP convention in Chicago was inspiring. Many comrades who heard it thought it must be the best speech he ever made, certainly the best they ever heard him make.

For reasons that I did not understand and could not explain to myself at that time, I did not share the prevailing feeling at that convention that the labor movement was entering a new phase of militancy and that the SWP was on the verge of rapid expansion. I had no direct conversations with Jim about this, and saw little of him during that convention.

It happened that I was on the elevator going down from the convention hall to the hotel lobby shortly after he had delivered his "Coming American Revolution" speech. He and several other comrades got in the elevator, and some were congratulating him on the talk. One comrade asked him if he thought it was his best or most important talk.

Like most people Jim appreciated compliments, but I don't think he was ever much taken in by flattery. And he always tried to keep the record straight. On this occasion he answered immediately and directly, "The best and most important speech I ever made was when the Stalinists expelled us."

This impressed me as a characteristic response, under the circumstances. It seemed to me that he was saying again, as he had said before the convention, that the 1946 American Theses were a continuation of the programmatic beginning of the Trotskyist movement in this country in 1928.

The U.S. Coast Guard was the agency charged with purging the maritime unions of Stalinist influence in line with cold war policy. This purge of seagoing personnel was conducted by a reissuance of seamen's certificates. Those seamen on the purge lists were not issued new papers, their old certificates canceled. In this process all radicals, militants, and "troublemakers" were eliminated. The bureaucrats in all the maritime unions went along with this, supplying names of those to be purged in many instances.

It was clear by 1950 that the days of the Trotskyist maritime fraction were numbered, but we thought it would be worthwhile to challenge the Coast Guard procedure in some cases.

As it developed, the leadership of the Sailors Union of the Pacific sought to take advantage of the government repression to carry out its own purge. It wanted to get rid of all critics within the union.

In Seattle a popular local officer of the union, John Mahoney, had been critical of SUP-SIU complicity in supplying strikebreakers and helping to destroy the Canadian Seamen's Union. Mahoney was expelled from the union by the officials in San Francisco, but he was almost unanimously supported by the membership of the Seattle branch.

I left an intercoastal freighter when it docked in Seattle and joined with Mahoney to organize the Mahoney Defense Committee.

We got the endorsement of several hundred seamen in the Seattle and Portland branches, raised funds for the defense, and prepared to publish a local newspaper that would tell the full story of the SUP purges. We enlisted the support of other maritime unions, the Marine Firemen, International Longshoremen's and Warehousemen's Union (itself under attack), and the Marine Cooks and Stewards (later destroyed and some of its officials jailed).

We had a pretty solid opposition movement within the Sailors Union in Seattle and there was a good deal of enthusiasm and optimism in the ranks even though we were being isolated from the rest of the coast by the Lundeberg machine that controlled the SUP through terrorist methods. Lundeberg had enlisted the support of Dave Beck and the Teamster union in Seattle on his behalf. We hoped the publication of our paper would help break our isolation and extend our fight to other maritime unions and other branches of the SUP along the coast.

Just as we were prepared to publish, I learned that our leading comrades in Los Angeles were opposed to the fight we were conducting and were advising our sailors to leave ship in San Pedro and not go to Seattle. They thought our fight was an adventure that could only lead to victimization.

I called the national office of the party and asked to talk with Bert Cochran who I thought was in charge of our trade union work. Jim came on the phone and asked how things were going. He was familiar with everything that had developed.

When I told him what the problem was and that we were prepared to bring out the first issue of our paper the next day but wanted to get the opinion of the national office on the whole matter, he answered without any hesitation or qualification. "You go ahead. I cannot speak for the committee here, but I think they will support you."

I never heard Jim talk about the personal traits or peculiarities of other comrades, or others he had known in the movement. Whatever he had to say in this respect was said publicly. Often his judgments were harsh. But in private conversation he only mentioned others by way of illustration, usually complimentary. He thought most people in the radical movement have to learn to relax. He liked Carlo Tresca, the anarchist, and said it was always a pleasure to work with Tresca. Even in times of most intensive work, Tresca always insisted on a leisurely meal with a bottle of wine.

Jim was critical of A. J. Muste's work in the mass movement because Muste, with his superior talents, always became the acknowledged public leader and speaker. Jim thought it was necessary to develop and train an indigenous leadership in the movement. In this respect he would sometimes contrast the leadership that developed in the Minneapolis strikes with the way Muste conducted the Auto-Lite strike in Toledo. He thought Muste spent too much time out on the picket lines making speeches instead of consulting more with the picket captains who could make more effective speeches, if given a chance to figure out what needed to be said and done.

Jim was at Mountain Spring Camp in New Jersey in the summer of 1951 or 1952, probably both summers for longer or shorter periods of time, and many comrades found an opportunity to talk with him in that relaxed atmosphere. I am sure he was troubled by the adverse turn of political events in this country, by the tendencies within the Socialist Workers Party, and by the traits of some of the European leaders of the Fourth International. But he was doing a good deal of writing then and was enjoying it. Some of what he wrote appeared in the *Militant* and in the evening before dinner he would come downstairs and talk about some of his projects. "I want to show the comrades what it means to get down to work," he would say in his half-joking way.

Once when I arrived from California and met him at the camp, he asked, "How do you like the new Ford?"

This was certainly an unusual question and something I knew nothing about. So I told him I hadn't yet heard about the new Ford but I had recently worked with a carpenter in San Francisco who bought a Kaiser as an investment, thinking cars would retain their value as they had during World War II when the auto companies stopped building cars and started building tanks. His response was that most people are myopic. And that ended our talk of cars.

But I noticed that in Jim's casual conversations with other comrades this question "What do you think of the new Ford?" kept cropping up. It turned out that Ford, like the other car makers, had recently brought out a "sensational" new model, radically different in style and performance from earlier models cast in the prewar mold. I suppose this was his way of finding out how much our comrades were in tune with the "new consumerism" and what effects this was having on the party at that time.

When Jim learned that I was working as a carpenter he expressed so much interest that it surprised me. I told him that after being expelled from the Sailors Union I had worked for a while in a sawmill and on the waterfront in Seattle, but that I needed to move around and the carpentry trade suited my purposes and besides I liked the work.

His father was a carpenter. But Jim said he was interested in what I was doing because he thought it was necessary for comrades who had lost their jobs in some industries or been victimized in their unions by the witch-hunt to make a proper adjustment. They would find that in some ways they might be better off.

He talked some about the shoddy products of capitalism and the alienation of labor. Under socialism, he thought, mass production would be vastly improved and the products would be better and last longer. But socialist men and women will take pleasure in making things for their personal use which are not mass produced. Everyone will have time to become an artist or craftsman and when we exchange gifts it will be those things we have made especially for someone else, the individual expression of affection.

These were some of the ideas that Jim returned to in *America's Road to Socialism*.

The 1954 convention of the SWP in Chicago was an important turning point for the party. It marked the adjustment of tHe party to the witch-hunt, the realization that the union movement was politically dormant and would be for the next period, and the beginning of our renewed attention to campus work at that time when students were called "the silent generation."

Jim took a big part in that convention, his last major operation in directing the course of the party's development. He pointed to the Detroit branch as a model of branch building because George Breitman who was then the organizer had successfully directed the attention of the local comrades to the students at Wayne State University and had managed to force the university authorities to officially recognize a socialist student club on campus. In one of his talks at the convention, Jim said that those who want to do trade union work in this period ought to turn their attention to the student youth because that is where the next wave of radicalization in the union movement will come from.

He did not intend that we should neglect our activities in the union movement, only that we should recognize the limited possibilities of party growth there. Fred Halstead, Ed Shaw, Bea Hansen, and others had been active participants in the Detroit Square D strike which was concluded just prior to our convention, and we thought we had contributed something to the success of that strike. Art Fox was also active in Ford Local 600 where he worked with opposition caucuses, sold *Militant* subscriptions, and brought militant unionists to our regular Friday Night Socialist Forum. Jim was careful not to underestimate the importance of this work or disparage in any way the efforts of those comrades who were trying to make some gains in the unions. But he tried to make us understand that it was all uphill work there and that we should not be disappointed if progress was slow in the next period. His opinion was that the party would have to look elsewhere and find other opportunities for socialist propaganda where the going would be easier and receptivity greater. This meant that some of our slogans would need to be changed, including our slogan "Build a Labor Party *Now*."

This slogan was out of tune with the political reality at that time and to underscore this for our benefit he sent a note to Art Fox which Art then shared with the Detroit delegation. It was a prediction that no union in the next two years would adopt a labor party resolution, something that several local unions had done regularly—largely out of habit—until that time. This personal note, submitted as a formal "prediction," was typical of the relationship Jim cultivated in the party. He often said that it is important for a leader to know the party membership, and to know what to say and how to say it in order to win approval and support for the party policy at every juncture in a constantly changing political environment.

> Prediction:—
> (and you can hold me to it)
>
> The Ford Local 600 —
> and all — or almost all — other local unions which have passed Resolutions for a Labor Party —
> — will keep absolutely mum on the subject during the next two years.
>
> Signed: J.P. Cannon
> (Subscribed and sworn to before me, a Notary Public, this 27th day of November, in the year of our Lord 1954
>
> John Doe
> Notary Public

Note to Art Fox, November 27, 1954

Milton Alvin

One of Jim Cannon's personal traits was modesty regarding his achievements in the political movement. However, in my opinion, he estimated what he had wrought, his contribution to the building of an American revolutionary party and an international organization, somewhat below where he should have.

His modesty requires a qualification which is hard to convey. Cannon really knew what he had achieved but he deliberately put a reserved estimate upon it. He had his reason for this just as he did for everything he did and said. He wanted to set an example of not taking himself too seriously in the hope that others would emulate him. This he referred to as his "Rule No. 5."

Cannon's political influence was widespread within the movements of which he was a part. These organizations remained small relative to the large working class in America even though the ideas upon which they were based corresponded to the historical interests of the workers. Material resources were usually in short supply in contrast to countless enemies on all sides. Trotskyism was heavily dependent upon ideas as the cement that held the movement together. That it persevered stands out as an accomplishment by Cannon and his associates who collaborated with him.

It was Cannon's method to work with leading comrades to build a team. He was not a "star" or synthetic hero such as

MILTON ALVIN was born in 1906. He joined the Workers Party in 1935 and spent much time with Cannon in Los Angeles from 1952 until Cannon's death. These remarks are based on a talk given in Los Angeles on September 3, 1974.

present-day society produces in politics, sports, films, and elsewhere. He was a team man and consciously worked as a member of the leadership team. This was an important part of his conception of how to educate and train a cadre of revolutionary leaders. He succeeded in doing this. I think he was universally regarded in the party as first among equals rather than as the "leader."

It was his constant desire to exchange ideas with others. He solicited the opinions of other comrades in order to know what they were thinking. This was his style. Other party leaders, of course, functioned in their own ways. There is room here for more than one way to work and Cannon's way was not necessarily best for others who worked in different ways.

An example from my experience occurred in the winter of 1953-54 when I went from Los Angeles to the Trotsky School in the East for six months. I received a letter from Jim dated February 9, 1954, in which he wrote, "I am enclosing copies of some political letters I have been writing recently, to keep you up to date on some of the matters discussed in correspondence between me and the center.

"If you and the other students at the school feel like expressing yourselves on some of these matters, or disagree with anything said, I would be glad to hear from you from time to time." There were fifteen letters in this group, covering various subjects.

It is worthwhile noting that the nine students at this session of the school were all local leaders in the areas from which they came but not one was then on the party's National Committee. Nevertheless, Jim obviously was interested in what they thought.

After he moved to Los Angeles in 1952 he often asked me if I knew or had any indication that the leading comrades in New York ever got together to talk informally, without the pressure of making decisions at meetings. He thought this type of thinking out loud was vitally necessary and he worried whether the leaders at the center were not doing this because all their time was taken up with practical work.

I said that he had a modest estimate of his own contribution. He put it this way,"All our generation can claim for itself is that we recognized the truth when we saw it and had sense enough to protect and defend it so it could be passed on to others." What he was referring to mainly was the political revelation that came as a result of his obtaining a copy of Trotsky's document, "The

Draft Program of the Communist International—A Criticism of Fundamentals" (since published in *The Third International After Lenin*). This occurred in Moscow in 1928 where he was a delegate to the Sixth Congress of the Communist International.

Reading this exhaustive analysis by Trotsky and absorbing the ideas in it changed everything for Cannon. He then understood what the five-year Trotsky-Stalin struggles in the Soviet Communist Party were all about as well as the distorted versions of these historical events that were exported to the American and other Communist parties.

His close ties to Leon Trotsky date from that event. He was grateful to Trotsky because his ideas shed light on the dark recesses of the never-ending factional struggles in the American Communist Party that neither Cannon nor anyone else on this side of the ocean had been able to explain and resolve.

He honored Trotsky and was certain that in the long run the great coleader with Lenin of the 1917 Russian revolution would be the best loved of all the Marxist masters because he fought so long and so hard against such great odds. Cannon also appreciated very much the work of other Soviet leaders almost all of whom eventually were victims of Stalin's murderous purges.

On the personal side, Jim was a very warm individual. He liked to have friends visit his house and enjoyed making drinks for them, serving them himself and sitting around just talking. I was present at many such sessions, some of which lasted long hours. These were of great educational value to me.

He was endowed with a good portion of Irish wit which he used freely. There was nothing of the long-faced pessimist about Cannon. He always had a few jokes and witticisms to offer.

The problem of friendship worried him during the long years when he was the central leader of the party. He told me that he could not take up with everyone who, for one reason or another, might have been a friend. He was compelled, because of his position in the party, to act cautiously in this respect and not give even the impression that any individual could become a leader in the party because of personal friendship with him.

The result was that some were kept at arm's length who, under other circumstances, would have become friends. This point is often not understood but it is important to give it some weight in order to keep proper relationships among comrades and to hold personal jealousies and envies down to a minimum. This problem was especially acute for Jim, who told me many years ago when we lived in New York that he was the kind of person who "needed friends."

Cannon was a down-to-earth fellow without any airs or pretensions. Everyone called him "Jim," even the newest and youngest member. There was little or no formality surrounding him and he was referred to as "Comrade Cannon" only when it could not be avoided.

Although he lived to an age very much beyond Trotsky's, eighty-four as against sixty years, he never expected to be known as the "Old Man" after Trotsky's death and was never referred to that way. He said that he never promised to be Trotsky, only to be Cannon. He did not want anyone to think that he was going to step into Trotsky's shoes. It was his opinion that there was no one qualified to do that in any event and the revolutionaries who survived Trotsky would have to get together and as a team, a group, do their best to carry on.

Cannon had a phenomenal memory, the best that I have ever come across. This applied not only to political events of the past but to other things as well. The historian Theodore Draper, in his preface to Cannon's book *The First Ten Years of American Communism,* paid tribute to Jim's ability to recall events of the past. Asking himself if Jim's memory was due to some inherent trait of mind, Draper goes on to say, "Unlike other communist leaders of his generation, Jim Cannon *wanted* to remember." The underlining of the word "wanted" by Draper was quite in order.

Jim remembered many old songs, of the Wobblies and even of his childhood, and he would sing them for us when he was in the mood. His recollection of his early days in the movement included not only important events and various people who took part in them, but even the addresses of headquarters and offices occupied by the early Communist Party and before that the Socialist Party and the IWW. He told many stories of meetings of various organizations in which he was active. They all had a lesson or two for those of us who were younger than Jim.

Cannon loved poetry, and Shakespeare above all other poets. He was fussy to a fault about quoting everyone correctly. Sitting together at a meeting one night we heard a speaker say, "This was the unkindest cut of all." Jim leaned over to me and whispered, "That's not the way Shakespeare wrote it. He said, 'This was the most unkindest cut of all.' Not correct grammatically, but poetic license, you know."

He had a good memory for poetry and one of his favorites was Robert Frost's "The Road Not Taken." In a way this short poem tells the story of Jim's life. It describes how a traveler in the woods comes to a fork in the road and decides to take the one less traveled by.

Jim had appreciation for the work of others in the movement. I will give only one example of many that I know. In Los Angeles, George Novack gave a series of lectures, more accurately seminar classes, on the origins of materialist philosophy. These have since been published under the title *The Origins of Materialism.* The attendance was confined to a small number, the members of the local executive committee. Cannon, busy with other matters and not a committee member, did not attend but was very much interested and asked me several times during the period the classes were given how they were coming and about the subject matter. I recall that when I once described the class at some length to him he remarked, "I would like to study philosophy with a man like George Novack."

It is only proper and necessary to say a word on Jim's relations with his wife and companion of forty-four years, Rose Karsner. Rose was a few weeks older than Jim and when their birthdays were drawing near he usually had a joke or two about having married "an older woman." Rose often met these sallies with the remark that Jim should be guided by her opinions more than he was since she was older and more experienced than he.

Rose died in 1968 at age seventy-eight. She spent virtually her entire life in the socialist movement beginning with the pre-World War I Socialist Party in Eugene V. Debs's time. A photograph of Debs with a message to Rose written in his hand hung on a wall in the Cannon home.

She was active in many capacities in the movement until illness prevented her from taking any part. But she never lost interest in what was going on and how the party was doing.

Cannon was without doubt the best public speaker I have ever heard, and I have heard Roosevelt, Churchill, and others from the capitalist side, and just about all from the radical and socialist side for over forty years. He made a special study of public speaking and had the art refined to the point of being a great orator.

However, political conditions prevented him from addressing large audiences as he deserved. Most of his speeches were given to gatherings of anywhere from a few dozen to several hundred listeners. Some of these have been collected in the book *Speeches for Socialism.*

Some of his speeches that have not been published and, unfortunately, have not been preserved, stand out in my memory. One was a short speech given at a large meeting of the New York membership of the Socialist Party not long before we Trotskyists were expelled from that organization for demanding the democratic rights that had been promised us and bureaucratically taken away. This was a debate in which Norman Thomas and other Socialist Party leaders participated.

Thomas, trying to score a point against our group, quoted Trotsky to the effect that the party was the locomotive of history. Other speakers took up the theme of railroads and locomotives. Finally, Cannon was recognized and went to the podium. Seated in the first row directly in front of him was one of the more obnoxious right-wingers in the Socialist Party whose name I don't remember. He had spoken before Cannon, used the railroad bit, and red-baited our group.

Cannon began his speech with approximately the following: "There has been a lot of talk about railroads here today. I have had some experience in this field myself. When I was a Wobbly I rode the rods many times." Then looking directly at the red-baiter he said, "And I know a railroad dick when I see one." This brought down the house and it took some time to restore order.

Another speech that seems to be lost was given at the 1939 convention of the Socialist Workers Party. It dealt with the coming war, then less than two months away, and what our duties would be under wartime conditions. This was a great oration, as I recall it, and had a big effect on me, at that time a relatively new and inexperienced member. It strengthened my resolution to fight back no matter how hard things became. I am sure that many others were similarly affected.

Although I joined the movement in 1935, I learned very little until after we were out of the Socialist Party and established as an independent organization, the Socialist Workers Party. Actually, I had not heard Jim or even seen him until the summer of 1937 when he spoke at the previously mentioned SP membership meeting. He was in California during the period when the Trotskyists were in the SP and returned to New York only on the eve of our expulsion.

The last time Jim spoke to a live audience was at a double birthday party given for. Howard Rosen and me. We were celebrating Howard's sixtieth birthday and retirement and my own sixty-fifth. We did not know that Jim would attend the party; he seldom went out of the house. And we certainly did not know that he wanted to speak. But he did both and caught us unprepared, without a tape recorder. This took place in March 1973, and for better or worse, it adds one more to Jim's speeches that no record of is preserved.

I mentioned earlier that Jim's estimate of his contribution to building the revolutionary party was modest. I think he made a significant impact, much greater than his own estimate. Many have called attention to his writings and speeches on various aspects of party organization. He certainly gave a lot in this field, clarifying the nature of the organization question, pointing out the correct way to select and renew the leadership, and to handle the problem of cliques and unprincipled groupings in the movement, and many other sides of the question.

But great as these were and valuable as they will be for those yet to come, his greatest achievement in our movement was not around the organization question but as a political leader.

It was constantly hammered home by Jim that the most important problem that faces the party is the formulation of a correct political program and the second most important is what to do next, that is, the question of tactics.

He taught that the organization question, with all its importance, was always subordinate to the political question. Organizational methods serve political aims and have no independent validity outside of these aims.

He stressed that a party, even with the best program in the world, if it made too many mistakes in orienting itself politically in the right direction, would eventually wear itself out and disappear. This calls for correct political analysis and selection of the right tactics within means available to the party and conforming to the reality of the situation.

The party that fails to distinguish between different periods and to adjust its tactics accordingly works itself into a sectarian corner from which it cannot exert any real influence. An example of this is the ossified Socialist Labor Party whose activities and propaganda are always the same regardless of what is taking place in the world and in the country.

Cannon moved to Los Angeles in 1952 and in the following year Farrell Dobbs replaced him as national secretary of the party. However, until 1963 Cannon participated in the leadership through letters to the center and attendance at National

Committee plenums and national conventions. After 1963 he attended no more national gatherings even though he remained a member of the National Committee in an advisory capacity. From that time his participation was markedly reduced.

Cannon had unbounded confidence in the successful culmination of the mission that history has assigned to the American working class. He often said that there was no purpose to our work, if it was to be mainly something other than preparation for the American revolution.

In his report to the 1946 Socialist Workers Party convention, where the Theses on the American Revolution were adopted, he said, "He who doubts the socialist revolution in America does not believe in the survival of human civilization, for there is no other way to save it. And there is no other power that can save it but the all-mighty working class of the United States."

Jim transmitted this confidence in the American workers to those of us who were fortunate enough to have worked with him and to have learned from him. We are richer for it. As he said many times, our cause has given our lives a meaning that they otherwise would not have. That has been our reward and it has been enough and more than enough.

James Kutcher

I have told how I became a socialist in *The Case of the Legless Veteran* (Monad Press, second edition, 1973). In 1935, at the age of twenty-three, I joined the Newark Circle of the Young People's Socialist League, affiliated to the Socialist Party, whose leader was Norman Thomas. At that point I didn't know much about politics. In the following two years I came into contact with the left-wingers in those two organizations, who were called "Trotskyists." When they were expelled in the summer of 1937, I protested and was informed that I must accept the expulsions or join the expelled. I joined them, later becoming a charter member of the Socialist Workers Party. My real political education began at this point, and it is connected in my mind with a speech by James P. Cannon that I still remember vividly almost forty years later.

The split in the YPSL took place at a national convention in Philadelphia over Labor Day weekend in 1937. It was preceded for two days by a heated National Executive Committee meeting and caucusing by the left and right wings. Since the overwhelming majority of the convention delegates supported the left wing, the right wing's strategy consisted of trying to prevent majority rule at the convention by disqualifying many left-wing delegates. I was present not as a delegate but as a rank-and-file observer. On the first day the person sitting next to me leaned over and said Cannon was sitting in the back listening to the debate. I

JAMES KUTCHER was born in 1912. He was strongly influenced the first time he heard Cannon speak, in 1937. His victimization by the government during the McCarthyite period is recounted in his book *The Case of the Legless Veteran.*

thought to myself, Who is Cannon? I had never heard the name before.

On the night before the right-wingers walked out of the convention to hold one of their own elsewhere, the left-wingers held a meeting at which Jim was the featured speaker. Up to then Norman Thomas had been my favorite speaker, but I now experienced a strong change of taste in such matters. I don't mean to belittle Thomas's oratorical abilities, but the two men were clearly not in the same league. Where Thomas was earnest, Jim came through as serious, although with touches of humor and witty invective. Thomas was sometimes a bit flowery, in a way that was not obnoxious to me, while Jim's remarks often had the ring of poetry although the words he used were ordinary and understandable by anyone. But the thing that struck me the most that night was Jim's ability to speak to young people, to appeal to their sense of idealism and to make touch with their aspirations for a better world, without even the trace of condescension that Thomas was not always able to control before such an audience.

What did Jim talk about that night? The split in the YPSL and SP, of course. But that became only incidental to his main themes—the characteristics of the revolutionist and how one learns to find a useful place in the movement; the great revolutionary heritage that was ours, from the pioneers of a century ago to the dissidents in Stalin's concentration camps; centrists and reformists, the pettiness of their outlook in the YPSL and SP, and the certainty of their speedy political disappearance; the current task of constructing a revolutionary party and the conditions that favored it; the program of the revolutionary party soon to be founded and the flexible, disciplined organizational forms needed to serve that program; the relations of the party and the youth organization and, above all, the need to bring about a solid and creative fusion of the youth and the "old guard" who were the custodians of the movement's theoretical capital, experience, and tradition (the main responsibility for such a fusion belonged to the old guard, he said); the Second, Third, and Fourth Internationals; the civil war in Spain; the meaning of the CIO, and much more. He ended on a note something like this:

We know that the struggle for socialism is the biggest thing in life, the only occupation worthy of the dignity of civilized people. In the comradely union of cothinkers fighting for socialism we overcome small and mean concerns for self, personal advancement, material comforts, money, and similar trivialities. The philistines can organize their little lives around such things—as for us, we aim to win a new world.

It was a speech that seemed to speak directly to me, to my hopes, doubts, and fears—as no doubt it did to many others in the audience. It was never published anywhere, like hundreds of others Jim gave, because in those years we lacked tape recorders and were too poor or backward to make stenographic transcriptions except on very rare occasions.

Jim spent some time in New York at the end of 1953 when the first copies of the first edition of *The Case of the Legless Veteran* arrived from England. In the following week or so several of the party leaders at 116 University Place spoke to me about the book, saying they liked it or thought it would be useful in fighting the witch-hunt. But Jim said nothing about it. On the last day before he returned to Los Angeles we exchanged some small talk but he still did not mention the book. I tried to work up the nerve to raise the subject myself, but I didn't succeed, and I left him discouraged by the feeling that either he hadn't read the book or thought it was so poor he couldn't say something polite about it.

But I was wrong. A few weeks later he not only had something to say about the book, but he said it in print, in the form of a letter to me, which he later included in his own book, *Notebook of an Agitator*. His expression of thanks to me as from one agitator to another was the most gratifying letter I ever got (although I thought it gave me far too much credit). But what was most satisfying about it to me was that it showed his warm concern and appreciation of the work of a congenital rank-and-filer.

Later in the 1950s, a number of us were sitting around the table at lunchtime in 116 University Place when Jim arrived for a meeting of the SWP National Committee that was to begin in a few days. He sat down with us and said that before he had left Los Angeles Rose (Karsner) gave him all kinds of instructions and orders as to what he should do and not do when he got to New York—like "Don't sit up too late"—and he laughed heartily as he told us about it.

Bob Chester

I first met Jim Cannon personally in 1937. The party was in process of moving into 116 University Place and an older comrade recruited me to work on putting up partitions. I was alone at one point when Jim, Rose Karsner, Shachtman, and a few others walked in. Jim came over and asked me, "Are you a carpenter?" I nodded although that was a gross exaggeration, a fact that I am sure Jim recognized. However, he went ahead, showing me where he wanted the entrance and exit doors to his office, checking on the light and other details of the setup.

I had considerable contact with Jim in the 1940-41 period. In the hectic days following the assassination of Trotsky I was assigned to the staff preparing the memorial meeting. The question of including the Shachtmanites, just four months after the split, was very touchy. An agreement was worked out that Albert Gates would be their speaker and that they would support the meeting. When we reported this to Jim, always the politician, he gave quick approval. "Whatever our differences, they still call themselves Trotskyists," he commented. "We can give a little in order to build support for the meeting."

Jim's speech to that meeting, "To the Memory of the Old Man," stands out in my mind as one of the most impressive of the many

BOB CHESTER (1912-1975) as a Trotskyist sympathizer joined the Socialist Party in 1936 after the Workers Party was dissolved and its members had entered the SP. He headed the Cannon for Mayor campaign in New York City in 1941 during the Minneapolis trial, and later served as Socialist Workers Party branch organizer in New York and in the San Francisco Bay Area. He was an active member of the Painters' union in San Francisco and was well known as an educator and speaker.

I have heard him give. All of our deep feelings, all of our political admiration for Trotsky, were expressed in Jim's special style—that is, in simple, colorful language that had powerful impact. I always regretted that the era of the tape recorder came too late to record that magnificent speech.

In 1941 the New York organizer, Murry Weiss, was incapacitated by a serious illness and Lou Cooper and I filled in at the city office. We were green but we did the best we could. One day Jim walked in and asked us how much the city would be able to pledge in the upcoming fund drive. Lou and I looked at each other in embarrassment since we had not even considered it. Catching the look, Jim, instead of lecturing, invited us to sit in on a fund drive discussion in the national office, thus giving us a clearer idea of what was needed. I always appreciated his perceptive method of teaching us without making us feel uncomfortable.

At the time of the Minneapolis indictments the New York local held a large public protest meeting. For decoration I painted a series of scrolls to be hung on the wall quoting some of the ludicrous legal gibberish contained in the indictments. When he arrived at the hall Jim walked around with an appreciative grin reading the scrolls. I was delighted when he referred to them in his speech, commenting that on the face of it the indictments made no more sense than those scrolls on the wall. It got a hearty laugh.

The national office decided to run Jim for mayor of New York City as part of its political counteroffensive to the indictments. The trials took place during the election campaign so that Jim was not available during that period. As campaign manager I often went to him for his signature on the legal documents. One day, just before leaving for Minneapolis, Jim leaned back in his chair and chuckled, "Only a Trotskyist would think of running a campaign with an absentee candidate."

Jim was very concerned about setting up a substitute leadership when the comrades went to jail. As part of the shifts, Tom Kerry came into New York from San Francisco to bolster the national office and as a result the San Francisco branch needed an organizer. I won the assignment. At the impromptu party held the night of the decision, Jim's comment, "That takes a load off my mind," was to me the highest form of praise.

Jim made several visits to San Francisco in the years 1945-49. On one occasion I took him to visit Warren K. Billings, of the Mooney-Billings frame-up case, at his watch shop on Market

Street. Jim had last seen Billings at Folsom Prison many years before. It was moving to see the warmth of greeting between these two old-time fighters in the class struggle. What Jim appreciated above all, and he said so to Billings, was Billings' impartial support of any class-struggle victim, and his refusal to give in to pressure from the Communist Party to keep hands off the Minneapolis case.

Jim was a political person to the fibre of his being. Even when he got emotional, the emotion had a political purpose, and was kept under control. The one time I remember him losing that control was in 1948 during the convention that nominated Farrell Dobbs and Grace Carlson as our presidential ticket. That was when Jim made his famous "Two Americas" keynote speech over national radio hookup. Jim stayed home to hear the acceptance speeches of the candidates. The impact of the speeches was so great, the idea that the Trotskyist program was being listened to across the nation, that he rushed back to the hall, charged in and embraced Grace and went back and forth, speechless. It was one of the few times that Jim could not find the right words for an occasion.

Jim was always able to see ahead and think things through faster than anyone else. This was graphically demonstrated to me at the time of the Henry Wallace candidacy in 1947-48. A tendency had developed in the party that wanted to give critical support to the Progressive Party and Jim was concerned about heading it off.

In California the branches had a sharp dispute in 1947 over a proposed tactic toward the Independent Progressive Party, an organization set up to promote the Wallace candidacy. At one point a conference was called in Los Angeles to discuss the question with Jim. He opened the meeting by asking each one of us whether we supported running our own presidential slate against Wallace. Only after each one expressed that support did Jim go into the pros and cons of the tactic, confident that it did not cover a move toward the support of Wallace.

Anne and I were able to visit Jim periodically over the years he lived in Los Angeles. In our visit in the spring of 1974, after a lapse of about a year, we noted his weakened condition which showed in his walk and the speed with which he tired. His mind, however, was as clear and sharp as ever. His parting words to us were, "Don't stay away so long."

Harry Ring

"Now I am back on my regular study schedule and am slowly reading [Trotsky's] My Life *in the brief periods of spare time I have. It is a political autobiography, but hardly a personal one. The Old Man is too reserved, too preoccupied with his struggle, to tell much about himself. One can get glimpses of Trotsky, the man, with his human contradiction, only by what he reads into the book; not by what is written there.*

"Strangely enough, nearly all those who came into personal relationship with him in the intimacy of his household feel impelled to write, more or less, in the same impersonal political way as though bound by the pattern of Trotsky's own memoirs. . . . Sooner or later, a biographer with real insight will undertake the task of writing the life of Trotsky, and he will not be content with the source material Trotsky himself had written (in My Life*) nor with the appreciations of him written by others in the same impersonal spirit. I hope he will be able to find more of the other kind of material than we now know of."*

—James P. Cannon, *Letters from Prison*

My first direct encounter with Jim Cannon was somewhat unnerving.

It occurred during the initial stage of a political faction fight in the Socialist Workers Party in 1939. A minority of the party, led

---

HARRY RING was born in 1918. He joined the Socialist Party and its Trotskyist wing in 1936. He has served as editor of the *Militant* and now heads the paper's Southwest Bureau. To gather information for a future biographer, he taped conversations with Cannon during 1972-74 about Cannon's early years.

by Max Shachtman and James Burnham, challenged the party's program on such fundamental questions as the defense of the Soviet Union from imperialist attack, and the party's characterization of the USSR as a degenerated workers' state. But the fight began—as most faction fights seem to—over much smaller issues. Party members were being recruited to the Burnham-Shachtman faction on the basis of organizational grievances and gossip— particularly gossip about Cannon.

There were tales about his personal habits coupled with charges that he dominated the party by bureaucratic means.

One of those who sought recruits for the minority faction on that basis was a man by the name of Ernest McKinney, who was organizer of the Newark branch of the SWP, to which I then belonged.

I had known and respected McKinney for several years before I joined the party and presumably for that reason was selected for the full treatment of horror stories.

McKinney was a member of the party's Political Committee and the morning after its meetings he would sit me down for a detailed account of Jim's latest offenses. One story about Jim allegedly turning up at a Political Committee meeting drunk sort of impressed me. But I found some of the other stories troublesome. McKinney offered vivid accounts of Jim dominating the Political Committee with the aid of a group of hand-raisers who blindly supported everything he favored.

I was especially disturbed when he described one meeting where a younger party leader for whom I had particular respect had assertedly spoken in favor of a proposal by Shachtman but then, after Jim opposed the proposal, voted against it.

When the faction fight developed to the point where the basic political issues in dispute—defense of the Soviet Union, etc.— were being debated I quickly decided I agreed with the Cannon-led majority. But I was still concerned about some of the "inside dope" stories McKinney had fed me. Particularly since I knew that members were being won to the Shachtman-Burnham group on the basis of these stories rather than the basic issues in dispute.

When a majority caucus was organized in Newark, Jim came to the initial meeting to report on the political developments in the fight nationally. After discussion was opened on the report, I stood up and presented a digest of some of the stories McKinney had told me. I asked Jim if he would respond to them since people were being won to the minority on the basis of these allegations and I considered it important to clear the air so we could get down to the main issues.

Jim looked at me—a bit frostily I thought— and said matter-of-factly, "We don't have time for that now. We'll discuss it another time."

I was somewhat troubled but I deferred. Even if the stories were true, I reasoned, they were still distinctly secondary to the central political issues at stake.

As the fight developed, and my own political understanding too, I acquired some comprehension of the "organization question." But the issue was not fully clarified for me until the very last days of the fight in the spring of 1940 when an internal party discussion bulletin appeared devoted in its entirety to Cannon's essay, "The Struggle for a Proletarian Party," the title piece of his subsequent book.

In this essay Cannon answered with devastating effectiveness the various organizational grievances and inventions so long circulated by the minority. At the same time he offered an exposition of Lenin's concept of political organization that won Trotsky's warm praise.

Jim's essay explained among other things why, if clarity is to be achieved, basic political and theoretical questions must be dealt with first. Important as they may be, organizational issues are really comprehensible only when considered as they relate to the key issues at hand. The lesson stuck in my mind.

In 1972, about two years before Jim died, I began doing taped interviews with him so that additional information about his life would be available to some future biographer.

There was no problem in getting him talking about his political experience over the years. But resistance was apparent when it came to questions about his personal life, particularly about his family relationships and his closest personal friends.

After several weeks of this somewhat frustrating experience, I read to him the section of his letter from prison about Trotsky's autobiography quoted at the outset of this article.

When I finished Jim seemed to wince. He puffed on his pipe for several moments and then explained that he had always been strongly inhibited about revealing deeply personal feelings. He thought he had acquired this from his mother who had instilled in him the notion that it wasn't seemly for people to make a public display of their feelings.

But after that he did make a greater effort to respond to such questions.

Not that he was aloof or impersonal in his relations with other people. Quite the contrary. But while he enjoyed many close personal relationships, there was always that element of reticence regarding some aspects of his personal life. Curiously, it was not a total inhibition. There were areas of his inner feeling—particularly what he regarded as failings—he would discuss quite freely.

One sensed that he wanted to avoid probing some things too deeply. Once, in explaining his reluctance to discuss too much of his early family life, he said, "It's too painful. At this stage of the game I don't want to start dredging up memories."

Because he was such a highly conscious person I think he realized the incongruities of some of his inhibitions and he sought to explain them away with the philosophical dictum he was so fond of citing, "Man, know thyself," to which he would add, "Man, forget thyself."

It was in the early 1950s that I first had the opportunity to know Jim in a personal way. It was again a time of difficulty for the party, with a new factional division in the organization. This time I found myself an early supporter of Jim's against a political opposition led by Bert Cochran and George Clarke which was rapidly moving away from the party's program and revolutionary perspective.

In addition to the inevitable political overhead of a faction fight within the party, there is often the added stress of a break in relationships among comrades who have been longtime friends and collaborators.

It was only later that Jim talked about it, but it was apparent that this was a painful aspect of the 1953 fight for him. Nor was it his first such experience.

George Clarke, for example, had worked closely with Jim almost from the day he had come into the movement in 1929 as an obviously gifted teen-ager. There were others besides George in the opposition who had been Jim's personal friends as well as political collaborators. A deeply sentimental person, it was no easy matter for Jim to enter into factional battle that cut through valued personal relationships. Yet throughout his entire political life he never seemed to have wavered once in doing what he regarded as his political duty without regard for personal considerations.

In discussions he would sometimes recall others with whom he had been forced to break because of deepgoing political differences. For instance, I had known of Hugo Oehler, a political sectarian who had left our movement in 1935. In his *History of American Trotskyism,* Jim had commented that prior to his break with our politics, Oehler had been a capable mass worker. What I didn't know was that for a number of years, beginning in the mid-1920s, Jim had regarded Oehler as one of his valued collaborators and close friends. Again, the political break meant a personal loss which was quite painful for him.

Jim, in the last days, would frequently mention Arne Swabeck, a pioneer Communist and Trotskyist who in the 1950s took a pro-Maoist course and left our movement in the 1960s. While Jim decisively rejected Arne's political line he was to the very end saddened by what had happened to him and would indicate how much he wished it could have been averted.

Often, in those last years, he would express a feeling of guilt about some of the people who left the movement, saying that if perhaps he had done more, tried harder, he might have been able to persuade them to reconsider their course.

Also, he began to talk about regretting his personal inhibitions. He felt that often they interfered with his saying and doing things he really wanted to.

Once he recalled waiting for a table in a downtown Los Angeles restaurant when he heard a voice that seemed familiar to him. Turning, he recognized the actor Walter Huston. Jim admired Huston and had just seen one of his pictures that he had liked.

"I thought it would be nice to simply tell him I had enjoyed the picture," Jim said. "But I just couldn't bring myself to do it."

He added wistfully, "It would have been a nice thing to do, don't you think?"

One of his greatest personal regrets, he said, was that he had been unable to offer personal friendship to Trotsky. He felt that Trotsky needed someone with whom he could have that kind of relationship and he felt that because he was closer to Trotsky's age than others in the movement he might have been able to play that role.

But he was just too inhibited to break the ice. (And, apparently, so was Trotsky.) Jim recalled with particular regret an experience while visiting Trotsky shortly after his son Leon Sedov had died under suspicious circumstances in Paris. Jim said he wanted very much to tell Trotsky about several hours he had once spent with Sedov in Paris in 1934. The only language they both spoke was German and Jim's was limited. Despite the language barrier they had found an immediate rapport.

Jim felt Trotsky might have appreciated hearing about that, but he found himself unable to tell him.

Despite that difficulty, Jim enjoyed many friendships. He quickly took to almost anyone who simply accepted him as a person rather than relating to him as a "leader." It was important to him that he be accepted and liked as an individual and he cherished every act of friendship extended to him.

Jim looked forward to each holiday or other occasions that provided the opportunity for a social get-together. To fully enjoy holiday occasions, he explained, they have to be thrice savored. "You have to savor the anticipation," he said. "Then you enjoy the occasion, and then you relish the memory of it."

In earlier years, one of his special pleasures was presiding over the eggnog at a Christmas open house. Another day he anticipated was Thanksgiving, with relatives and comrades over for a traditional dinner.

While some of Jim's notions of family life were rendered a bit antiquated by the rise of the women's movement, he was an enthusiastic supporter of that movement. He was proud that Rose Karsner had been an early feminist and he would note with pride that from the outset back in the 1920s they had referred to each other as companions rather than husband and wife. He said he had been stimulated to such awareness by the anarchist Emma Goldman, a feminist he admired.

In the recent years, Jim often expressed his gratification at the new, leading role being played by women in the SWP and YSA. A skilled journalist who read our press with a practiced, critical eye, he frequently mentioned how especially impressed he was by the abilities of the women writers on the *Militant*.

One of Jim's special capacities as a party leader was his ability to assess people in a rounded, objective way. In some cases one might think that his attraction to the particular virtue of one or another individual led him to develop blind spots regarding their shortcomings. But in the overwhelming majority of cases it was astonishing how well he could separate out people's strengths and weaknesses and see to it that the party had the benefit of their positive qualities. He incorporated into the party team many people who could have easily been passed over or rejected by others.

Discussing this question with him once, and trying to draw him out to the maximum, I finally closed off the questioning with the somewhat superfluous comment, "In other words, you're saying you have to work with what you've got."

Jim responded laconically, "You have to. That's all there is."

But his rounded approach to people represented a good deal more than simple "practicality." He could be extremely intolerant of some people. But when he decided someone possessed character and integrity, he could forgive a lot of faults.

I think this was particularly true of his attitude toward serious intellectuals. In his *Struggle for a Proletarian Party*, Jim responded to the Shachtmanite charge that the workers who constituted the base of the party majority in 1940 were "anti-intellectual." If anything, Jim observed, revolutionary workers have an exaggerated respect for intellectuals.

I think that perhaps this applied to him.

Growing up with the intellectual poverty of a small town like Rosedale, Kansas, Jim was hungry for knowledge and he deeply appreciated those who could provide it. Years later, he would wax eloquent in describing the impact of the radical magazine *The Liberator* at the time of the Russian revolution. Featuring radical poets, artists, and political writers, Jim said it illuminated the house with each arrival.

When the Communist Party assigned him to New York in the early 1920s, the first thing he did was to head down to Greenwich Village to meet the staff of *The Liberator*. He became good friends with a number of them as well as with the people around them. These included Max Eastman, Joseph Freeman, and others.

After Eastman broke with the socialist movement and went far to the right, Jim often recalled his talents and his contributions to the movement—contributions which he clearly felt outweighed Eastman's later break with the movement.

Jim lived his entire adult life under intense, unrelieved political and personal pressure. He was not afraid to accept the responsibility of political leadership, but it sometimes depressed him. I recall once in the early 1950s, during the period of the fight with the Cochran grouping, stopping by to visit with him one afternoon and finding him pretty glum. He tried, a little reluctantly I thought, to explain what was bothering him. He described his reaction when he first came to New York to participate in the central leadership of the early Communist Party. He tried, he said, to appraise the principal leaders of the young organization, with their pronounced sectarian tendencies. And as much as he might be inclined to leave the decisions to others, he recognized that despite personal abilities they were politically unqualified to lead the party. "I knew then," he said, "that I had to fight for the leadership."

There was not a trace of boastfulness in the statement. He was simply trying to explain that over the years he had been compelled to accept substantial responsibilities and sometimes the burden weighed down heavily.

Jim was stubborn, but it was not the product of a dogmatic mind. Jim was a politician with a consummate capacity for tactical flexibility. But, he stressed in discussions, you can only be flexible in your tactics if they are clearly designed to serve well-delineated principles. And, he added, the firmer and clearer you are in your commitment to principles, the greater will be your capacity for flexibility of tactics. His concept of principles was broad, including the basic ideals and vision which inspire people to join the movement.

In this connection, I recall vividly the speech he made at the sixtieth birthday party held for him in New York in 1950. In a manner appropriate to the occasion, he engaged in a bit of self-examination. "I didn't do the best I knew how," he ventured. "But I did the best I could. And that's all you can ask of anyone."

He added: "The mark of a man's life is his capacity to march to the music of his youth."

Jim Cannon passed that test with flying colors.

Charles Curtiss

Cannon several times compared his working methods with those of Trotsky. With Trotsky, Jim said—surely he made this observation to others—there was little free-ranging, easy-flowing, let-the-talk-wend-where-it-will, no-agenda discussions; everything was formal and "structured" and organized; every moment was utilized, and as soon as the agenda was completed, L. D. left for other work. Jim, on the other hand, delighted in these "bull sessions," with pipe or cigar and a glass of beer. He felt that this type of discourse was useful and productive, and that L. D. was missing something. (It may be that the latter, among his own contemporaries, was not quite so formal.)

These discussions with Jim included episodes from class struggles, particularly American; individuals participating in them; the radical movement; the factionalism-pervaded Communist Party and events and individuals connected with it; and, of course, the Socialist Workers Party in its development. And literature, too. I don't remember any other art form being discussed, but a great deal about novels, poetry, and drama. He would listen attentively while others spoke of philosophy and science but seldom took part in these discussions.

Cannon did not frequently talk about individuals apart from their politics; that is, the virtues or faults of individuals. But he

---

CHARLES CURTISS was born in 1908. He was among the earliest members of the Communist League of America and worked with Trotsky in Mexico in 1938-39 as a representative of the International Secretariat of the Fourth International. He left the Socialist Workers Party in 1951 and joined the Socialist Party, but maintained friendly relations with Cannon.

170

reserved a special antipathy for Jay Lovestone. In law, Jim said, pornography is forgiven if the work has "redeeming social value," but on this test Lovestone was completely beyond forgiveness—from the time the two first met to the present. This contempt for an individual was very unusual for Jim.

One afternoon in 1972 Jim told me that he had received a telephone call. A voice had asked, "How about a cup of coffee?" followed by a chuckle. I looked blank, and Jim explained that when he, Shachtman, Abern, and Spector first formed the Left Opposition, their former Communist Party colleagues would call them on the phone and question them about the Left Opposition, but were reluctant to come to the office to talk with them; fraternizing with Trotskyists was grounds for expulsion from the CP. Therefore, these questioners would be asked, "How about a cup of coffee?" at some cafe, in order to continue the discussion, and "How about a cup of coffee?" became a byword.

It was Shachtman on the phone, in Los Angeles for a visit, and he and Jim got together. What they spoke of I don't know, and Jim never said, but it must have been, below the surface humor and wit which surely flashed again and again, sad; one very sick with a faltering heart and knowing it, and the other old, frail, and ebbing fast, and knowing it, too; so estranged and so much sharing warm memories of past hopes and battles—saying farewell. I was bitterly denunciatory of Shachtman—and I believe with just cause—but Jim said not a word as I voiced my condemnation—just listened with a quizzical look. Jim, I felt, was glad the visit with Shachtman had taken place.

Cannon avoided "expletives" of a scatological type, whether referring to people, horses, or bulls, in his conversations and public talks. He also deliberately avoided sexual allusions. In the late 1940s, at a meeting of the National Committee, Cannon was absorbed in developing, from the rostrum, a theme in the course of a debate when he used an image that could be understood as risqué. There was laughter from the audience, and Cannon hesitated, obviously puzzled as to the why of the laughter. After a moment he continued.

Later during a recess, he told me that he had been somewhat confused and chagrined at the laughter and it had taken him a moment to realize its cause, for he made it a policy never to use sexual figures of speech or images in his talks, and above all, not suggestive ones. That the image could be understood two ways was inadvertent on his part; the *double entendre* was all in the minds of the auditors.

If Jim was reserved, Trotsky was even more constrained in this regard. Possibly among people of the same native language as his, and of the same age group, he may have been more relaxed, but I doubt it. When people used words or phrases as regards sex that were even somewhat coarse, L. D. sent out vibrations of being ill-at-ease and disapproving.

Surely, it need not be said that neither Cannon nor Trotsky were prudes; they did not meddle in others' lives nor were they censorious. They did not want sex made the subject of grossness and ribaldry. Besides, the average "dirty joke" is an expression of masculine domination, and this too they rejected.

The era of Cannon's boyhood, and many decades thereafter, was the period in American history when the foulness of child labor was much more widespread than now. His anger at child exploitation surely must have been one of the reasons for his ardent championship of the rights of youngsters to a happy and carefree childhood, an advocacy he frequently expressed. From the occasions when he spoke of his own childhood in Kansas I gather that his boyhood was happy, despite the straitened economic conditions of his family. He rejoiced in the company of children. In the months and years before his death, he was much taken by the visits, as an example, of Jo-Jo, the nickname of a four- or five-year-old, the daughter of a comrade, a sprite of a child, whose tongue seldom ceased wagging. But for Jim it was more than just amusement; he derived a reinvigoration from children and youth.

I was a witness at a poignant scene with Trotsky. A. Zamora, one of the editors of *Clave,* invited the entire editorial staff to his home in Mexico City for a meeting and social gathering. I do not remember if Natalia attended. It was a quiet evening, with good talk, some banter, much wit, as well as the business for which the meeting was assembled. But, in the early part of the evening, just after L. D. arrived, Zamora had a father-and-son quarrel with his teen-age son, over some incident—maybe a chore unattended, but anyway of the kind that takes place in millions of homes all over the world any day of any year. Zamora came down the stairs, shaking his head, and said something like: "What a trial children are!" Very quietly, and with deep sadness beyond words to convey, Trotsky said: Please don't say that. Children are very important. I know.

We were all silent; what could we say as we thought of the deaths of all the children of Natalia and L. D. at the hands of the murderer Stalin, and what unending grief and emptiness they faced?

Jim never made an issue of the use of "obscenities" by others; the use of foul language in L. D.'s presence seemed to be just unimaginable. However, both L. D. and Jim were aggressive in confronting the use of insulting and brutalizing terms and epithets of ethnic, racial, and national bigotry, arrogance, and oppression, terms which deny full dignity to people.

One of the American guards in Mexico, V. T. O'Brien, originally from Salt Lake City and a long-time friend of Reba and Joe Hansen, bore the nickname "Irish," a nickname used in complete innocence. But Trotsky raised the query: Are not the Irish people the objects of discrimination in the United States, and is not the nickname offensive? He did not raise this with me; the incident was recounted to me by others, possibly Joe or Reba.

But there was one occasion at which I was present. While on a visit to the household, L. D. asked about the Mexican comrades. I replied, and thought the topic closed, when suddenly L. D. warned me against any feeling of "big" nation superiority toward the Mexicans. I was astonished at the admonition, since my feeling toward the Mexican comrades was comradely and of high regard.

Trotsky continued, "Please don't feel hurt, Charles." He went on, "big nation" (in this case "Yankee") feelings of superiority toward small, colonial, or semicolonial people could infiltrate the thinking of the best-intentioned people, even on an unconscious or subconscious level. He said that the socialists of Russia had a vast experience in this regard, and again warned me I should be wary of the pitfalls of "big-country" arrogance. I assured him I had no such feelings, but would bear the warning in mind.

I dismissed this at the time as a piece of well-meaning fussiness, absolutely unnecessary. Yes? Six or seven years later, as an infantryman in World War II, the fortunes of war brought me to the French town of Digne, in Vichy France. There was a brief engagement with the rearguard of the retreating Hitler army, and when the firing stopped the townspeople poured into the streets in relief at the end of the gunfire, in celebration of their freedom from Hitler and his French collaborators, and in welcome to the "liberators."

One Frenchman spoke excellent English, and we held a long

conversation, alongside a military vehicle. He told me of life in France, and specifically in Digne, during the years since the fall of France.

Among the throngs I noticed a small man and woman, with Jewish features, followed by a brood of children. If an artist would have sought models for drawings of Jewish needle-trade sweatshop workers, the man and woman, no longer young, near-sighted, with stooped backs, would have been perfect. They stood out. I asked my acquaintance about them. Sure enough, they were Jewish needle-trades workers, Parisians, originally from Eastern Europe, who on the capitulation of Paris had been able to escape the Hitlerite pogrom and make their way to Digne. In Digne, ruled by the racist Vichy regime, collaborators with the Gestapo, the family was still in danger, however.

Here, my French friend told me, they had been hidden in a farmhouse, brought food and medicine for the youngsters. In return, they mended the patched garments of the inhabitants of Digne. Of course, I expressed my admiration at the act of solidarity; the people of Digne could well be proud of their courage, for those so shielding this family exposed themselves to arrest and possibly torture and death. I then told my new French friend a "joke" I had heard many years before, that when Jewish people go to the synagogue their prayer is: "Please, dear God, choose some other people."

The Frenchman thought this very funny and apt, and immediately hurried to the Jewish couple, standing some forty or fifty feet away, surely exulting in the feeling, for the first time in years, of not being hunted. He repeated the joke—but they didn't think it funny. They smiled uncertainly, but the look that leapt into their eyes seemed to say: The terror and anguish we endured should not be the subject of even kindly jests. They hurried away into the crowd. And L. D.'s warning came to my mind.

Although spurning luxuries—most of which are burdens imposed by the requirements of upper class conspicuous consumption anyway—both Cannon and L. D. theoretically defended the amenities and physical comforts of life, but in practice lived in a spare manner. Primarily, they wanted books, newspapers, periodicals, a pleasant and well-lighted place to work, read, and write, and people.

Jim enjoyed his pipe or cigar, whether the cigar was a four-for-a-quarter stogie or a more expensive weed. Trotsky not only did not smoke, but frowned on smoking in his presence, at least indoors. Possibly he simply frowned on smoking, but didn't make an issue of it.

Jim, for whom alcohol could be a problem, when in good health physically and psychologically could safely drink a beer, and did so with gusto. In the Trotsky household, on gala occasions, such as a welcome to a comrade or friend from abroad, brandy would be served. But I felt that for L. D. this was a concession, of which he did not completely approve, made to custom and possibly Natalia's sense of hospitality. I paid no heed, but it could well be that the brandy in L. D.'s glass went unsipped.

Jim delighted in people and discourse. As his strength waned, visits had to be rationed. He seldom expressed impatience with people, maybe it could be said that he suffered fools and bores patiently if not gladly. Trotsky, living under conditions of siege and constant peril, still wanted, insisted on, contact with people from the outside.

Lillian and I did not live in the household; she worked there days, while I only occasionally visited. I was sometimes asked to talk to someone who wanted an interview or discussion with L. D. to evaluate whether the visit would be safe and worthwhile from the point of view of security and L. D.'s time limitations. One such would-be visitor was a young American Lovestoneite. After a long conversation with him I concluded there would be little benefit organizationally or politically to be derived from such a visit with L. D. I so reported to either Joe or Jean van Heijenoort and the matter was closed with them.

But L. D., who had heard of the possible visit, was not satisfied, and cross-examined me. Was I sure? Was I not overly solicitous? He finally conceded, but I sensed that some doubt lingered— maybe we were too cautious. He explained to me—and others— more than once, that Stalin and the fascists wanted to isolate him; that each time security precautions cut him off from human contact represented a small victory for reaction, whether Stalinist or in any other form.

Still, in the L. D. household, as with Jim, there was a constant stream of visitors, and it was my privilege to attend some of the discussions with them. Both wanted people to talk with, to win over to socialism, or to their own viewpoint as to principles, tactics, and strategy for the socialist movement; people to give information and opinions, people with whom, in the course of presentation and counterpresentation, to test, corroborate, reinforce, adjust, modify, and maybe even to completely revise their own ideas.

(Democracy and democratic rights, the right of each human being to freedom of speech, press, religion, and assemblage, are hard-won achievements of humanity, restricted and inhibited as these rights are in actuality by the class structure of society. These democratic rights are particularly precious to those who challenge the structure of class and bureaucratic privilege, root, branch, and bud. Consequently, the challenged privileged strata constantly strive to further curtail democracy, a primary function of the FBIs or CIAs of all lands, or outlaw democracy, which is the function of the Gestapos and GPUs of all lands. Democracy is generally valuable in and of itself, and as a means of human progress; it is concretely and specifically essential in selecting the best course in building the socialist movement and building the good, rational—and democratic society. Democracy is both an end and a means.)

Both Trotsky and Cannon were very aware of the importance of writers and artists to socialism, not only because of the nature of their work, which has to explore social questions, but also because of the prestige such individuals add to the socialist movement. With Jim particularly this was extended to individuals in the sciences and professions; I know how he valued Harry Fischler and other medical practitioners, either in or close to the party, and serving the party not only in their professional capacities, but also enhancing the appeal of the organization. And Jim valued very much such writers as John Dos Passos, Max Eastman, and James T. Farrell, and grieved over their waverings, and finally their repudiation of socialism. He was pleased when Farrell retraced his steps, at least part way, back to socialism.

Occasionally Trotsky raised topics which I regret I didn't ask him to elaborate. One arose out of a briefing he gave me about Diego Rivera, a briefing made necessary as I was called on to be an intermediary in the differences between L. D. and Rivera. My role as intermediary, fact, if not modesty, compels me to state was not important. The differences have been recounted elsewhere; I will only repeat that L. D. tried earnestly and with great forebearance to keep Rivera in, or at least close to, the Fourth International. He expressed himself in the course of the briefing thus: With my writings I can convince people in the ones and fives. Rivera with his paintings can draw thousands to socialism. But in detailing the evolution of the differences, L. D. said that Rivera began by referring back to an incident of twenty years before, at the time of the formation of the Third International, when, Rivera held, the International, and Trotsky, had made a mistake as regards the fledgling Communist Party of Mexico. In the beginning of the rupture between the two, Rivera tried to soften the assertion by saying: Trotsky, or the Third International, could not be expected to be cognizant of the problems of "little" Mexico, being preoccupied with the problems of "big" Russia. Trotsky's somewhat wry comment was: You know, we made plenty of mistakes regarding "big" Russia, too.

I was tempted to ask him what these mistakes were, but knowing the demands of his work, and knowing he was planning to write books on the Soviet Union after the revolution, I didn't. Stalin's pickax decreed that the books were not to be written.

But an even more important question came up when Trotsky was discussing a Belgian comrade, of whom Trotsky observed: He is a worker but has the faults of a petty bourgeois. On one level, came to mind: How is it that a worker could adopt a middle-class viewpoint, while Trotsky, by origin middle class, felt he was upholding the working class viewpoint? An interesting question, but even so, subordinate to a more important question: How does an entire working class, while constantly pressing to improve its status within capitalism but never challenging the validity of capitalism itself, free itself from capitalist ideology and adopt a working class, that is, socialist viewpoint? In this country, the term "blue collar," at least for white workers, has become synonymous with reaction and racism (an imputed attitude not completely justified, but with enough substance to cause socialists to wince). How does this working class become class conscious, that is, socialist, in its aspirations? What can socialists do to accelerate the process? An important question.

This is a question I wish, now more than ever, I had asked. I may not have agreed with his answer, but what he would have said surely would have been wise and illuminating.

Both Jim and L. D. encouraged efforts at independent theoretical work. This scene, after the passage of decades, is understandably vague but is told as an example of Jim's deliberate encouragement of work in theory. A small group of young people were seated at a table in a Chicago restaurant, either during a break in an all-day meeting, or after it had ended. Jim came in, picked up a cup of coffee at the counter, looked for a seat, and saw us. He was plainly fatigued, and probably would have preferred to sit alone, but as that would have been a slight, he joined us.

We stopped our conversation but he asked us to continue (he protested against the respectful silences that met his entrance into a room or into a group). One young comrade was telling of a visit he had paid that day to a picnic of a group of Socialists— probably to sell *Militants*. Anyway, this young comrade was somewhat outraged. These Socialists, who prided themselves on their knowledge of Marxism, had taken an "inevitableistic" (he didn't use this term) attitude toward socialism; they had counseled him somewhat patronizingly not to be so intense, since socialism was "inevitable." And with dramatization, and maybe exaggeration to make his point, he described a group of pinochle players, and one telling him, "Don't get excited, young comrade; socialism is inevitable. Marx proves it. I bid 300."

Then this young party member went on, developing a train of thought to this effect: There are two mistakes; one, that socialism is inevitable regardless of what people do or don't do, which he called the pinochle-playing Marxists; and the other, that socialism could be achieved by will and activity, regardless of conditions, and of the ideas and feelings of the working class.

Jim at first only half-listened, but as this young comrade expressed himself with verve, humor, and earnestness, Jim became attentive. Jim gave a brief extemporaneous dissertation on the subjective and objective conditions for socialism and urged the comrade to further study, and to speak and write on the subject as it was of great importance.

I wish I could recall Jim's remarks more sharply; all I remember is the young comrade relating the events, his awkward attempts to generalize from them, and Jim's vigorous encouragement of theoretical endeavor.

As with Jim, L. D. was constantly alert to foster theoretical research and study. Here I can cite a little incident. Lillian and I made a trip to Vera Cruz by bus, and on our return, stopped in the city of Orizaba, staying overnight in a hotel patronized by tourists. On the day we came to Orizaba, a textile town, a general strike had been declared. Our fellow guests at the hotel were astounded by our intrepidity in leaving the safety of the hotel to visit the town. We talked with strike pickets, to whom we expressed our solidarity. The pickets proudly took us to the strike headquarters, the athletic field and stadium the union had built, the union cooperative store, introduced us to union officials, and conducted us to the home of one of the older members of the union, a very impressive man, who spoke some English and was a devoted musician—a grand piano nearly filled the tiny living room of his home. And as a gesture of fraternity he played a classical piece for us. It was a thrilling, unforgettable experience, and on returning to Coyoacán, we enthusiastically told the guards about it, and Trotsky learned of it. He termed our adventure a "study," and used the term completely without irony and although we demurred at what we considered a grandiloquent term for a sight-seeing experience, he insisted on the term "study" possibly to encourage us.

Alas, this desire to encourage theoretical work by younger socialists led to Trotsky's murder, for the assassin used the pretext of a paper on occupied France to gain entry to Trotsky's study and while Trotsky was reading the paper, to deliver the death blow.

In this connection of theoretical work, I have the duty to relay a tribute Trotsky paid to Usick Vanzler (John G. Wright). While we were in Mexico, L. D. was working on his biography of Stalin, but had few facilities to verify data and dates. In New York, Usick proved invaluable, and Trotsky expressed himself to me with deep gratitude for Usick's conscientious research work. And even more: Trotsky said that Vanzler was not only a valuable aide, he was an equally valuable colleague, "it could be said a coauthor," for Usick made valuable suggestions and critiques and even proposed lines of development for the book, many of which L. D. accepted. This warm tribute by L. D. is doubly worthy of being recorded because of the special bond of friendship between Cannon and Vanzler. To the day of Jim's death, on the wall of his workroom, there was a photograph of Usick.

But it has to be admitted that on one occasion when L. D. sought help, I and the other Americans couldn't deliver. He was a target of attack by some U.S. senators, and was drafting a reply. He asked me if I could verify a quotation from Shakespeare which he wanted to use, from *Coriolanus* he thought, that went something like this, as L. D. remembered:

"Roman senator: . . . 'You are a liar.'"
"Roman citizen: 'Yes, but you are a senator.'"

I could not verify the quotation. I didn't even recall it and had to confess I had never read *Coriolanus*. L. D. expressed himself rather scathingly about my, and the other Americans' ignorance of the literature of our language.*

He didn't say so on this occasion, but often said and wrote that a Marxist, as with Marxism, must stand on the apex of the best of all previous culture and from this position develop culture, in the full sense of the word, even to greater heights.

Now if L. D. had asked Jim Cannon about Shakespeare he might have received the information he sought: play, act, scene, and line; for Jim loved to read aloud from Shakespeare. When there was an outstanding cinema production of *King Henry V,* with Olivier, Cannon saw it, possibly a number of times. He read to us with feeling the stirring rallying call of King Hal to his soldiers on the eve of the battle that was to take place on the day of Crispin-Crispian (Saints Crispinus and Crispianus):

Rather proclaim it, Westmoreland, through my host,
That he which hath no stomach to this fight,
Let him depart; his passport shall be made
And crowns for convoy put into his purse:
We would not die in that man's company
That fears his fellowship to die with us.
This day is called the feast of Crispian:
He that outlives this day, and comes safe home,
Will stand a tip-toe when this day is named,
And rouse him at the name of Crispian.
He that shall live this day, and see old age,
Will yearly on the vigil feast his neighbours,
And say 'Tomorrow is Saint Crispin':. . .

And Crispin Crispian shall ne'er go by,
From this day to the ending of the world,
But we in it shall be remembered;
We few, we happy few, we band of brothers. . . .

Jim reveled in the swing and ring of the words. And above all, surely, wasn't there a real if unspoken transference when Jim read the words: "we band of brothers"?—to which only should be added "and sisters."

---

* Is not the quotation in *Othello,* opening act and scene?
  "Brabantio: 'Thou art a villain.'
  "Rodrigo: 'You are a senator.'"

Evelyn Reed

I first met Jim Cannon thirty-five years ago in 1940 at Trotsky's house in Coyoacán, Mexico. A more likely way to have run into him would have been at the SWP headquarters, then at 116 University Place, which was only about five blocks from where I lived at the time on Tenth Street in Manhattan. However, through a series of somewhat bizarre circumstances, I had taken off for Mexico City and arrived there in January 1940. By the time Jim came down that June I had become a friend of Natalia and L. D., visiting them daily and helping the household.

Jim arrived shortly after the May 24 night attack on the household by a band of Stalinist assassins armed with machine guns, headed by the Mexican artist Siqueiros. They kidnapped Sheldon Harte, one of the guards, who was later found murdered. On that occasion they failed to assassinate Trotsky. Since no one knew when or how the next deadly attempt would be made, the first order of business was to reinforce the security of the little fortress.

After attending to that, Jim and the contingent who came with him settled down to a series of discussions with the Old Man. Among the participants were Farrell Dobbs, Antoinette Konikow, Sam Gordon, and Joe Hansen. Their discussions covered a variety of topics on the issues of the day, such as the impending war and its perspectives for revolutionaries, the Shachtman-Burnham fight, party organization methods, policy toward the Stalinists, youth, and racial minorities. A stenogram of these

EVELYN REED was born in 1905. She met Cannon in Mexico in 1940 and worked with him closely in the following decades in New York and Los Angeles. She is the author of *Woman's Evolution: From Matriarchal Clan to Patriarchal Family*.

talks can be found in Pathfinder's *Writings of Leon Trotsky (1939-40)*.

Natalia and L. D. lived such a closed-in existence that they were always eager for an opportunity to leave the place, see the countryside they loved, and collect new specimens of cactus plants to take back for their garden. They felt that Jim and the other guests from the States should be treated to such a festive event, which they called a "picnic."

Such excursions were hazardous and not taken very often. The most elaborate precautions were made to ensure secrecy about the time of departure and destination. Usually two cars, each with armed guards, "slipped out" and sped down the roadway from the house. I rode with Natalia in one of these cars. Once we were well away from the house and assured we were not followed, it was relatively safe to explore the countryside.

On this occasion, as I recall, Farrell drove one car and Joe Hansen the other. Our destination was the top of Toluca Mountain, some 15,000 feet above sea level. The long, narrow, winding dirt road, with a yawning precipice on one side and corroding rocks and gravel slithering down from the mountain wall on the other, seemed bloodcurdling to me. Didn't anyone else realize how dangerous this journey was? Apparently not, for the others just kept on talking and enjoying "the view."

All except Jim, as I learned later, since he was in the other car with Trotsky. Jim was far from the athletic type. His most strenuous exercise consisted in walking his dog down a pleasant lane for a short distance on a sunny afternoon. On occasion, when he was surrounded by more energetic people, he would willingly remain in the house, seated near the hearth fire, fortified by pipe and beer can, waiting for the sports-minded to come back and regale him with their day's exploits. In addition he disliked great heights. So a rugged expedition to a mountaintop was not exactly Jim's dish of tea.

When we finally arrived up there it was cold and damp. Natalia and L. D. enjoyed every minute of the outing, red noses and all, and the hot lunch we prepared tasted very good. But the rarefied atmosphere that affected breathing, as well as other discomforts, were not for Jim. Although he did not utter a word of complaint, he "hibernated" somewhere in a corner until we were ready to make the descent trip.

I first met Rose and became better acquainted with Jim after returning to New York, a few months after Trotsky's assassination in August 1940. In fact, Rose and Jim became my two oldest and closest friends. I believe it was through Jim's suggestion that I was asked to work with George Novack, which resulted in our becoming not only colleagues but husband and wife.

In the spring of 1941 George and I were asked to go to the Twin Cities where the union conflict with Teamster President Tobin was brewing. The branch required reinforcements for that struggle. George was to teach classes on American history and other subjects and we would be available for contingencies.

That was the period when President "I Hate War" Roosevelt was dragging the American people down the road toward the Second World War. His antagonism toward the Socialist Workers Party for its outspoken opposition to the imperialist slaughter coincided with the Teamster officials' determination to get rid of the militant Local 544's leadership. Roosevelt was conspiring with Tobin to victimize both the antiwar Trotskyists and the union militants. Under these circumstances contingencies were bound to occur.

A house had been rented for George and me in St. Paul from a professor who was away on a sabbatical. Before long Rose and Jim came out from New York and stayed with us. The house soon became the center for informal sessions where moves to meet the assaults of Tobin and his goons were discussed. We never completed our tenure in that place because more than the anticipated contingencies piled up to send us back to New York.

In June 1941 Tobin appointed a receiver over Local 544 and in July the FBI raided the Minneapolis SWP headquarters. Shortly afterward indictments were handed down which resulted in the eventual conviction and imprisonment of eighteen leaders and members of the SWP and Local 544. Jim was not intimidated by these blows. "They have lined practically everybody else up for the war," he said in one of the public statements, "but they couldn't line us up. We are against it and will continue to be against it even though confined to prison."

These events cut short our stay in Minneapolis. George took a train back to New York (it was still train, not plane, travel in those days!). He had to rally sponsors and supporters for a national defense committee. I followed by automobile, driving Rose back with me—after assuring Jim, who looked uncertain, that I was a duly qualified driver. In New York George and I set up and administered the Civil Rights Defense Committee (CRDC) with headquarters at 160 Fifth Avenue.

The CRDC had local branches in many cities but because so

many men were in the army or in war industries it was primarily the women members who carried on the struggle to gain support and raise funds for the case. They did well. At its peak more than 200 unions representing 1.5 million workers gave their support to the campaign. Jim, an old hand at defense work, was very satisfied with the results achieved by the members of the CRDC.

We carried the fight up to the Supreme Court—which three times refused to hear the case. So on January 1, 1944, Jim and the others indicted under the Smith "Gag" Act went to prison for standing by their antiwar views. In his speech at the New York farewell banquet Jim said defiantly: "Our party didn't sell out. It didn't lie. We told the truth. That is why we are being railroaded to prison."

Years before, in 1926, when Jim was national secretary of the International Labor Defense, he said that the path to freedom leads through a prison. "The door swings in and out and through that door passes a steady procession of those fools too stubborn to bend, who will not turn aside from the path because prisons obstruct it here and there."

Jim did not waste precious time in prison; he decided to "bone up" on a lot of subjects that in the normal course of political life he would have little time for. So the prison term was converted into a university course for Jim and the others who were behind bars with him. They requested the CRDC to send them books, magazines, newspapers. Science, history, philosophy, poetry, and languages were read and studied in prison.

It was a vexing, laborious task to get the books into prison since Attorney General Biddle insisted on approving every single item that went in, which created much stalling and red tape. But if the books didn't get to Sandstone on time, according to Jim's study schedule, I heard about it plenty—through Rose! Jim's letters to her were our principal means of communication, as his book *Letters from Prison* testifies.

In January 1945, seven months before the war ended, Jim and eleven others were released from Sandstone (six had been let out earlier). Now on a new job as reporter for the *Militant*, I was assigned to go to Minneapolis to cover the "homecoming" story. As I leaned over the railing in the railroad station, I saw some of the younger men bounding up the stairs. Jim was somewhere behind, not yet in sight. He's getting on in years, I thought, but that hasn't altered his fighting spirit. I remembered the photo taken upon their surrender to the federal marshal in Minneapolis when Jim and Vincent Dunne proudly marched to their prison terms at the head of the brigade.

After Jim came back to New York and the war ended, life returned to normal. George and I were back in our Tenth Street apartment where we had many lively dinners and convivial discussions late into the night with Rose and Jim and many other comrades. Various ideas were sounded out and some good ones carried into execution. The two that came up over and over again were our need for a Rest and Recreation camp and our need for a cadre school.

In the previous years I would sometimes rent a summer house where Rose and Jim would stay and many of us on our day or weekend off would go for a rest and some good conversation. While Jim was in prison Rose stayed in a house at Seacliff on the north shore of Long Island, from which a long flight of stairs led down to the sea. Later there was a little cottage for Rose and Jim at Armonk, where visitors could swim in a tree-surrounded natural pool—icy-cold but delicious—while Jim walked his dog Wong. But these were improvised arrangements that were quite inadequate for any number of comrades.

Meanwhile Jim was pressing for a school for SWP organizers and other activists who carried on the daily work of the party but had to secure their education as best they could on the wing. Thanks to Connie and George Weissman a happy combination of cadre school and summer camp was established at Mountain Spring, New Jersey. In the summer months adults and children took their vacations at the camp; the rest of the time it became the Trotsky School, educating comrades selected from all over the country. George Novack was resident "dean" of the school, and among the regular and occasional instructors were Tom Kerry, Joe Hansen, Farrell Dobbs, George Weissman, John G. Wright, and Murry Weiss.

Rose and Jim moved out to Los Angeles around 1952. In 1954 George and I also went there where we remained until our return to New York in 1964. We saw a great deal of Jim and Rose while in that city, and usually spent time with them on their periodical visits to the desert. Jim liked the desert because of its warmth and enjoyed watching the changing purple shadows and brilliant lights on the mountains that surrounded the desert.

Through all these years I became fairly well acquainted with Jim's personality and character. Publicly he is best known as a political person, tough and canny in any kind of political or labor fight. But he was also a very humane individual, sensitive to the needs or distress of any of his comrades. He had very little patience with chronic complainers who thought the world revolved around their petty egos and could not distinguish between "the world's agony" and their private pains. But he was keenly perceptive of any genuine appeal for help even when it was mute—and spared no efforts to remedy the situation where he could. Jim understood the difficulties of keeping going in capitalist society which systematically undermines the self-confidence of people. He had the gift, through word or gesture, of restoring some assurance and fortifying resistance to those who were temporarily shaken.

In addition to compassion, Jim had a lively wit and ready sense of humor. He knew we were "transitional people" living in the lights and shadows of a convulsively changing world. History had placed upon us the colossal task of helping to guide the course of social and political change to victory. But this was no excuse for adopting a pained posture or living like martyrs. On the contrary, Jim found much to enjoy and poke fun at on the way to liberation.

This is evidenced by Jim's taste in the popular humorists of his day. He was delighted by W. C. Fields, the satirist with the bulbous nose, whose caustic comments exposed capitalism's most sacred institutions. He appreciated Mae West who held up Victorian puritanical mores to ridicule. He relished the picturesque slang used by Damon Runyon. Along with his frequent quotations from Shakespeare and what he called the "Good Book," Jim would sometimes display Runyonesque humor of his own.

Jim had no use for reverence. So I feel he would not object to this tale of what happened after he reached the pearly gates guarded by St. Peter, venerated by his Catholic forebears:

Saint Peter: Well, Cannon, you didn't do so good down there but seeing as you're white and Irish I guess I'll give you admission to heaven anyway.

Jim: Listen, bub, they put me on the wrong train going in the wrong direction. I want a ticket to where my friends are—the Jews, the Poles, the Blacks, the women. . . .

Saint Peter: The women? The good ones are up here, dressed in white, playing their shiny harps and praising their lord and master. . . .

Jim: That's what I mean. I want a ticket to where Rose is—raising hell and organizing for the biggest jailbreak in the history of the heavens.

Photo by Joseph Hansen

Arne Swabeck, James P. Cannon, Rose Karsner, Sam Gordon, Oscar Coover, Sr., and Carl Skoglund. Mountain Spring Camp, New Jersey, 1949.

Max Geldman

I shall confine the greater part of my remarks on the memory of Jim Cannon to an account of an experience I shared with him—that is, the imprisonment of the eighteen Trotskyists and leaders of the Minneapolis Teamsters union for our opposition to World War II. Most of those gathered here tonight are familiar with the events leading up to the trial, conviction, and sentencing of the Trotskyists and Minneapolis Teamsters leaders. We represented a threat to the government's desires for a passive working class stripped of militant union leadership. Those who are not familiar with these events can obtain books and writings relating to the trials, and describing the vicious nature of the Smith Act under which we were convicted and imprisoned. The sentences ran from twelve to sixteen months. I shared the sixteen-month sentence with Jim, which we served in the federal prison called Sandstone, in northern Minnesota.

But before I tell you about the kind of prisoner, the kind of convict, Jim Cannon was, I cannot help but pause because the faces of the others who served time with us, both the dead and the living, come before my eyes. Particularly Vincent Dunne, so staunch, so full of courage and wisdom; and Carl Skoglund and Oscar Coover, Sr., class-struggle fighters all, with total commitment to the party and the socialist goal. But, back to Jim Cannon

MAX GELDMAN was born in 1905. He joined the Communist League of America in 1930 and was a fellow prisoner with Cannon at Sandstone penitentiary in 1944-45 after their conviction in the 1941 Minneapolis trial. He was a Socialist Workers Party branch organizer in Philadelphia and Newark in the 1940s and 1950s. This is an excerpt from a talk in Los Angeles on September 3, 1974.

as a prisoner. At that time federal prison regulations were based on segregating the so-called offenders of the law. The American Criminal Code did not have, and still does not have, a category for political prisoners. So, since we were not what the authorities termed at that time "draft dodgers," we were in the dormitory with the thieves, bank robbers, drug peddlers, addicts, and you name it. Black inmates were segregated into one dormitory; COs (conscientious objectors) were in another dormitory; Jehovah's Witnesses (who claimed they were preachers and therefore exempt from the draft) were in still another dormitory; and Black Muslims (from Chicago) were in another dormitory. All were segregated on the basis of police-type thinking which believed that this makes for law and order.

Jim, as all who knew him well recognized, was a shy man outside of the political arena. He did not advertise himself as the political leader of the American Trotskyist movement. He conducted himself as a prisoner, demanding no special privileges.

Jim was assigned the job of dormitory orderly. His duties were to sweep, mop, and dust his side of the dormitory floor and surroundings. I can tell you that he did a good job keeping his side of the dorm spic and span. He had a real good stroke with the mop, and although I asked him where he learned it, he never told me—just smiled and continued the rhythmic swing of the mop. An example of his competence in carrying out the Trotskyist slogan of "being the best worker on the job" is he was never called down by the authorities for negligence. Friday was the day of the week when the prison brass made the rounds to inspect the sanitary conditions of the dormitories. The doctor, wearing white gloves, was followed by the captain of the guards, and a retinue. They went through the dorms looking for dust and other evidence of neglect. Jim never got a "shot." That means he was not given a demerit. (Demerits meant loss of privileges.)

Jim, along with the rest of us, did what is called "easy time." We did not generally butt our head against prison regulations. We organized our time and took on study projects. Jim took on the study of Greek history and philosophy. His quotations from the Greek philosophers show he studied well. His most significant contributions from that period are in the published volume *Letters from Prison*.

All inmates of Sandstone knew that the Trotskyists were a "different" type of prisoner. We had the reputation of being "good cons." That meant there was no fear of anything being said to us getting back to the authorities, and there was a general respect shown us. One particular conversation I recall was with two other inmates of our dormitory. I don't remember their names, but they had been involved in some graft operation in the Hollywood Stage Hands union. They expressed to me the respect they had for the Trotskyists, and how they wished that they could have been in prison for the reason we were. The Black Muslims talked with no one else but us; and we also talked with the COs and the Jehovah's Witnesses.

A typical day in prison went something like this. I worked in the kitchen, which meant working a split shift. After the breakfast shift I returned to the dormitory where Jim, who by this time was all through with his sweeping and mopping, would be in the wash-up room shaving and cleaning up. We would exchange greetings and a few short comments on what we heard or knew inside or outside the walls. Then we would go back to our small bed-spaces to continue our studies, write letters, or read. The afternoons, after work hours, were spent walking in the prison yard, or in warm weather watching the ongoing baseball game. We also spent our time visiting with other comrades, and holding fraction meetings. We had a Sandstone fraction where we discussed political questions and matters regarding our appeals and defense. In the evenings, after dinner, we were locked in after 6:00 p.m. Jim and I would play two games of checkers. I never did win a game. Years later he told me I never won because he had gotten hold of a book on checker strategy and was always able to make the necessary moves to swamp me. I remember very well how after wiping me off the board he would use that well-known hand gesture that was part of his speaking technique, and say: "Pay attention. Practice without theory will get you nowhere." We never played more than two games because there was studying and reading to be done.

On weekends we relaxed with light reading, and some of us were fortunate to have visitors. Unfortunately, during the entire period of Jim's imprisonment Rose was only able to visit him once. Sandstone was a long way from New York, and the trip was a hard and costly one.

The high point of Sunday was the Sunday night movie which Jim really enjoyed. He was a movie fan from way back. Such was the routine of the greater part of the time we served at Sandstone.

As I remarked before, we all did "easy time"—but there was one time when Jim blew his cool. The incident took place around a

CO who buckled under the pressure and lost control. The prison authorities threw him into the "Hole" to cool off. In Sandstone, the Hole was a bare cement cell where the prisoner was kept in total isolation with food restricted to bread and water. This CO had become sympathetic to our ideas, and Jim had gotten to know him and had established a friendship with him. Jim went wild when he heard what had happened to the CO. As I recall it took all the efforts of the rest of us in the dormitory to calm Jim down before the guards arrived. We sure didn't want Jim sent into the Hole also.

One more note on our prison life. Through the efforts of our defense committee we were able to get the *Militant* into the prison, and we followed with feelings of excitement the accounts of the rising circulation of the paper and the growth of the party.

Photo by Joseph Hansen

Cannon and Rose Karsner, Sutton Island, Maine, 1949.

Karolyn Kerry

Tom Kerry and I first came to New York as part of the substitute leadership after Jim, Farrell Dobbs, and the other party leaders had been railroaded to prison in 1944 under the Smith "Gag" Act.

We stayed with Rose Karsner, Jim's companion, collaborator, and a long-time party leader in her own right, while Jim was in prison.

Prison regulations required that the "inmates," as they are called, limit their correspondence to members of their immediate families. Rose, therefore, served as the link for Jim's correspondence with the party leadership.

There was one aspect of Jim's correspondence that had Rose and the rest of us completely mystified. When Jim entered prison he was suffering from ulcers. His customary diet was milk and bananas. Under the circumstances, food, as such, was of little interest to him.

When, therefore, his letters began to deal at great length about the most esoteric menus, we were convinced he was attempting to communicate with the party leadership through a code of his own design. Unfortunately, neither Rose nor anyone else in the party leadership had been provided with a key to the code.

KAROLYN KERRY was born in 1910. She joined the Communist League of America in 1934 in San Francisco where she was active in the trade union movement. She came to New York in 1944 to help strengthen the Socialist Workers Party national office while Cannon and seventeen other party leaders were imprisoned under the Smith Act. She worked with Cannon in the late 1940s and early 1950s before he moved to Los Angeles. This talk was given at the Socialist Educational Conference in Oberlin, Ohio, on August 23, 1974.

Here is a typical example of one menu from the Pathfinder Press book *Letters from Prison* (letter number 30): "This," wrote Jim, "is Sunday morning and I am thinking of a breakfast of soft-boiled eggs with creamery butter, orange juice (iced), milk, crepes suzette and rightly made coffee with cream."

We puzzled greatly over Jim's menus only to learn later that there was no code, and therefore no key, but that Jim, like all the others, was driven to improvising imaginative menus by the spartan diet imposed by the prison authorities.

In fact, a key to the solution to the puzzle was provided in letter number 125—ninety-five letters later—which reads: "You can tell the friends who inquire about my health that I am all right. I continue to stick strictly to my diet of boiled eggs and milk three times a day, seven days a week, and will stick to it until January 22. Then I think, I will be entitled to a little variety and *I am beginning to look forward to the special menus previously sent to you.*"

But this subject was only incidental to Jim's *real* concern, his constant preoccupation with problems of party politics, strategy, tactics, and especially education. I recall, for example, several very important areas of party activity, which received their initial impetus from Jim's letters.

1. The proposal for a mass *Militant* subscription drive to be aimed at new readers. Jim thought he was being optimistic when he projected a tentative quota of 3,000 for a 25-cent six-month sub. I can't remember the exact figure of this subscription drive— our first since the war—but I know it exceeded the 3,000 figure. What I *do* remember, however, is that soon after, in 1945, we were achieving goals of more than 20,000 in our *Militant* subscription campaigns.

This drive to make the *Militant* a paper of mass circulation was aided by the work of our first trailblazer team, composed of Eloise Booth and Rudie Rhodes, who traveled by bus from city to city and state to state, selling *Militant* subs to new readers.

2. Party education. In this area Jim conveyed many new ideas of expanding party education for party members and party leaders. He urged us to apply, in this area of party work, the same Bolshevik spirit that animates all of our party-building activities.

It was through Jim's prodding that the first Trotsky School was organized and continued for a number of years thereafter. In a sense we can justly attribute the past several annual educational conferences of the Young Socialist Alliance and the

Socialist Workers Party to his reiterated emphasis on organized and systematic educational activities.

I cannot in these few minutes even begin to summarize all of Jim's thoughts on the ways and means of building the party and making it a more effective instrument of revolutionary struggle.

If there is any generalization I can make about Jim Cannon's character, it was his total commitment, his total immersion, his total concern about the party and with the party, first manifested for me in his letters from prison. That was true of the Jim Cannon I first met in San Francisco in 1934, until the day he died last Wednesday.

Jim Cannon's life as a revolutionary fighter—as a leader of the IWW, as a founder of the American Communist Party, and as a founder and leader of the American Trotskyist movement—will, I am convinced, provide an inspiration and a guide to all members of the SWP and YSA. And to those yet to come, who will dedicate their lives to the task of carrying forward the struggle—to which he contributed his entire adult life—to overthrow this monstrous, outworn, and decaying capitalist system and to establish a new order, the world socialist society.

This is why we will forever love and cherish the memory of our beloved friend, our comrade, and our peerless leader, Jim Cannon.

Tom Kerry

I knew the invitation to speak at this meeting would present a problem: How, in the brief time allotted, would it be possible to deal adequately with the many aspects of Jim Cannon's kaleidoscopic personality; or even to recite but a small portion of the store of biographical reminiscences; or to list, let alone expatiate on, the countless contributions made in his lifetime of service to the working class struggle for a world socialist society?

Having long ago learned not to attempt the impossible, I decided to address myself to what I consider the dominant trait of Jim Cannon's political physiognomy (understanding by that term the external manifestation of a compulsive inner drive), namely, the building of a Leninist combat party on American soil capable of leading the working class struggle for socialist power in this citadel of world imperialism.

The building of a Leninist party and Leninist international was a major preoccupation of Cannon's political life. Jim had been convinced, by the experience of the October 1917 revolution in Russia and its repercussions in Europe and the world, that the combat party was an indispensable prerequisite for the conquest of proletarian power—at least in the industrially advanced countries of the world.

From that time forward Cannon considered himself a Leninist.

TOM KERRY was born in 1901. He joined the Workers Party of the United States in 1934 and met Cannon in San Francisco in 1936, collaborating closely with him in the leadership of the Socialist Workers Party until Cannon's death. He has been an editor of the *Militant* and of the *International Socialist Review*. He made these remarks at a meeting in New York on September 18, 1974.

"Lenin's greatest contribution to his whole epoch," Cannon wrote, "was his idea and his determined struggle to build a vanguard party capable of leading the workers in revolution.

"And he did not confine his theory to the time of his own activity. He went all the way back to 1871, and said that the decisive factor in the defeat of the first proletarian revolution, the Paris Commune, was the absence of a party of the revolutionary Marxist vanguard, capable of giving the mass movement a conscious program and a resolute leadership."

Jim then underscores the paramount importance he attached to what he considered Lenin's primary contribution, by concluding: "It was Trotsky's acceptance of this part of Lenin in 1917 that made Trotsky a Leninist."

Although Jim Cannon became a convert to Leninism in the period following the October revolution of 1917, it was not until 1928, eleven years later, that he became a Trotskyist. Through a fluke he came into possession of a copy of Trotsky's "Criticism of the Draft Program of the Communist International" at the Sixth World Congress of the Comintern.

A study of that document convinced Jim that Trotsky was advocating and defending the Leninist line in theory, strategy, tactics, and party organization. The rest is history. The "Criticism of the Draft Program of the Communist International" was published in the very first issues of the *Militant* and became the platform of the American section of the Trotskyist Left Opposition. From that time forward, to Jim Cannon, Leninism and Trotskyism were synonymous.

It was to this central question of the party that Cannon devoted much of his time, his energy, and his considerable talents. It commanded the unstinting application of his mental and physical resources to the very day of his death.

Much of Cannon's published work is of a polemical character. His opponents can testify that in internal party struggle he was a redoubtable faction fighter. But that was just one aspect of his character, albeit a very important one.

Jim was a great admirer of Eugene Victor Debs. He considered him to be one of the greatest orators, agitators, and propagandists that the American working class radical movement had produced. He wrote a pamphlet paying tribute to Debs's single-minded commitment to the workers' struggle for emancipation from wage slavery.

He remarked on Debs's readiness to respond to the call for aid from any battlefront in the class war. This was the side of Debs that Jim admired without stint.

After Jim left the party center in New York to live in Los Angeles, he decided to write an essay on Debs, which had been long germinating in his mind.

"My projected essay," he wrote, "would have two sides. First, I would undertake to show Debs in all his grandeur as a proletarian hero; as the prototype and exemplar of the revolutionary man of the masses, the trade union organizer, the strike leader, the inspirer of the youth.

"That side of the project will be a labor of love for me, for I dearly love the memory of Debs."

"But," Jim added, "I would feel obliged also to deal with another side of Debs; what I consider the weaker side, which has never been adequately examined and explained by other biographers and evaluators. In fact, it has never been touched; and the true picture of the real Debs, 'the man with his contradiction,' with his weak side as well as his strong side, has never been drawn."

"Debs," Cannon observes, "was a man of good will, if there ever was one; a giver, a constructive worker, a builder."

"But he was just a little too 'good' to be the leader that a revolutionary party requires.

"Debs couldn't stand quarreling. He fled from 'brawlers' as from a plague. He couldn't abide embroilments in controversies, especially if they were tainted with conniving and 'maneuvering,' which unfortunately are not always absent even in party disputes.

"He feared faction fights and splits above everything, and simply ran away from them. As a result of all that, Debs turned his back on the internal affairs of the Socialist Party of the United States.

"He, the most influential leader, poured out all his energy, and eventually his life, in popular mass agitation, organization, and struggle, and allowed lesser men than he—lesser in all respects, in my judgment, and especially in revolutionary temperament— to run the party machine and shape the party policy."

There was no such contradiction in Jim Cannon's makeup. He was equally involved in internal party affairs and, when the occasion required, in mass action.

Jim, as you know, was convicted and imprisoned, along with a number of other Socialist Workers Party and Teamsters Local 544 leaders, under the Smith "Gag" Act for opposition to Roosevelt's war for the "four freedoms."

He matriculated at Sandstone penitentiary, at government expense, where he was provided the luxury of an ample amount of free time—which he proceeded to put to constructive use. He thought up plans, projects, and party campaigns. He proposed mass *Militant* subscription drives. He elaborated educational prospectuses and study systems, etc., etc.

I cannot think of a single change in Jim's physical mode of existence that wasn't converted into a launching pad for projecting party-building schemes, plans, and designs.

Those of us at the party center, who were responsible for directing and supervising the day-to-day activity of the party, were sometimes irritated at the profusion of ideas, proposals, suggestions, and, sometimes, criticisms that emanated from Jim's fertile mind. His life was a graphic application of Trotsky's memorable aphorism: Without the party we are nothing; with the party we are all.

Jim Cannon not only practiced this creed, he preached it. And how eloquently he did so!

I note in the September 20 issue of the *Militant* a transcript of an interview with Cannon by a young Mexican revolutionist just a week before Jim's death. The editors' foreword to the interview concludes with the information that "at the time of his death Cannon was national chairman emeritus of the Socialist Workers Party."

According to my copy of *Webster's Collegiate Dictionary*, "emeritus" is defined as, "Retired, as for age, with a title corresponding to that held in active service; especially of a clergyman or college professor."

Now Jim was no clergyman, although he preached some powerful sermons against capitalist exploitation and oppression and for the socialist emancipation of the working class through revolutionary action. Nor could he qualify as a "college professor," although as a teacher of revolutionary theory, tactics, strategy, and party building he had few peers.

I recall that it was Jim himself who proposed the title "emeritus" in preference to a title such as "honorary national chairman." He became "emeritus"—with the understanding that it carried no implication of withdrawal from politics—as part of the planned leadership transition initiated by himself.

Jim had some very strong views on the question of party leadership. In one of the numerous speeches in which he dealt with this subject, he affirmed:

"The problem of the party is the problem of the leadership of the party. I believe, that just as the problem of the party is the problem the working class has to solve before the struggle against capitalism can be definitively successful—the problem of the party truly is the problem of the leadership of the party."

In consonance with the importance he attached to this question, the problem of leadership selection, training, and transition on all levels was not to be left to chance or accident, but was invested with conscious organization and planning.

If you will permit me I should like to reminisce, at this point, about another facet of Jim's character. In order to make room on our leading committee for younger party leaders coming to the fore, it was agreed that a number of older leaders would voluntarily accept the status of "advisory" members with voice but no vote on the National Committee.

Jim had spoken at our convention on the need for investing the process of leadership transition with the element of conscious planning. There was general agreement. But the process seemed to have bogged down. We concluded that the problem arose because Jim had neglected to follow the word with the deed, and others seemed to be waiting for Jim to set the example.

When the matter was broached with Jim, he chuckled and said, "I never thought anyone would use against *me* what I was saying to *them*. Aren't they familiar with Rule 15, which reads: Don't do as I *do*, do as I *say!*"

Jim had all his maxims codified into rules and listed according to number. No, we said, in this situation it is Rule 22 that applies, to wit: Do unto others—or others won't do either! Well, Jim saw the point, set the example, the others followed, and the logjam was broken.

The question of the party, Jim declared, "is the most important of all questions." But he was always quick to add that this truism was based upon the premise that the party was armed with the program of revolutionary Marxism.

The program came first. Without the revolutionary program there could be no Leninist combat party. That was Lenin's credo. It became Trotsky's view. And Cannon was their disciple.

Jim Cannon was a remarkable orator. One of the best that the radical movement in this country has produced. That is why most of his published work appears in the form of transcriptions of the spoken word.

And the work that best illustrates and underscores the theme of my remarks this evening is the Pathfinder Press book entitled *Speeches to the Party*. The book has the most revealing subtitle: "The Revolutionary Perspective and the Revolutionary Party."

The revolutionary perspective. That means the program! The projection of the course of historical development culminating in the third American revolution—the socialist revolution. It is the granite foundation upon which the party rests.

While the many speeches and letters published in this volume are replete with argument and affirmation of the revolutionary perspective in this country, the SWP's program is codified in written form as an appendix to the speeches, in the form in which it appeared in 1946, as the "Theses on the American Revolution."

That was almost thirty years ago! And what years! These have been years of war, revolution, and colonial uprisings; of advances and retreats, of victories and defeats of the world revolution.

The "Theses on the American Revolution" have withstood the test of time. That is the acid test of any program. In one of his letters to Farrell Dobbs, dated October 14, 1952, published in *Speeches to the Party*, Cannon wrote in reply to some critics:

"The Theses are a fundamental document. . . . What is needed is merely amplification, expansion, and concretization of the probable line of development (insofar as this is possible)."

These words, written twenty-two years ago, can be repeated today without the change of a single word. With perhaps some amplification, some expansion, and some concretization of the probable line of development.

Are there any other changes required in the light of the present situation in this country and the world? I don't think so. Changes in tempo, perhaps. But not in analysis or perspective.

Here we have an Earl Butz, our exalted secretary of agriculture, who advises those who have the temerity to protest the bounding inflation, which imposes an ever more meager diet on the working people, to "tighten their belts." That's his solution for all problems.

And in the White House, surrounded by counselors, advisers, consultants, and various and sundry experts, we have another mental midget who, when asked what his solution was to the problem of runaway inflation and rising unemployment, cheerfully opines that there is nothing to worry about—things are going to get a lot worse before they get better.

And in his solution, the Nixon-appointed and Nixon-anointed occupant of the White House proffers a plagiarized prescription from fellow cabinet member Butz: Tighten your belts.

And this in the richest country in the world, with the highest level of agricultural productivity, and with the potential of providing food in abundance for all under a rational system of production for use instead of profit.

What is the perspective of world development today? In many of the underdeveloped countries, in which reside the bulk of the world's population, hunger, starvation, famine, devour men, women, and children like an apocalyptic plague.

In the advanced capitalist sector, galloping inflation and mounting unemployment give rise to the specter of economic prostration. To characterize its incipient stage the bourgeois pundits have coined a new word—stagflation. Which means that the world capitalist system is sick, and getting sicker.

You don't have to take my word for it—read the financial pages of any of the metropolitan dailies. Pay heed to what the bankers and financiers, the stockjobbers and money changers, the cabinet ministers and high government officials, are saying. Their system is sick and none of their medicine men have a remedy for what ails them. They can't even agree on what medicine to prescribe.

We can tell them what's wrong. And we can prescribe for them a remedy to cure what ails them. But I am afraid they won't find our kind of medicine very palatable.

As a matter of fact, to put it very bluntly, the world capitalist system is afflicted with an incurable disease. It is a terminal case of historical incompatibility. The bourgeois parasites have simply outlived their usefulness and outworn their obnoxious presence on this terrestrial sphere. Or, as Trotsky put it more succinctly, they are in the throes of their death agony. What to do about it?

I can only repeat the truth, as set down by Jim Cannon, in his draft of the "Theses on the American Revolution," in Thesis 15, the rousing climax and conclusion of this historical document:

"The hopeless contradictions of American capitalism, inextricably tied up with the death agony of world capitalism, are bound to lead to a social crisis of such catastrophic proportions as will place the proletarian revolution on the order of the day.

"In this crisis, it is realistic to expect that the American workers, who attained trade union consciousness and organization within a single decade, will pass through another great transformation in their mentality, attaining political consciousness and organization.

"If in the course of this dynamic development a mass labor party based on the trade unions is formed, it will not represent a detour into reformist stagnation and futility, as happened in England and elsewhere in the period of capitalist ascent.

"From all indications, it will rather represent a preliminary stage in the political radicalization of the American workers, preparing them for the direct leadership of the revolutionary party.

"The revolutionary vanguard party, destined to lead this tumultous revolutionary movement in the U.S., does not have to be created. It already exists, and its name is the SOCIALIST WORKERS PARTY.

"It is the sole legitimate heir and continuator of pioneer American Communism and the revolutionary movements of the American workers from which it sprang. Its nucleus has already taken shape in three decades of unremitting work and struggle against the stream. Its program has been hammered out in ideological battles and successfully defended against every kind of revisionist assault upon it.

"The fundamental core of a professional leadership has been assembled and trained in the irreconcilable spirit of the combat party of the revolution.

"The task of the SOCIALIST WORKERS PARTY consists simply in this: to remain true to its program and banner; to render it more precise with each new development and apply it correctly in the class struggle; and to expand and grow with the growth of the revolutionary mass movement, always aspiring to lead it to victory in the struggle for political power."

That is our perspective; that is our platform, and that is our aim. We are confident that the party, the living embodiment of the ideas and ideals for which Jim Cannon fought, will successfully carry through its historic mission and thereby provide the most fitting monument to the memory of our teacher, guide, and leader, Jim Cannon.

Harry Braverman

I remember when Jim Cannon spoke at a meeting in New York which welcomed him and the other Smith Act defendants back from a year in prison during World War II. There were quite a number of speakers that night, but Cannon was of course always a favorite on the platform, and his appearance was eagerly awaited. When he came to the rostrum there was much applause which grew in volume for several moments, and Jim looked with a smile. When the clapping died down he began, "As I was saying when I was so rudely interrupted. . . . " Well, Jim Cannon has been rudely interrupted again and his long and honorable fighting career brought to an end.

Jim had an impact on many who no longer share his views. In my own case I have tried to assess as honestly as I can just what that impact was. And I think what I can say to you tonight is this: First, he persuaded quite a few of us to devote our lives to the struggle for socialism. It wasn't that we heard of socialism from him or that he made Marxists of us. Socialism and Marxism were in the air in the 1930s. Capitalism was putting on a pretty bad performance. But he did inspire in us the idea of devoting ourselves to a life lived in the service of this cause rather than to a conventional career.

He spoke to us in the accents of the Russian revolution and of the Leninism which had gone forth from the Soviet Union in the

HARRY BRAVERMAN was born in 1921. He was a political associate of Cannon from 1937 to 1953, when he left the Socialist Workers Party. He is the author of *Labor and Monopoly Capital* and is the director of Monthly Review Press. He made these remarks at a New York meeting on September 18, 1974.

203

twenties and the thirties. But there was in his voice something more which attracted us. And that was the echoes of the radicalism of the pre-World War I years, the popular radicalism of Debs, Haywood, and John Reed. And he spoke with great force and passion. I have thought of this from time to time in recent years when I have been struck by the contrast between the cool style popular with academics and the older style of oratory of which Cannon was an excellent practitioner. It's true that he was raised on Shakespeare and the Bible, from which you get a much better training in rhetoric than from Henry James and Henry Kissinger. And he had the kind of respect for language that used to be much more common in America before it was destroyed by Madison Avenue and higher education. I once heard him say, "Do what you like to the queen, but don't murder the king's English."

But it was not only the oratory of the old school that I have in mind when I speak of the passion he brought to his politics. Cannon invested the full force of a not inconsiderable personality in his convictions, as if to say that one could not hope to convince others of ideas which inspired in oneself only lukewarm feelings. This, I think, is useful to remember at a time when the ideas of socialism and the critique of capitalism are too often treated as mere mathematical exercises, the outcome of formulas, or the comparison of alternative models. It seems to me that the ruling force of Cannon's political life, insofar as I know it, was this passion for the political principles spread by the Russian revolution in its early years. He lived by these principles and by these alone, and he became expert at separating every other impulse that plays a role in socialist politics from the thing that mattered most to him—adherence to these principles. Now, I would not pretend that this kind of dedication to principles, taken by itself, and without reference to all other requirements, theoretical and practical, is a sufficient basis for sound socialist politics. It can also be the basis for sectarianism, and usually is. But without it the politics of even the best-meaning people can become a swamp and a tangle.

Cannon's adherence to the principles that inspired him in his youth was a manifest thing that shaped his whole life and life's activity. The emphasis that he gave to what he called principled politics was clear in every speech and every article. He tried to have his every political act and association reflect his principles and reflect them clearly and unambiguously. He was not a particularly assiduous practitioner of the personal wiles of flattery and attention and the hearty cordialities of courthouse politics. In that sense he was not—and I think I may use the phrase in spite of the national typing it implies—he was not an Irish politician. Someone once taxed him with this and told me about his reaction. He said to Cannon, "You have a reputation as a political organizer, a machine builder, yet you have none of the habits of the type in personal matters. Quite the contrary. But haven't you ever thought that a bit more attention to people and their peculiarities, a bit more care about feelings, might be a good thing?"

"Well," Cannon answered, "I can say this in my defense: I am the only man of my generation who has remained a revolutionist and kept his health."

Now that was a typical Cannon quip. But there was more to it than that. There was something in him which shrank from accepting support on a personal basis. Thus, within the framework of his politics he was generally concerned to clarify every matter that he saw as a matter of principle and not to have the advantage of misunderstanding.

An incident that happened in one of my earliest contacts with him made a strong impression on me. During the dispute in the Trotskyist organization of 1939 and 1940 almost all of the youth organization in New York sided against Cannon. But two of us were surprise exceptions—surprise, since we had never had any contact with the Cannon group. Later on, as the dispute progressed, my friend decided to switch sides, and I went in to tell Cannon about it.

My friend, I mentioned, had said that he had no intention of ending up as a wheelhorse for James P. Cannon. Cannon interrupted to ask whether I knew the meaning of the word "wheelhorse." And indeed there was something about the way I had used it in my narrative that considerably softened the meaning of the word to give myself a break. He then painted for me in biting language an unvarnished portrait of a political wheelhorse. He obviously didn't want me to be under any illusions about what I was being accused of. And then he let me continue.

In this small instance I felt the force of his resolve not to gain support through misunderstandings, and by and large I found the same to be true thereafter. There's a lot to be said about Jim Cannon because when you're talking about him you're talking about a big man. But you're also talking about small group politics in the American socialist movement. If I say too much I'm going to start to quarrel with him and that wouldn't be right when he can't answer back. He was a fighter, he was a trouper, he was an inspiration to many of us that made us, perhaps, better people than we would otherwise have been. My respect and admiration for him outlasted many years of separation from him and his organization and I don't believe I'm the only one who'll say that.

Photo by Joseph Hansen

Cannon and Reba Hansen, Mountain Spring Camp, New Jersey, 1949.

Jean Y. Tussey

Despite years of political collaboration with Jim Cannon—beginning when I joined the Socialist Workers Party in 1942 and continuing until his death—my recollection of *personal* experiences with Jim is limited to two incidents: one when he bawled hell out of me, and the other when we discussed my assignment to Cleveland.

The first was during the fourteenth national convention of the party in New York City November 24-26, 1950. We were meeting in the Grand Ballroom of Central Plaza at Second Avenue and Seventh Street.

The major political debate of the convention was on Yugoslavia and related questions. There was a majority report and minority reports and a stormy discussion.

I was thirty-two years old, a young party activist in charge of the convention arrangements committee, and missed much of the discussion because I was busy handling problems of rooms for panel discussions, housing, registration, food, etc.

Many of our well-laid plans were disrupted by the fact that New York City was experiencing one of the worst blizzards in its history. Transportation delays. Power failures. Accidents. Huge plate-glass windows of stores and public buildings blown in. Theater and hotel marquees crashed to the ground.

But in the Grand Ballroom the delegates continued their

JEAN Y. TUSSEY was born in 1918. She joined the Socialist Workers Party in 1942. She has been a member of the party's National Committee since 1952 and has been a member of various unions, including the International Typographical Union, the United Steelworkers, the International Association of Machinists, and the Newspaper Guild.

intense political discussion, oblivious to the storm outside except for occasional wrinkled brows when noises on the roof made it difficult to hear a speaker.

That was when someone told me Jim Cannon wanted to see me.

Jim was national secretary of the party, the central organizer. He told me angrily that as the person in charge of arrangements I should get the manager and find out what was causing the racket on the roof that was interfering with the delegates' discussion.

I went to the manager with the complaint. He explained that the noise was caused by the high winds blowing against the vents on the roof and there was nothing he could do about it.

When I told Jim that, he flipped his lid. He was furious. We had paid for a hall for a party convention. *Nothing* could be permitted to interfere with the delegates' discussion. "You go back and tell the manager that noise has to be stopped!"

I went back and gave him the message. The poor man sputtered. Didn't we know what was going on outside? The worst blizzard in history, a catastrophe. There was no way he could get anyone to go up on the roof to stop the clatter. "It's an act of God!" he protested.

Telling Jim that was more than I could handle. I just decided to stay out of his sight the rest of the day.

Six months later, under entirely different circumstances, I had my other discussion with Jim.

I had been attending the Trotsky School in New Jersey, where party leaders and activists were assigned for six months' education in Marxist theory.

The political climate in the country following the period of McCarthyism, the cold war, and economic recession had increased the problems of building a revolutionary socialist party. Union militancy had subsided, conservatism dominated the Black and youth organizations, and socialists were swimming against the stream.

The national office of the party was attempting to provide reinforcements for branches that had become isolated and were struggling for survival.

Several of us at the school were asked to consider transferring when our session ended in June. I was asked to go to Cleveland and was told Cannon wanted to discuss it with me.

We met in his apartment. Just Jim and I. Our talk was a little strained at first. I had been active in the Socialist Workers Party since I joined in 1942, in California, but I had never talked with Jim alone.

It soon became apparent, however, that he knew much more about me than I had realized. As soon as he ascertained that I had no personal blocks to making the move, we got down to the business at hand, which was what was needed in Cleveland.

Jim talked about the traditions of radicalism in Ohio, and about the solidarity of Wobblies and Trotskyists in repelling the attacks by Stalinist goons in the early days of our movement there.

He described some of the problems of a small group of Trotskyist workers trying to build a party branch, the pressures of a long period of isolation; how unrewarding effort can make them turn inward, exhaust their limited time and energy on internal discussion and disputes.

The main need at that time, Jim said, was to turn the face of the party outward, reach new people with our ideas, our socialist program. Sell the *Militant* wherever you can. At public meetings. House-to-house. At union meetings.

As soon as it's possible, get a headquarters. Hold public meetings, forums, classes. Get involved in election campaigns.

You won't be able to do it overnight, he warned. And you won't be able to do it alone. But if you do a good job, reach some new people, sell some subs to the *Militant*, bring a few new faces into the branch, begin to get some results, other comrades will see that it's worth the effort again, and will join you in the activities.

Jim reminded me that I was going to Cleveland to function as an active rank-and-file member of the branch, not as organizer, and would have to earn the authority to influence branch policies and practices. But the one thing you can do right from the start, he said, is sell the *Militant*.

"Jim makes sense," I thought as I left his apartment.

It worked.

Fred Halstead

Jim Cannon's name first came to my attention when I was a
child because my parents were socialists and used to mention him
occasionally. My father was an old Wobbly and a Trotskyist. I
wish I could say he was a Cannonite, but it wouldn't really be
accurate. He was generally in a different faction. As a matter of
fact the first time Cannon's name registered on my mind—while I
was eavesdropping on an adult conversation sometime in the
early 1930s—it was followed by a string of epithets not meant for
a child's ears. But I do know my father respected Jim as a fighter.

I didn't get to know Cannon well until he came to Los Angeles
to live in the early 1950s. He was a little over sixty then. He and
Rose Karsner needed some help moving their belongings from the
freight depot to a temporary apartment they had found. I had a
truck so the SWP branch organizer asked me to do the job. As it
turned out the truck was much too big for the few boxes that held
what appeared to be all their worldly goods. When I commented
on this to Jim he seemed pleased to have this noticed and
proceeded to give me a lecture on the origin and meaning of the
word "impedimenta," and how important it was for a soldier of
the revolution to be free of it. Sometime later, Rose and Jim
moved into a permanent house, and once again I brought the

FRED HALSTEAD was born in 1927. He joined the Socialist Workers
Party in 1948 in Los Angeles. He knew Cannon after his and Rose
Karsner's move to Los Angeles in 1952. He was the Socialist Workers
Party's presidential candidate in 1968 and a prominent leader of the
movement against the Vietnam War of the 1960s and early 1970s. He is
the author of *Out Now! A Participant's Account of the American Antiwar
Movement.*

truck. Their books had been shipped in the meantime and they had also picked up a lot of odds and ends. It took two trips and I worked up quite a sweat moving everything. When it was done, and Jim was handing me a can of beer, I said: "Looks like you've picked up a little impedimenta, Jim."

But he wouldn't retreat an inch on the point he had made before. He just replied: "You know, I used to carry everything I owned around in a big red handkerchief—and I got along all right."

In general, Jim was sparing of words around me. Virtually everything he said seemed calculated—not unnatural, not strained, but calculated to make some particular point. In my experience he was not given to idle chitchat, and even on those occasions when he conversed at length, it was always to a point, some lesson, some piece of experience or history he wanted to pass on.

Jim was a study in contrasts. I got the impression he looked at the world like a child, totally open to it, wide-eyed; at the same time sophisticated and, unlike Hamlet, thoroughly inured to the slings and arrows of outrageous fortune—always ready to accept the best in people, never hurt if he got the worst. Angered, perhaps, especially at injustice but not hurt. No sentimentality about it. Nothing in his character dragged him down. He was a fighter and he fought to win. I think this was his central character trait.

When things went well, he'd sometimes say: "Never underestimate the human race." He was an optimist, which wasn't easy for a revolutionary in the United States in the years of the McCarthy witch-hunt and reaction. In a sense this was the last great political fight of Cannon's life, the fight to help keep the party alive and kicking through that extended period of lull in the class struggle. The Cochran fight (analyzed in his book *Speeches to the Party*) was an essential part of it, of course, but it really extended over the whole period.

I remember a talk Jim gave in Los Angeles toward the end of 1949 in which he said that in the future we would look back on 1949 as "the hard year." What he said wasn't false. We *would* reach a time when things were not as hard, and when we would look back on that period and realize it was worth sticking through it. But he didn't tell us there were going to be ten or twelve years like that, all in a row, and that before it got better we were going to become more and more isolated. He didn't tell us that, of course, because he had no way of knowing it. As it became clear that the reaction was a long-term affair, some tactical and even strategic adjustments had to be made.

But personally I still look back on Jim's attitude in those days as the essentially correct one. It wasn't a question of prophecy, it was a question of line. He simply refused to be pessimistic about the prospects for the party, and he never missed a chance to instill some of that historical optimism in the young rank-and-file comrades who he knew were fighting rearguard actions in the unions and having a difficult time spreading the socialist word in an indifferent or hostile atmosphere. What made this effective— it's no trick to be foolishly optimistic—is that Jim had a reputation as the most hard-nosed realist.

In 1954, for example, some of us in Detroit had been involved in the Square D strike in which an attempt by the company to use the witch-hunt to break the union had been beaten back by a mobilization of workers from other plants. At the party convention later that year there was some talk—on the floor and in the corridors—that this indicated a change in the objective situation. Jim came down hard on this idea. We've got to be able to tell the difference between the beginning of an offensive and a rearguard action in a general retreat, he said, and this was strictly a desperate rearguard action. We knew Jim's optimism was not based on illusions.

I left L.A. in 1953 and after that would see Jim only briefly at conventions or on visits. Sometimes on those occasions, after a little conversation about the situation in the unions, he would look me in the eye and say something like, "Well, Fred, what's the condition of your soul?" By which I knew he meant: was I still optimistic about the revolution in general and the prospects for the party in particular?

In those years we had an institution called the Trotsky School, where a dozen or so activists at a time would be sustained for six months for full-time study. It was part of the party campaign of intensive educational activities that helped get us through. Actually, the party took advantage of the period to do some exceptional educational work.

Once I was driving in a car with Jim past the camp where the Trotsky School was held during the 1950s. Jim pointed to the entrance and said: "Some day there'll be a historical marker there that will say, 'This is where they studied.'"

Now Jim was not at all pompous. I looked in vain for a hint of a smile or a sparkle in the eye. But it wasn't meant to be funny. It had nothing to do with ego-building either. Personal credit was not involved in what made Jim tick politically. What he was telling us, and he made the point many times and in many ways, was that what we were doing was of historical importance to the future of humanity. And in truth we had to believe that. Otherwise we couldn't have gone on.

In the period of isolation he was also constantly warning against the habits of a sect. "A small group," he once told me, "can get themselves in a room and talk themselves into almost anything. You always have to test against the real world, the one out there with all those other people in it."

Later when things opened up and we were able to relate to broader forces, it was a special pleasure to Jim to see the role the party played in the anti-Vietnam-war movement. Our line in that situation did not fall from the sky. It was part of an old tradition. I particularly appreciated Cannon's intervention in the L.A. branch discussion in 1965 just after the first national convention of the new antiwar movement where we had fought a knockdown drag-out battle with the Stalinists involving the slogan of immediate withdrawal of U.S. troops. Not everyone was sure we had done the right thing.

"This slogan appealed to me right away," said Jim, "partly out of nostalgia." Then he described how the Socialist Party had used it against the U.S. invasion of Mexico in 1917. "That was all the situation called for," he continued, "and it created both the basis for organizing the broadest opposition of people who were really against the monstrous attack upon the Mexican people, and at the same time made no concession whatever in principle because the withdrawal of the troops signified the victory of the Mexicans."

At the beginning of the Korean War Cannon had put another brick in the structure of our antiwar stand, in an open letter to the president and members of Congress which began:

"Gentlemen: I disagree with your actions in Korea, and in my capacity as a private citizen I petition you to change your policy fundamentally, as follows: Withdraw the American troops and let the Korean people alone. I am setting forth my reasons for this demand in detail in the following paragraphs. But before opening the argument I beg your permission, gentlemen, to tell you what I think of you. You are a pack of scoundrels. You are traitors to the human race. I hate your rudeness and your brutality. You make me ashamed of my country, which I have always loved, and ashamed of my race, which I used to think was as good as any."

That statement made a big impression on the party cadres back in 1950. I know it made a big impression on me. Unfortunately, during the Korean War we were still too isolated, the situation too unfavorable, to make a material difference in opposition to the war. It was different with Vietnam. But the line was the same. It did Jim and all of us a lot of good to find ourselves in a position where there was more power behind our punch in the movement against U.S. intervention in Vietnam.

On a more personal note. Jim Cannon was easy to like as an individual, though it was certainly not his way to work only with people he liked, or who liked him. Political agreement was the criterion there. But he was easy to like personally. One reason was his sense of humor. I liked him also, because he was not a puritan, not an ascetic. He knew the value of an occasional good time for the long haul, and that appealed to me.

Photo by Joseph Hansen

Carl Skoglund (left) with Cannon, Mountain Spring Camp, New Jersey, 1949.

Ethel Lobman

I first got to know Jim in 1953 when I was the organizer of the Youth Branch of the New York local of the SWP. Jim was visiting New York and I was introduced to him at a social at 116 University Place. We sat and talked and I remember feeling very flattered that he was interested in how I had come into the party and in my opinion on the situation in the local. At the time we were engaged in a struggle with the Cochranite faction.

After that we would occasionally have lunch or dinner together when he visited New York. After I had written a few times for the *Militant*, he spent one evening encouraging me to write on a regular basis. He told me how difficult it was for him to discipline himself in order to write for the party. He suggested one method he used, which was to force himself to write each day. The topic did not matter. Sometimes he wrote about newpaper items which interested him, especially human interest stories. At other times it was about something that had happened in the past and the memory had been triggered by a recent incident.

The last time we had lunch together was during the 1963 convention, which was held in New York. I was feeling guilty because I had recently had a baby and was not as active as I had been in previous years. I told Jim how I felt. He told me that was nonsense and that there was time to do many things in a lifetime. Then he described the pleasure he had when his children were little. "No matter how awful the day had been, no matter what back-breaking work I'd done or humiliating experience I had had, when I opened the door to my house it would all vanish as he children flew into my arms screaming, 'Daddy, Daddy.' Those were some of the most joyful moments of my life."

ETHEL LOBMAN was born in 1924. She joined the Socialist Workers Party in 1943 in New York, where as a contributor to the *Militant* she worked with Cannon.

Matthew Ross

I'm often asked by Trotskyists and independent revolutionaries who are familiar with American radical history and are interested in the personal side of Jim Cannon what it was like being the grandchild of an important and lifelong active revolutionary. Often I must apologize for my anecdotes which show much less of the heroic, tireless militant subordinating family and person, as my inquirers expect, and more of a gentle grandfather treasuring Christmas dinners with his family and silly hide-and-seek games with his grandchildren.

I know, of course, that my grandfather made great personal sacrifices, especially in the early, more difficult years. And my perceptions of Jim were always colored by the awareness that my grandparents were deeply involved in momentous events far more powerful than the course of family affairs. Still, my memories of Jim are of a loving grandfather, much as many grandchildren remember their grandparents, only more enriched by a humanism and vitality they drew from other quarters of their lives. I hope this side of Jim Cannon will be remembered along with his contribution to the revolutionary movement.

My memory of Jim is infused with the strong image of my grandmother, his close comrade Rose Karsner. Others can speak with experience of their long political collaboration. I can add to our remembrance of these two that their personal life was as supportive and caring as their political life's intimacy. Their respectful love was always felt by their family and friends, but

MATTHEW ROSS was born in 1948. He is Cannon's grandson. He was active in the Berkeley antiwar movement and is a member of the National Lawyers Guild.

never was the depth of that love so clear to me as in the period after Rose's death in 1968. I remember conversations with Jim in that period filled with painful silences surrounding frequent references to Rose, mutual friends, and a shared history. He desired that our family remember that love and provided my sister, Lorna Ross, and me each a copy of a love letter he wrote to Rose years before. Jim's wit and revolutionary optimism survived to his last day, but his family and old friends know that much of Jim died with Rose.

Jim and Rose had a personal relationship not obvious to those who knew only of their political collaboration. Their different personalities complemented each other and in family settings often expressed themselves in playful teasing. Jim had a sharp humor and wonderful sense of irony. Rose was a literalist, taking his punch lines at face value. After one of Jim's jokes or double entendres Rose would delay and offer a straightforward explanation of the joke, often missing the spontaneity of Jim's wit and artful language. He would chuckle and throw up his hands as if to say, "What can one expect from a Romanian materialist?"

Jim earned family smiles with his deadpan traditionalism. Christmas dinner was incomplete, he would insist, without plum pudding. Great ceremony was made over Jim's arrival at a family affair in a new sport coat. He paraded the discount garment as if it was a Brooks Brothers item, taking pleasure in our deep appreciation of his Midwestern sense of propriety!

Although Jim could offer an occasional haircut joke, he welcomed the swift cultural changes of the sixties, recognizing the political dimensions of my generation's concern for a "life style" and sex roles. Jim was *never* judgmental or admonishing in his relationship to me or Lorna. My grandfather's traditionalism, it seemed, was much less a concern for ritual than a humorized expression of his Rosedaleian sense of roots, history, and native ways.

Rose was much more of a modernist. She had a fine curiosity about the cultural changes of the sixties. Rose was particularly concerned with the history of the women's movement. I accompanied my grandparents to their last party summer school in 1966 in the Santa Cruz mountains. Rose led the workshop on women. I remember distinctly how confident she was in her prediction that a new wave of feminism was drawing near. My great regret about the untimeliness of my grandmother's death is that she could not have lived but a few more years to have witnessed the overwhelming confirmation of that prediction and the strong effect it would have in the movement.

Rose and Jim made efforts to accommodate this consciousness in their personal lives which were necessarily hampered by the limitations of their age and tradition. Certainly in their late years it was always Jim who did the dishes and he cared for her in her illness tenderly and competently.

To my sister and me Jim and Rose were "Bam" and "Nana"— affectionate names that survived from our childhood. Bam and Nana were always easy marks for some attention. Bam could be conned into a game of hide and seek or later, checkers. Neither was much concerned with material possessions, but they frequently gifted little items. Nana kept a little treasure trove of bubble gum or cookies in a special drawer. They gave one gift that delighted more than the fanciest toy. Between visits Bam saved his cigar bands and presented them to me with obvious delight. It is hard to say if I enjoyed the cigar bands more than Jim's pleasure in seeing me run around with plastic rings on my fingers.

Jim had a strong attachment not only to his own children but to all the comrades' kids. I'm told that in his last weeks he began to coach the marbles game of the son of an L.A. comrade. Jim noticed that the young player lacked an "aggie"—an agate marble used by serious players as the primary shooter. History can rest assured that he made certain the child was provided with the equipment for a proper game of marbles.

One of my favorite stories of Jim and Rose surprises some people, usually friends that are unfamiliar with them and expect revolutionary leaders to be intellectuals without the silly affections that keep most of us going. In my memory they were not big movie goers, but they watched TV. Their greatest passion was Perry Mason. They competed with each other guessing who "done it," and expressed mock sympathy for the pathetic DA who lost every case.

Being with them during the unfolding of a Perry plot was plenty of fun, but the best moments came during commercials. Jim hated the advertisements and asked a friend to install a special "blab-off" switch to turn off the volume. He delighted in the power thus won over Madison Avenue. I have an image of Bam sitting in his favorite chair, surrounded by mounds of correspondence and journals, concentrating on the Perry Mason denouement with the blab-off switch held ready to stop some jerk's intrusion into an evening's entertainment.

Friends who know about my family background are usually interested in the political nurturing of a red-diaper baby. To be sure, my childhood was unlike most kids! One early difference concerned TV programs. While some friends were prohibited from watching "adult" movies or discouraged from reading certain books and magazines, I could take in as much sex or violence as I wished. Only *I Led Three Lives*—a 1950s, viciously anticommunist TV show, glorifying an FBI spy who infiltrated the Communist Party, was banned.

Still, I think my childhood was not unlike most kids'. Jim did not take me on his knee and teach me to hate the capitalist warmongers. All I knew about Trotsky until late in high school was that he was a leader of the Russian revolution, which was good, contrary to my civics class instructor.

Rather than a course of instruction in the ABCs of Marxism, Jim and Rose sought to encourage the growth of my curiosity about their politics. I will never forget my first introduction to Marxism. I went with Jim and Rose to a party summer camp. All the comrades would take their kids and we would have a ball playing while the grown-ups talked all day. I spent one afternoon with Nana and watched her prepare a very pretty chart. It had many big words, like FEUDALISM AND CAPITALISM, separated by black lines and the word PREHISTORY in heavy script written along the side. I asked Nana what the words meant. She started to explain, but gave up after a few sentences and told me that I would understand one day.

The most recurring theme taken by Jim in our political discussions was the importance of a sense of history. Jim had an extraordinary memory for names and events. Discussions of current politics were filled with detailed reminiscing, not limited to socialist history. He always insisted in our conversations that American revolutionaries had much to learn from the history of different societies. He had a special fondness for the Greeks and inscribed my copy of *The First Ten Years of American Communism*, "To be read when you return from Greece."

My sharpest memory of political discussions with Jim centers on my visits with him during a period when I was intensely involved in the Berkeley antiwar movement. I returned to Los Angeles for a visit, anxious to share with Jim my impressions and political judgments of events in that maelstrom of student activism. Jim was eager to hear my reactions and always prepared with an historic parallel, but he was just as interested in the details of my course of study at Berkeley. He always inquired about my classes; what I was reading; what I intended to study. At the time, this took me aback and left me wondering whether Jim was being overly paternal. I had abandoned many of my classes, regarding a "liberal arts" education at Berkeley as a deposit of bourgeois ideology, or at best, a drain on other commitments. At first I was puzzled by Jim's concern for my formal "education."

In the course of these college visits I gained the understanding that Jim valued a college "education" because it represented to him the chance that he never had to spend a period of years surveying the broad contours of history and human experience. Jim was more than sympathetic to my complaints about the *content* of most of my classes. Still, he was capable of finishing a discussion of campus politics with the suggestion that I take more history courses and later was supportive of a personal decision to use my degree to obtain a special skill.

Some visits with Jim in this period had awkward moments for both of us and put into conflict the two characters Jim demonstrated to his grandchild. Despite some good friendships with YSAers in Berkeley and a significant agreement with elements of the SWP's program, I was critical of certain aspects of the party's practice and program. I felt the need to explain these disagreements to him but I found it very difficult acknowledging these disagreements—after only several years of experience and modest study—to a man who had spent his entire active life grappling with these issues. Jim's attention was also centered during this period on Rose and family affairs. I remember once feeling that a lively discussion in Jim's presence with the young comrades who lived with him after Rose's death was a substitute for the dialogue I wanted with my grandfather.

I know Jim felt a similar reluctance to challenge my distance from the party. I am sure that he would have been very pleased if I expressed my intention to join the YSA, but I always felt that Jim and Rose never took for granted that I would join the party and were not "disappointed" by my political development. Jim's reluctance to discuss the character of my political direction was more a product of his strong desire not to let the political turbulence that had cost him friends during his life unsettle family relations.

In this way my experience with the personal character and

intimacy of the grandfather who never missed a Christmas dinner with his family came in conflict with a complete exposure to the figure of Jim Cannon the principal builder of American Trotskyism.

Jim largely resolved this conflict by resorting to his favorite idiom. Wanting to respond to some observation I would make, but equally desirous of not sounding instructive with me, he would reach back into his memory for an event or political debate parallel to my observation. The meaning of these historical references, and more so, the motivation behind this measured approach, was never lost on me.

Jim's death and the request for the present contribution has caused me to review my memories. I have come to recognize how much I benefitted politically and personally from the fact that they did not force-feed politics to their grandchildren. I think Jim and Rose hoped that their grandchildren would translate their own experiences into the revolutionary tradition they so outstandingly represented.

I know from my own experience that many persons once active in the antiwar movement of the sixties now counterpose present attempts to live and exemplify socialist and feminist values with the active, certainly difficult work of defeating capitalism. Many believe that the life of the "organizer" necessarily deforms some of the humanist values they identify as the nucleus of their hatred of capitalist social relations. Jim and Rose gave me a personal refutation of this fear. They provided a political environment, without intimidation, in which I grew to identify their great love for me and confidence in the future as products of an active and fulfilling life in the revolutionary movement. I felt in their love, in their wonderful stories about the past and concern for my future, the great vitality of those who have touched history. We can only struggle to live with the same satisfaction in life and confidence in our collective future.

Shortly before Rose's death in 1968, I returned from Berkeley for what was to be my last visit with Nana. She was under heavy medication and had difficulty understanding all that was said to her. Rose asked why I had come to Los Angeles, knowing full well the gravity of the hour. I offered the transparent answer that I came home to celebrate Washington's birthday. She looked at all of us and replied: "That's right! Celebrate! Don't commemorate! Celebrate!"

Peggy Brundy

Living and working with Jim, we came to know him as a revolutionary leader and as a human being. We also learned a great deal about the party and about politics. This was no accident. Jim worked at it. But his method of educating was very, very different from the pompous, alienating variety found in colleges.

He worked at eliminating all barriers between himself and his comrades. I think we were all awe-struck when we first met him. When I was part of the household, comrades meeting him for the first time would sometimes ask me, "How do I address him? 'Comrade Cannon'? Maybe even, 'Mr. Cannon'?" Well, Jim wanted to be called. . . "Jim."

Education, for Jim, was a give-and-take situation, whether he was talking with a leading cadre of the party or a brand-new recruit. Anyone who worked with Jim became part of his team.

He outlined this approach toward education in a letter he wrote while he was working on his book *Letters from Prison*. He wrote: "A prime obligation of a revolutionary leader is to explain the reasons for what he proposes and does, thus enabling the entire movement to participate in his thinking."

This kind of education was an integral part of the household routine. It took place through casual conversations at the dinner table, meetings with visitors, books and papers he urged us to

PEGGY BRUNDY was born in 1944. She joined the Socialist Workers Party in 1965 and was active in the antiwar movement. In 1968-70 she worked as Cannon's secretary in Los Angeles. Since 1974 she has been the managing editor of Pathfinder Press. These remarks were made at the Socialist Educational Conference in Oberlin, Ohio, on August 23, 1974.

read, and even jokes he told us while we were watching television. It was a continuing process. Jim didn't just give us the right answers. He tried to teach us how he approached problems.

Most of the essential lessons he drew for us are recorded in his books and are available for everyone to read and study. But occasionally he would remember a new incident in the class struggle, or a story about an individual that illustrated an important lesson. He worried about how these unrecorded anecdotes would be preserved for future generations. He sometimes said that our only hope was that the FBI had the house bugged, so that after the revolution we could transcribe the tapes. We plan to do just that.

One of the projects he carried out over the past year and a half was a series of interviews with comrades and friends—conducted largely by Harry Ring—in which he tried to pass on these previously unrecorded incidents.

He eagerly welcomed visitors. This was one of the ways he sought to keep abreast of current developments in the class struggle.

He spent hours reading each day. He studied the internal bulletins and the press of the party, and he followed the capitalist press. He subscribed to the *New York Times Book Review, The Nation,* and *New Republic,* as well as the papers of other tendencies. He considered this very important for keeping in touch with what was going on in the world and with how the different classes and political currents were reacting to it.

He was always thinking about ways to improve the party. His concerns ranged widely, from the problems of building the Fourth International to ideas such as the prepaid subscription card to the *Militant.* He carried out all of these activities, and more, in spite of failing health.

Jim was a long-time supporter of women's rights. His first public speech was a debate with another Rosedale, Kansas, high school student on the question, "Should women be allowed to vote?" Jim defended the affirmative—and he won. Over the next seventy years he never changed that position of support.

In an interview he gave just last month, he said, "The party has recruited women comrades on a scale never seen before in the radical movement. Forty percent of our members are women and, I think, about 40 percent of our staff members are women. This takes place not as a quota policy, but just naturally. So many talented women have come forward to fill this or that position."

Most of all, Jim educated us by his example. When I first met him in 1968, he had been a leader of the revolutionary movement for around sixty years. *Letters from Prison* had just been published, a book that passes on to our generation many of the most basic lessons he had to teach about party building. But he was seventy-eight years old. He was deeply shaken by the recent death of Rose Karsner.

By anybody's standards, he could have retired. He had already given the party a tremendous amount. And he could have decided to just sit back and take it easy for the rest of his life.

But he didn't. With the help of those who worked with him, he organized his life so that in his remaining years he could continue functioning as an *active party member*—to the maximum degree that he was able.

That, I think, is the primary legacy of the last years of Jim's life. In spite of personal hardships—and he suffered many during those years—he remained steadfastly true to the principles that had guided him all his life. He remained convinced that there *can* be a better world if we are willing to *fight* for it.

He once said, "I came out of Rosedale, Kansas, forty years ago looking for truth and justice. I'm still looking, and I won't give one percent discount."

Jim Cannon's approach to life and to the party was summed up by Rose Karsner in 1962 in some remarks she made at a banquet celebrating the publication of *The First Ten Years of American Communism.* I'd like to close by quoting from what she said:

"From the moment we threw our lot in with the socialist movement, more than fifty years ago, we have never wavered in our conviction that a socialist world will come into being. Whether we live to see it or not. That's immaterial. We never faltered in our devotion to this conviction, or in our allegiance to the party we believed was working toward that end. In times of personal difficulty, and we all had them, we sometimes took out time to straighten these matters. But never with the idea of dropping out.

"Never did we feel that we were sacrificing for the party. On the contrary, we were always conscious of the fact that to have to give up the party, that would be a sacrifice. Because through activity of the party, we got fulfillment of life and satisfaction and the confidence that we were working not merely for our own little selves, but for the entire human race. We feel the same way tonight. We recommend that way to you all."

Andrew Pulley

Jim Cannon was too old to formally join the Young Socialist Alliance, according to our constitution. But we didn't let that stop us.

He was over eighty in years. But in his optimism in the socialist future and his determination to realize it, and in his sense of humor, he was as young as any of us in the YSA.

Jim was like a member of the YSA. He was our senior consultant. Whenever YSA leaders would visit Los Angeles we would meet with him. His door was always open to the YSA.

It is only natural to be a little nervous when you first meet a person of Jim's stature. But as soon as he began to speak, he would relax you. I was amazed, in one of the meetings I had with Jim, at his familiarity with the work of the party and the YSA, his deep interest in the YSA, and his sharp perception of the events of the class struggle, the youth radicalization, and the general political reality of the day.

Jim Cannon appreciated the YSA as a Leninist youth organization. In one of his last interviews, printed in the July-August *Young Socialist,* Jim stated, "The Young Socialist Alliance of today is an entirely new phenomenon, as far as my

ANDREW PULLEY was born in 1951. He was a leader of GIs United Against the War at Fort Jackson, South Carolina, in 1969, and joined the Young Socialist Alliance shortly after his release from two months in the stockade for his antiwar views. He was the 1972 vice-presidential candidate of the Socialist Workers Party and later served as national chairman of the Young Socialist Alliance. He made these remarks at the August 23, 1974, meeting in Oberlin, Ohio.

experience can judge, by its composition, its general activity, and in practically every other way."

Jim was a big partisan of founding the YSA. He felt the YSA had an important role to play on the campuses, in the high schools, and among the youth in general: to lead young people in struggle to change society, and to train young revolutionists for membership in the revolutionary party.

In a speech presented to the West Coast Vacation School in 1964 titled "What It Means to Be a Young Revolutionist Today"—a speech that recruited to the socialist movement a number of people sitting here tonight—Jim spoke of the danger of nuclear annihilation and said: "So we have come to the conclusion that time is shorter. When you join a socialist movement now, you're joining the battle which in your own lifetime—not that of your children, not that of your grandchildren, but in your own lifetime—and even before you reach an advanced age, is going to be settled.

"You have got to be the vanguard of the people who are going to settle it. So being a socialist becomes the central purpose of your life and your activity."

You know, Jim was a YSAer when he was young. They just didn't call it that then. Jim joined the fight for socialism while in high school. One of his first activities was in the defense campaign against the frame-up of Haywood, Pettibone, and Moyer.

As a youth Jim was a footloose rebel. He became a socialist and spread the socialist word, speaking on street corners and selling the *Appeal to Reason,* the popular socialist weekly. That was almost seventy years ago. He stayed with that fight for way over half a century, and that's a *long* time.

How many of you have been told, by your parents, teachers, bosses, parole officers, or lieutenants, that you'll outgrow your socialist views when you grow up and get wise?

Well, Jim Cannon grew up, and he *did* get wiser—and that's why he stayed true to his rebel ideas *all the way.* As he explained in the recent *Young Socialist* interview, "If I can convey any suggestion to you it's this—the longer you live in this fight, the more determined you are to try to win it and the more confident you are that the human race will survive."

In one of his letters written from Sandstone federal prison in Minnesota in 1945 Jim wrote, "The young relate the word to the deed. They are moved and inspired by *example.* That is why they demand *heroes;* nobody can talk them out of it."

Those words could not be truer. The Young Socialist Alliance has found the greatest inspiration in the example set by Jim Cannon, one of its heroes.

Photo by John Gray

1968

Joyce Meissenheimer

When I was privileged to meet Jim Cannon in January 1973, the first thing he said to me was, "Well, it's very exciting meeting you, comrade." And I said, "Well, Jim, it's very exciting meeting you. What can I tell you?" He said, "Tell me about yourself."

I told him about my participation in the liberation struggles in South Africa, and particularly I told him why I felt so privileged to meet Jim Cannon. Because you see, in South Africa in 1946, the movement I was in, the Unity Movement, started a newspaper, the *Torch*. I became editor in 1948. We used to exchange copies of our paper with papers from different parts of the world, and one of these papers was the *Militant*. And this is where I first got to know about Jim Cannon, from reading the *Militant*.

Afterwards, I ceased receiving the *Militant,* and instead, I got in the mail pieces of paper from the South African government, saying that they had confiscated the following subversive material in my mail, and the list included the *Militant.*

Other comrades here have spoken about the internationalism that Jim knew was so important to the struggle for world liberation. He wanted to know everything that had gone on in South Africa during my experience, a lot of things I couldn't even tell him, things that had happened before I was born even. And then he told me things that had gone on in my country that I didn't know about.

JOYCE MEISSENHEIMER was born in 1922. She is a long-time socialist and was a leader of the Unity Movement in South Africa. In recent years she has lived in Canada. These remarks were made to a meeting in Vancouver, British Columbia, on September 6, 1974.

He said, it's so important for people like us to get together, because we can gather together all this information—what I know, what you know, what somebody else knows. That is one of the most important aspects of an international movement. People can collectively gather their history, and he said how important this was.

We followed this with a discussion of Canadian politics, and I told him something about our labor party experience in the NDP. And he was intensely interested in this; he had always followed it very closely.

We talked about the youth radicalization. We talked about the rise of political consciousness among people who are racially oppressed: Black people, Chicanos, and so on.

When it was time for me to go, Jim got up and said, "I want to show you this picture." On the wall there was a picture of a little baby.

He said, "That's Bernadette Devlin's baby." This was when there was a terrible scandal because this young woman had a baby without benefit of wedlock. Jim had a picture of Bernadette's baby on the wall.

He told me that his granddaughter was a close friend of hers. Bernadette was shortly to be married, and he was going to send her a wedding present, his book *Speeches for Socialism*. As I left I told him I thought it was a good wedding present, and he should send her all his books, because I was sure that they would be very useful to Bernadette Devlin, and all revolutionaries in Ireland.

Reba Hansen

I worked with Jim for more than ten years, off and on, and it's pleasant to think back over that experience.

I first met Jim in San Francisco in 1937 when he was editing *Labor Action*. He was interested in the fact that I'd had lots of experience working in offices in Salt Lake City, San Diego, San Francisco, and the Pioche, Nevada, mining district. I had even been an office manager for Shell Oil. I felt flattered at Jim's questions but thought no more about it.

In January 1939, I came to New York and went to work as a statistical typist with one of the biggest accounting firms in the Wall Street area. Later I shifted to a secretarial job with another accounting firm in the Chrysler building.

After I had been in New York for a while, Jim asked me if I would work for the party full time. I jumped at the chance.

First I was assigned to Pioneer Publishers (a predecessor of Pathfinder Press). From there I went onto the *Militant* staff as business manager.

Jim would drop into the business office frequently. Generally he had a suggestion or two about circulation, about a subscription campaign, about the "Militant Army," the column I wrote each week. Or he might just ask how things were going.

One day he came into the business office asking what the hell

REBA HANSEN was born in 1909. She joined the Communist League of America in 1934 and first worked with Cannon in San Francisco in 1937. She was Cannon's secretary in New York from 1948 until Cannon retired to Los Angeles in 1952. She has served as business manager of the *Militant* and of *Intercontinental Press*.

we thought we were doing, changing the column-head on the "Militant Army" like that.

It was clear he was upset. What was our reason for changing it? The old one was good. It had been used a long time. A change like this should never be made light-mindedly.

The old drawing showed a turnout of marchers with flags and banners. I had been working in the business office several years before it occurred to me that maybe a new drawing would be an improvement.

A good artist in the Canadian movement, Joe Rosenthal, sent in some sketches from which we could make a selection. We decided on a drawing of workers streaming out of a factory with enthusiasts hawking the *Militant*.

I tried to explain how good the change was. It was a stormy session, and Jim remained unconvinced. But we continued using the new drawing.

One thing Jim always stressed about the "Militant Army" was that the space belonged to the comrades in the field who were selling the paper, that it was one column where these comrades could tell about their experiences. He said "Let the comrades speak." He didn't think it was necessary to sit at the desk and try to think up something profound with which to fill the column. He felt there were enough comrades on the writing staff to do that elsewhere in the paper.

Even when he was in prison, Jim kept track of the "Militant Army." He wrote Rose Karsner, his companion, asking her to clip the weekly column and send it to him.

In 1949, after I had shifted from the *Militant* to work in the national office, Jim suggested the same approach for fund-campaign stories.

He asked if I would direct the $12,000 Party Building Fund to finance a program of expanded activities, to build and strengthen the party, and to increase the circulation of the press and publications.

Jim launched the campaign with a signed article in the *Militant*. "The life of the branches of the Socialist Workers Party during the fall and winter months," he wrote, "will be dominated by an intensive party-building campaign outlined by the National Committee and enthusiastically greeted by the party membership. . . ."

He added that "the party members have pledged themselves

. . . to make all the necessary personal sacrifices to raise their quotas IN FULL AND ON TIME." I think this was the first time we used that slogan. It came to represent a party attitude—take realistic goals, but meet those goals precisely and on schedule.

Jim ended the article with a promise; at least that was the way I interpreted the word "celebration." "We all confidently look forward to a Happy New Year's celebration of 100% success in this great endeavor."

After the kickoff, the weekly column was turned over to me. But Jim always checked the story before it went to the *Militant*; he liked to read the items sent in by the directors in the branches.

The final story carried the head "SWP FUND CAMPAIGN COMPLETED IN FULL AND ON TIME."

It was last-minute though. The steelworkers were out on strike and the comrades in the Youngstown Branch, who had been confident of completing their $400 quota by the deadline, were now on the picket line and feeling the financial squeeze. They told us they could see no way of completing their quota in full.

The Detroit Branch heard about this and decided to do what they could to help their hard-hit Youngstown comrades. This wasn't easy because they had already increased their own quota from $800 to $1,100. But they turned their pockets inside-out and a day before the deadline sent this telegram: "$100 to aid Youngstown complete fund quota. Detroit Branch is eager to express its revolutionary solidarity. We remember assistance Youngstown Branch and others gave us when similar need upon us."

In 1951 Jim launched another fund campaign with an article in the *Militant* to raise $18,000. He wrote: "We know that our organizational budget for 1951 will be provided, the press deficit will be guaranteed, and an emergency sum for legal expenses, if we need it, can be set aside. We know this because the party branches have promised it in the acceptance of their quotas, and their promises, which are never made lightly, have always been as good as money in the bank. It will be that way this time too."

And that's just the way it was.

I single out these two campaigns, models in my opinion, because it wasn't always just that way—in full and on time.

During those years Sylvia Caldwell served as secretary in the national office, a job that included working with Jim, who held the post of national secretary. She was the second full-time secretary the party had. The first was Lillian Roberts.

Jim often told us about how it was "in the old days," when it was difficult to get things done because of having no secretarial help. He said he was grateful for any help he could get and he never failed to show his deep appreciation for the aid that Sylvia gave.

Jim was fond of telling the story about how Sylvia went to a business school to learn shorthand when it was proposed she work in the national office. This was before the days of the tape recorder, and shorthand was essential to taking adequate minutes at meetings and dictation for letters and articles. Sylvia learned fast and well. Her Gregg characters were like copper-plate engravings, her typing without strikeovers, and no messy erasures.

When the load in the national office was heavy and Sylvia needed help, I gave her a hand, working very closely with her. Her efficiency impressed me. She knew how to do everything that was necessary to keep a one-person office running smoothly. Her devotion to the movement and her readiness to put in long hours of hard work inspired all of us.

Sylvia and I became close collaborators and good personal friends. She was a warm human being.

When Sylvia left New York in 1947 because of family obligations, Jim asked me to take her place in the national office. Since this included working closely with Jim, I felt a little nervous, but Sylvia helped me through the transition from business manager of the *Militant* to my new assignment.

At that time Rose and Jim lived at 126 West Eleventh Street, seventh floor. The apartment building was modern—it had an elevator—and the rooms were large by New York standards. The front room, facing on Eleventh Street, was big enough for two desks, several filing cabinets, and a worktable. Sylvia took me there to work with her and learn the ropes.

But Jim didn't shift easily from one secretary to another. And it was only after Sylvia had been gone some time that Jim felt enough at home with me through working together in the national office to ask me to come over to West Eleventh Street.

During the next months I spent only a few hours there each week, keeping the periodicals filed, the articles clipped that Jim had marked in the daily newspapers, and the desks dusted. Also I tried to familiarize myself with the correspondence files. If my work in the national office at 116 University Place was pressing, I skipped going to Jim's altogether.

Then one day early in 1948 he telephoned and asked if I would come over. He explained that "we wouldn't work, not today, but would just get a few things cleared out of the way." He wanted to talk with me.

Rose had gone to California to be with Walta, her daughter, who was soon to have her first baby.

Jim talked about himself, and I jotted down occasional notes in my shorthand book.

In Rosedale, Kansas, he was "what they called a cardsharp, a pool player." When the high school was built in 1907, however, he quit work in the packinghouse and enrolled.

He said his "desire for knowledge was so keen" that he saved $200 while he was working, then sold some of his clothes for $90. The $290 helped him go to high school.

This was "the bravest thing" he had ever done because he had to "run the gauntlet of his former chums," who scoffed about his going to school. He had to show them that he "would take nothing but respect from them."

He joined the high school debating team in 1908. He said he became "one of the best debaters in the high school," and that when he had a debate, his former pals would show up, and cheer.

Lista Makimson was one of Jim's teachers. She taught him English and History. Jim was seventeen: Lista, thirty—"some odds." She was "blonde, fair, beautiful."

Jim told me he "couldn't complete high school." He managed about three school years on that $290, plus what he could save from jobs he hustled during the summer. Then he ran out of money, and never did graduate.

Jim mentioned that he joined the Rosedale local of the Socialist Party when he was seventeen. But, he added, "I committed myself when I joined the IWW in 1911. I was twenty-one. That was in Kansas City. Before that I was a sympathizer. I make a distinction. When I joined the IWW, my way of life was decided."

"When I became a revolutionist," he said, "I threw off my early training, both in money and in sex. Since I became a revolutionist, I haven't had a bank account."

It wasn't until Jim left high school that he went to see Lista to tell her he wanted to marry her. That was "impossible," she told him.

Then in 1913 Jim "had to go away to Chicago." Before leaving, he met Lista and they went to Swope Park, a big park "where you had absolute privacy." This "was supposed to be the farewell."

Jim's labor activities in the Avery Manufacturing plant strike led to his being arrested and indicted in Peoria, Illinois. He said that since he might be jailed, Lista came to Chicago to visit him, bringing two of her girl friends. Jim and Lista were married, with $14 between them. "A brave thing to do," he said, but Lista agreed fully with his ideas about revolution and the future of mankind.

This was the first time that Jim talked to me about himself. I think he opened up because he realized he worked best with someone he felt knew him, who would try to understand his moods, who wouldn't expect him to produce on a nine-to-five workday schedule, although I must say there were times when Jim worked so intensely for long hours that it was tiring.

After a time a close working relationship was established between us along with a warm, lasting friendship. Sometimes when we reached a good stopping place in our work, Jim would tell me more about himself and reminisce about those he had known.

For instance, he spoke often of Vincent St. John, one of the leaders of the Industrial Workers of the World. His memory of the "Saint" seemed very fresh, reminding Jim particularly of how the great Wobbly leader handled young rebels. The Saint, Jim said, had confidence in him. He recalled the time St. John sent him to Akron during the rubber strike. That was in 1913. "See what you can do," he remembered the Saint saying. "Just like that!" Jim snapped his fingers. In Akron he "worked with Trotter and Speedman. I became a leader." Jim was twenty-three.

Another time Jim told me about the Saint's asking him to go to Rock Island where they needed help in a strike. He asked Jim if he thought he could handle the job. Jim thought he could.

Remembering the self-confidence St. John inspired in him when he was "a green kid," Jim on many occasions would say: "You've got to have confidence in people."

Frank Little, one of the founders of the IWW, was another name that became familiar to me soon after I started working with Jim. But it was some years before I saw a copy of the August 1926 "Frank Little Memorial Number" of the *Labor Defender* with Jim's tribute to "Frank Little, the Rebel."

"It is nine years, this month," Jim wrote, "since they hung Frank Little to the trestle's beam in Butte. They put Frank out of the way and thought they were through with him, but they made a mistake. The things Frank Little stood for—and that was the real Frank Little—are still alive. The things Frank Little did in his lifetime are not forgotten and the memory of them is not without influence even today."

Jim's tribute to Frank Little is included in his book *Notebook of an Agitator*.

Jim made his first trip to New York in 1919 to attend the Unity Conference of the left-wing Socialists. He was a delegate from the Kansas City faction. "I was just what they were waiting for in New York—an Irishman from Rosedale!"

The party "devoured" him; he didn't push himself. He was "a green kid—like you and Joe—from out of the West," he said. But when he looked around at the people leading the party, he made up his mind that he "would take the party over and run it honestly, put it on an honest footing."

The party pushed him, sent him around to speak everywhere.

After several weeks, Jim returned to "the West," but from now on, he "hit the road" more than he stayed in Rosedale or Kansas City. He became known as a troubleshooter and his travels took him wherever there was a "situation."

Jim remembered a miners' meeting he had to go to. "I left New York on a bus at twelve o'clock one night and arrived in Chicago about nine the next night. I got off the bus and went to a social where I had to speak. Then I had to take a bus to Gillespie for the miners' meeting. This bus business was routine."

Going to a social after traveling on a bus for twenty-one hours and then speaking, sounds questionable to me now. But when you're young and fired with enthusiasm for the struggle, you can do these things.

I don't think Jim ever mentioned when he met Rose. But in a letter he dictated to me for Rose when she was in Los Angeles, he used the phrase "When I first met you up on the mountain. . . ." Rose, in an interview with Evelyn Reed, said that she met Jim at the 1921 Unity Convention of the Communist Party and the United Communist Party. This was in Woodstock, New York, in an old hotel building on top of Mount Overlook. Jim, laughing, said it was an underground convention on top of a mountain.

One of the "hardest things" Jim ever had to do in his "whole life was decide between Lista and Rose."

He told me he was "so honest, so frank," that he "had to tell Lista about Rose. Do you know what her reaction was? She said, 'Jim, let's go to bed.'" But it didn't work out; "Lista's pride wouldn't let her take it." The final break, however, didn't come until some time in 1924 or 1925.

Jim returned to Chicago. "I was there a whole year without a woman. A principled bastard then," he said.

Before the break with Lista, Jim was in Cleveland editing *The Toiler,* the paper of the Communist Labor Party, which later became the *Daily Worker.* When *The Toiler* was moved to New York in 1920, Jim moved with it. During the next several years he worked at moving Lista and the two children, Carl and Ruth, from Cleveland, where they had moved from Kansas City to join him. No small feat to move a family from one city to another on party wages. But finally they were all together in New York.

Jim had bitter memories of how party functionaries were treated in the Communist Party. He said: "As soon as the Stalinists expelled us, and we could organize things our own way, we made sure the functionaries got enough to live on. Those goddamned sons of bitches didn't give a damn about anybody but themselves."

"You can't keep going on starvation wages," he said, "a dollar here, a dollar there. You begin going into debt. You wear out revolutionists that way, and they quit."

Not long after I started working at Jim's West Eleventh Street office on a regular schedule, he telephoned me at the national office one morning and asked me to come over early. He was worrying about his speech.

This was the keynote speech to the Thirteenth National Convention in July 1948, which would be broadcast over radio network ABC on Thursday the next week at 11:15 p.m.

Jim complained that he had "to say everything in thirteen minutes," and he hadn't been able to even get started.

He said he thought he would "do a bold thing." He would "deal with the first American revolution, the second, and the third."

A few days later, when Joe and I were having dinner, Jim telephoned. He wanted Joe to write the speech for him and asked if I would take down some notes to give to Joe.

The theme was to be "the third American revolution." "The first was necessary to establish the independence of the country and to assure the possibility of the development of this great country. The second revolution was necessary to break chattel slavery and to establish freedom of production. The third revolution is what the country needs."

The next morning Joe went over to Jim's. They worked on the speech until almost the following morning, but they came up with a good first draft. By the next Thursday the speech was polished and tailored to fit within the thirteen minutes allowed by ABC.

Jim worried about a lot of things, although he generally didn't show it.

One day when he wanted to relax, he moved from his desk to his easy chair, and resumed worrying about Grace Carlson, remembering the time she was in prison. "Our Grace, who went down there to prison, who was concerned about those girls down there when nobody else gave a damn for them. Grace looked after them, the whores down there. That's all those poor girls were, whores."

Jim used the word "whore" not in a derogatory sense, but rather to express his sympathy for the young women sent to prison for things in which males were just as responsible and which were their own concern after all. At times Jim expressed himself among friends in language that was rather shocking in those days but which now seems to have become the custom rather generally. Usually, however, Jim used very proper English.

Thinking about Grace Carlson led Jim to thinking about Henry Schultz who also lived in the Twin Cities. "Those comrades out in Minneapolis . . . " he said. "Look what Hank Schultz is doing now. He has two trades and has been blacklisted from both of them because of his devotion to the party. And Dorothy [Henry's wife] with four kids, and probably all of them with whooping cough right now, and Dorothy out slinging hash while Henry is out in Colorado.

"Do you know what he is doing? He's putting the party on the ballot in Colorado.

"They make me feel so ashamed."

Jim didn't really mean that he felt ashamed. At bottom he always felt that he should be doing more for the movement and he expressed this as feeling ashamed when he talked about how much others were doing. Actually, Jim was working at top capacity.

At the same time, Jim knew how to relax and thought there should be more to life than just work. The task at hand should be done, and done well, no "horsing around." But then there should be a time to play. And he insisted that vacations be taken. How else, he would say, can a comrade keep going for the rest of the year?

In August 1949 when it was time for our vacation, there wasn't much money around. We consoled ourselves with the many advantages of an August vacation in New York City. Thousands of people come to New York each summer for their vacations; we were already here. All we had to do was act like tourists.

Our plans changed when Lou Gordon offered Rose and Jim the use of his automobile, and Freddy and Lyman Paine suggested that the four of us spend our vacation in the Paine house on Sutton Island, one of the Cranberry Islands, just off the coast of Maine.

The only access from the mainland to the island was by motorboat. From the dock to the house you followed a footpath between cranberry and blueberry bushes.

After checking the house, top to bottom, we decided to use only four of the ten rooms or so—two bedrooms, the living room with a big fireplace, and the kitchen.

We seemed to be the only ones on the island, except for a massive bulldog that lunged at the end of a chain and barked ferociously each time we wandered within hearing distance. Jim always found bulldogs, especially big ones, distasteful and carefully led us in a big circle around the dog's territory when we went exploring.

During our stay we decided on a certain division of labor. While Rose, Joe, and I dug for clams, or fished for flounder, or gathered wild blueberries, Jim got the daily New York weather report on the portable radio in the kitchen. He talked a lot about the comrades left behind in New York who were sweltering in the heat and humidity while we had to keep logs burning in the fireplace and the kitchen oven going—even when Joe wasn't making blueberry pies—just to stay comfortably warm.

Jim and Joe talked about the beauty of that oven. It was an old-time eye-level oven, and Jim claimed that one day every kitchen would have just such an oven, an oven at eye level so that you didn't have to get down on your hands and knees to see if the top crust of the pie was turning brown.

Between weather reports and an occasional trip to the woodshed for another log, Jim played a complicated game of solitaire. It demanded concentration if you wanted to win. Jim won often—and without cheating. He would visualize fifteen to twenty moves ahead. Sometimes, seeing it was hopeless, he would not even try to play the cards but would gather them up, reshuffle them, and try again. "It's a waste of time to play if you're licked. It's as important to know when to quit as when to go ahead."

Whenever Jim was mulling over an idea or thinking about a problem, he sometimes occupied himself playing solitaire, not only when he was on vacation but in his apartment. He always broke up his game, of course, when I came in to start working.

Jim was still thinking about that vacation the following year. In a letter from Hollywood, June 6, 1950, he asked: "Are you going to Maine again for your vacation? Or, have you discovered another island?"

His letter wasn't sent just to kid me about vacations. He had a helpful suggestion to make about how we might solve the problem we were having with the national office tape recording project. He wrote:

"I suppose Murry [Weiss] or others will report on our Western conference last Saturday. I thought it was very good on the whole. Both the Frisco and Seattle delegations took recordings back with them to be played at local membership meetings.

"By the way, Bob Chester's tape recorder gave a much clearer and truer recording than any I have yet heard. The tape recorder in N.Y. always seems to come out with a slightly blurred or muffled sound, but Bob's is clear as a bell. It is an 'Eicor,' put out by 'Eicor, Inc.,' Chicago 7, and only cost $110.00 wholesale. Joe should investigate the possibility of switching to this brand.

"The wire recordings of [George] Clarke's speech helped me in preparing my report. However, I should inform you that, despite the excellent packing, the containers were banged up in transit and the ends were broken off. You should consider getting metal or plastic containers, if they are to be had, for future shipments of recordings.

"If you are in the mood, and have time, let me know what's going on in N.Y. once in a while. We are a long way from home, and the purely political reports we get, important as they are, and so highly appreciated, don't give any information about the people we know who are also important, don't you think?"

Some years later, in a letter from Los Angeles, Rose also spoke about our Maine vacation.

"Do you know what, Rebe?" she said. "The two best vacations we've had in our life were with you and Joe. One on the Cranberry Island, never to be forgotten, and the second at Carpinteria [California]. No comparison between the two as far as the countryside is concerned. But an indefinable something; an unspoken, easygoing agreement between the two couples in spite of gap in ages. A sort of feeling of knowing each other forever as tho of the same family where love is the driving force that makes each member appreciate the other's virtues and sympathetically tolerate his vices. At the same time each individual of the group feels free to do what he wants without encroaching on the freedom of the others. Actions that have to be taken together are easily disposed of by a short conference of all involved. That is what made our vacations with you so wonderful. At least that is how I feel and I dare say Jim does too. And all this in spite of the gap in age."

When Jim and I were on our regular work schedule, and had finished the week around five o'clock on Friday, we relaxed, had a martini, and talked. This became a tradition and even now, when it comes five o'clock on a Friday, I begin to think of a good, dry martini.

During the next period, Rose and Jim moved from West Eleventh Street to 92 Jane Street in the west part of Greenwich Village. Their apartment was on the second floor in a walk-up building. The front room facing on Jane Street was large and was made into a work place for Jim.

After they were settled, Jim suggested that we go back on a regular work schedule, Tuesday through Friday, three o'clock to five. In the morning I would do my work in the national office.

One afternoon when I arrived, Jim was in "the dumps," as he put it. He explained that the previous evening he had gone to visit a comrade who was going through a difficult personal situation. When he tried to talk with her, she burst into tears. He was despondent. "She's taking psychiatric treatment. She never told me, but she told Rose that each visit is torture."

Jim asked if I had read much Freud. He said that he had read him only superficially but that he intended to read him more thoroughly.

"I have never been able to disclose my personal self to anyone. I could never confide in my first wife or my children. But with you I feel a compulsion to tell you. The things I told you last summer I've never told anyone. Not even Vincent [Dunne]—and I dearly love him. Do you mind if I talk with you? Just tell you my experiences. Neither to condemn nor to praise."

One day while I was clipping articles Jim had marked in the daily papers, he sat, chair tipped back, bare feet on the windowsill. He mentioned that he had read an article in the *New York Herald Tribune* about some men who gave their skin to help another. But he had thrown the paper out, and he couldn't think of another topic he would like to write a "Notebook" piece about.

Jim had not done a Notebook column since Sylvia left. And I was eager to get going.

I dashed uptown to the *Herald Tribune* office where I knew back copies were kept for people like us who toss out the paper too soon. I was back in "jig time," Jim said. "Jig time" is very fast as anyone who has danced an Irish jig knows.

We went to work. The Notebook piece was about Robert A. Sullivan, a boilermaker with Consolidated Edison Co., who entered Bellevue Hospital with burns covering 70 percent of his body. He lived only because fourteen of his fellow workers "gave two grafts each of skin taken from their own bodies." This column was printed in the *Militant* of April 30, 1951.

That was the beginning. The pace from then on was steady. Each week a Notebook was finished and delivered to the *Militant*. Every week during the next eight months.

The Notebook column wasn't the only thing we worked on. In June, Jim began a series on the Stalinist peace program, eight articles, that appeared in the *Militant*. These were later published as a pamphlet, *The Road to Peace*.

Jim autographed a copy of the pamphlet for me. It made feel good, after I found the meaning of the Latin phrase in the dictionary. The inscription read: "To Reba—*sine qua non*—Jim."

In 1958 he autographed a copy of a compilation of his columns, *Notebook of an Agitator*, and used almost the same words. "To Reba, *sine qua non*. In grateful remembrance. Jim Cannon." I don't know if he had forgotten using the same words seven years before, or just wanted to emphasize the category he had put me in.

Arrangements had been made for Jim and Rose to stay at Mountain Spring Camp, in the foothills of the Poconos near Washington, New Jersey, during the summer of 1951, where work space was available. The plan was that I would spend three days a week at the camp, the rest in the national office.

Jim was so enthused about the prospect of working out of New York City during the summer that he began firing on all cylinders. In this note you can hear the revving up:

"Mt. Spring—Monday. Reb [short for Reba]: Please make three copies of this Notebook ["From Karl Marx to the Fourth of July"]. Give one to Jules [Geller, who was then editing the *Militant*], bring one with you when you come out Tuesday night. Send the third copy to Art [Sharon] and tell him I am sending him this advance copy as a reply to his note.

"Tell Jules I will check the copy you bring out over the Fourth and will phone him at *noon sharp* on Thursday to give him any last-minute corrections. This Notebook piece should run *ahead* of the Stalinist series *in next week's paper*, as it is more timely.

"(There are so many corrections in the handwritten manuscript, you had better proofread the typewritten copy.)"

Jim was always careful about final drafts sent to the editorial office. He wanted clean copy. From his own long experience as an editor, he knew that sloppy copy invites typographical errors, besides being an imposition on the workers who have to set the copy and make corrections.

Jim's note went on: "I fell right back into the routine Friday morning just as if there had been no interruption. [I had gone to camp, but had to leave Thursday evening because a virus hit me.] I worked two shifts Friday and another Saturday morning and finished the draft of this 'Incident at Little Rock.' I am right back in the groove this morning, and will have something for you to work on when you arrive. It looks like a productive summer for us.

"All the equipment arrived in good shape. I tested out the dictaphone and found it in working order. Till Tuesday."

Our plans for the summer were changed. I was laid up, but Jim continued his work.

In the fall of 1951 Rose was nominated for the student body at the Trotsky School. In discussing her nomination, some of the comrades voiced certain reservations. First of all, Rose was sixty-one years old and this was well above the age considered ideal for the school. Second, if Rose was away from home for six months, this could upset Jim's work schedule.

But Rose was enthusiastic about the prospect of becoming a student. She felt that it would give her a new lease on life and was sure to show in whatever contributions she could still make to the party. Jim, while he was at first surprised at the idea, thought it was good because of what it showed about the party's attitude toward women and toward counteracting the generation gap, one of the divisions fostered by capitalism that finds its reflection even among socialists. Both of them thought they could manage living apart for six months.

The comrades felt reassured. And Rose became one of the students at the Trotsky School session of 1951-52. While she was away (she came in to New York on some weekends, on others Jim joined her at the school), we continued on our routine.

When we finished the Notebook on "Crime and Politics," I told Jim I was glad to see another piece finished, that this would show the "skeptics." I meant only to encourage him to keep up the good work, but Jim said he knew there were some who thought the writing wouldn't continue, who thought that because Rose was studying at the Trotsky School everything would go "to pot."

"Ever since I was a boy," Jim said, "people have expected me to go to the dogs, but I haven't."

Then one day a leading comrade asked if I would arrange an appointment with Jim for eight o'clock any evening. He wanted "to make sure Jim was O.K."

Jim said: "Tell him I'm going out for dinner and will see him in the office Saturday. All my life I have been fighting to be free. I've done what I wanted to do. It has caused some trouble for me, but like the blind horse, I just don't give a damn.

"Foster [William Z.] always served his office. The most I'll do is have lunch with someone, but not dinner. After a day's work is done, I choose the people I want to be with, not people I need or people who need me. That's the worst—people who need me. I don't like that. It takes too much out of you."

He added: "The comrade doesn't have any faith in people. That's one reason he isn't a leader. He looks like a leader, but he isn't."

Then we worked on a Notebook column about Georgie Flores, Brooklyn welterweight, who died five days after a knockout in Madison Square Garden. The death of this twenty-year old, who left a young wife and a month-old baby, upset Jim. He thought about it, talked about it, then wrote his savage indictment of the "sport" called boxing. He entitled it "Murder in the Garden."

A week later he wrote "A Dead Man's Decision," which begins: "Dead men tell no tales; but sometimes, as is well known, the memory of what they did, or the way they died, exerts an authority over the living and affects their actions and decisions."

Because of Georgie Flores's death, the life of Sugar Ray Robinson was spared in the Turpin-Robinson fight for the middleweight championship at the Polo Grounds. The referee stopped the fight with only eight seconds to go in the round because Robinson was bleeding "like a stuck pig from an eye cut."

The referee stopped the fight because he hadn't forgotten the Georgie Flores scandal.

Jim pointed out that "Cock-fighting is illegal; it is considered inhumane to put a couple of roosters into the pit and incite them to spur each other until one of them keels over. It is also against the law to put bulldogs into the pit to fight for a side bet. But our civilization—which is on the march to be sure—has not yet advanced to the point where law and public opinion forbid men, who have nothing against each other, to fight for money and the amusement of paying spectators."

I mentioned to Jim that another leading comrade wanted to talk with him about our policy toward the Stalinists. He was wondering about the possibility of entering the American Labor Party clubs or supporting a couple of ALP candidates.

Several of the comrades were agitating each other about this. "I guessed as much," Jim said. "Let them flounder. . . . I want them to flounder."

He pointed out that "the Stalinists in the United States are a different proposition than the Stalinists in France or England, and we've got to decide if they can lead us to the masses, if they have any influence with the masses. We've got to go slow."

At this time differences had begun to develop in the top leadership of the SWP that were to evolve into a full-fledged factional struggle. Comrades who had fought side by side with Jim for many years began to challenge his leadership, claiming that his positions had become outmoded. The leaders of this group included Bert Cochran, George Clarke, and Mike Bartell. At the time it was not known that they had the backing of Michel Pablo in Europe.

A few days later Jim continued on the point about supporting ALP candidates.

"Clarke has gone Parisian on us," he said, "but he'll bounce back. After twelve years training in our movement, he goes Parisian on us after one year in France. That's a characteristic of his, going off half-cocked.

"Tonight Clarke and Bartell went up to hear I. F. Stone who is speaking under the auspices of this new committee for civil rights. We'll have a discussion on it. They have a brainstorm about joining the ALP. I think I'll mention in passing tomorrow night [at the Political Committee meeting] that they made an error in joining this outfit on their own.

"I don't know whether they will learn from it or not. It is like someone who makes an indiscreet error; they hope nobody will notice. I may mention that tomorrow night.

"Whenever the movement is stymied, they look around. That's good, but you must be cagey."

From Jim's desk he could see what was going on down the street. When we were at work on the Notebook piece "They Strain at a Gnat," Jim jumped to his feet. He said an old man had just stumbled and fallen into the gutter across the street.

We watched.

Two men came out of the garage, picked up the old man, and sat him down against the wall of the garage.

"Poor old fellow—he's pretty sick," Jim said.

The old man began to move, and tried to get up. He couldn't make it. One of the garage men helped him up, but seemed to be trying to convince him to stay down. The old man struggled. The garage man gave up and turned away.

The old man reeled. Jim shouted, "Catch him!" The garage man caught him even though he could hardly have heard Jim. "I've got to go down." Jim changed from slippers to shoes, and rushed down the stairs.

He placed both hands on the old man's shoulders and talked to him. Then he put his arm around him and led him down the street and around the corner.

When Jim returned, he said, "I took him home; he'd been drinking."

The day we finished "Strain at a Gnat," we decided to celebrate our first six months of steady work by eating out. Jim put on his best suit. "I might as well be a good sport," he said.

I don't remember where we ate, but I do remember that during the dinner Jim said: "Do you know that the last six months have been the most productive for me—the most sustained working period?"

A few days later, Jim seemed disturbed. A comrade who had previously visited him and talked about her psychoanalysis had called again the evening before. She was down, in a mess, and wanted advice. "I don't know why people go to others for help when they are down. I am just the opposite. When I am in the dumps, I like to be by myself and not see anybody—except certain people."

He added: "I've put up a constant struggle not to let people change me. Be yourself . . . don't try to be what you think people want you to be."

One Sunday, "just for a change," Jim agreed to climb up to our fifth-floor apartment at 19 Stuyvesant Street for "brunch." We had sourdough pancakes and sausages with maple syrup— genuine homemade syrup from "Mapleine (Imitation Maple Flavoring)" and sugar.

After breakfast while we had our coffee, Jim fished a clipping from his pocket about hospitality by Ralph Waldo Emerson; he thought it was good, and he read this part: "Hospitality is a little fire, a little food, and an immense quiet." He said he "didn't feel at home until there is unrestrained quiet."

He saw a copy of Heine's *Poetry and Prose* in our bookcase and pulled it out. He found "The Lorelei" and read it out loud. "Isn't that beautiful?" He read it again.

He said that when he was in Sandstone prison, he "read Heine's poems in German." He turned the pages of the book until he found a poem about a child that he had read in prison. "I thought of my little Lorna," he said, and asked if I would like to hear it.

> You're lovely as a flower,
> So pure and fair to see;
> I look at you, and sadness
> Comes stealing over me.
> I feel, my hands should gently
> Cover your head in prayer—
> That God may always keep you
> So lovely, pure, and fair.

Then he repeated part of the poem from memory in German:

Du bist wie eine Blume
So hold und schön und rein;
Ich schau' dich an, und Wehmut
Schleicht mir ins Herz hinein.

Jim's German sounded good to me, and I wondered why he didn't continue.

"Heine was a revolutionist," he told me. "He knew Marx."

That afternoon Jim wanted to see *A Streetcar Named Desire*. I never did like going to movies during the daytime, especially on Sunday, but I went. Jim thought the play "was powerful, well done. It pays to save up and see a good movie, better than seeing a lot of them that aren't good."

On the afternoon we were to begin working on the Notebook series about the Catholic Church, Jim was in an angry mood. "Like a fool I didn't go to sleep until six this morning. Just before I went to bed I read a piece by [Alfred] Rosmer in the *New International*. Do you know who he is? The piece is about Natalia's [Sedova Trotsky] break with the Fourth International. It made me so mad I mulled over the idea of writing the Notebook column about that. But I'm so mad I'm afraid I wouldn't do a good piece. We'll do the column we talked about, the Catholics. What do you think?"

We went to work. Three articles were written on the Catholic Church.

To relax, Jim had been reading *Footloose in Arcadia*, but he asked me to take it back to the library. "It made me feel bad," he explained.

The book was about Jack London, George Sterling, and Ambrose Bierce. The author, Joseph Noel, knew the three intimately from 1897 until they drifted apart.

Noel describes the ideals of the three, follows them through many seamy experiences, and tells about their deaths—Jack London's from a doctor-prescribed opiate, from which "he kept out enough that was not missed" for three nights "to join with the fourth night's full allowance to put an end to it all." Ambrose Bierce, Noel claims, was shot in Mexico. And George Sterling took cyanide of potassium.

Jim said he had "been in the dumps. I know I only go so far, and then come out of it. It is sort of an indulgence on my part. I'm not like others who get in the dumps and don't come out.

"When you came over, I wasn't in any mood to write. You're good for me, good medicine," he said.

Since "good medicine" generally goes to work right away, we settled down and broke the back of next week's column.

This was the first in a series on the Stalinists and the unionists, entitled "Some Chickens Come Home to Roost."

Later Jim said: "When I get in the dumps I wonder if the stuff we are writing is good. I wonder if I should write anymore. . . . But when I'm in the dumps I don't know it's good, and nobody can tell me it is."

He asked: "Do you think they're satisfied with the work we're doing? One column a week? Or do they expect more?"

Jim never did anything by halves, so when it came to public speaking, he really studied the art. In the American revolutionary movement he was considered to be one of the best speakers who ever "came down the pike."

He was very thorough in his preparations. In working with me, he would sometimes write out the first draft of a speech in longhand, sometimes dictate notes. Then this material would be typed, always triple space, allowing plenty of room to rework it. He would go over the draft carefully, cutting, splicing, rearranging. The second draft would be typed. And gone over again. A third draft would be typed, a fourth, until finally Jim would say it was getting close. But it wasn't until he was more or less satisfied with the draft that he would mark the paragraphs, sentences, clauses, words in the way he would deliver them.

Then the final copy would be typed.

One of the first speeches I remember working on with Jim was "The New Situation in the Trade Union Movement and the Tasks of the Party."

An early draft of this is a good example of the way Jim worked. Sometimes, though, he would make changes even after the final draft.

Jim generally underlined phrases with a red or blue pencil. The blue wasn't used as much as the red, and seemed to indicate a shift in tone, sometimes the insertion of parenthetical material. If the blue line was double, this indicated a pause for emphasis or a shift in thought.

When I heard Jim give this speech, I couldn't believe it was completely written out. He seldom looked down at the podium, or,

Reba: This copy of the speech is rightfully yours. You did at least half of the work on it

THE NEW SITUATION IN THE TRADE UNION MOVEMENT *Jim*

~~AND THE TASKS OF THE PARTY.~~ *11/3/47*

(Speech by James P. Cannon to New York Membership Meeting of the
Socialist Workers Party, Sunday, November 30, 1947).

I.

During the war the trade union bureaucracy *in the United States*

completely revealed its role

as an agency of the bourgeois government in the labor

movement. Its assigned task

was to restrain and discipline the workers

within the strait-jacket of the no-strike *pledge* ~~formula~~ and

the wage freeze.

It must be recognized that the *bureaucracy in all its sections* performed this task with the

greatest efficiency.

The Stalinists, who are a part of the *trade union* bureaucracy,

did even more than their share ~~on~~ *of* this dirty job.

In return for this service

as a disciplinary police force over the workers,

the governmental machinery protected

if he did, it was just a glance. He did not turn the sheets over, but slipped them to one side, one after another, in a way that was not noticeable. He was a master at free and easy delivery, with seeming spontaneity. I don't believe anyone in the audience would have guessed that he was following a written text almost word for word.

Money didn't mean much to Jim personally and if ever he did get a few "shekels in his jeans," he managed to get rid of them long before they could burn a hole in his pocket. He was generous with his friends and thoroughly enjoyed sharing with them.

In a letter to "Gabe, Ernest, and Pierre" (Michel Pablo, Ernest Mandel, and Pierre Frank) on February 17, 1950, he wrote:

"Dear Friends,

"I have finally become a rich man, and have some extra money which I am free to dispose of as I see fit. As I recall, Marx, like Engels, once wrote that one should wish for worldly goods only to be able to fly to the assistance of his friends. This is my disposition too.

"On the occasion of my sixtieth birthday celebration in New York, the rank and file comrades of the New York organization presented me with a purse of $400. The Party Plenum, which was held at the same time, unanimously approved the initiative of the New York comrades and decided to make the fund a national one. The comrades of all branches throughout the country, as well as friends and sympathizers, will be given an opportunity to contribute to this fund on a purely voluntary basis. So, in a few weeks I will have even more money.

"But in the meantime, in order to protect myself against the conservatizing influence of wealth, I want to dispose of the $400 now in hand and have decided to divide it among the three of you as my personal gift to you. Please let me know right away how to send it. I wish to divide this money into three equal parts among yourselves.

"However, I make one absolute stipulation as to the use of the money. I want you to understand firmly that it is for your *personal* use, to be put into your own pockets and used only for your *personal* needs. Under no circumstances is it to be turned in to the organization treasury or to be spent for any of the regular items of the budget. With this strict limitation, I don't care what you do with the money. Buy food with it if you are hungry; or, if you are thirsty, you can spend it all on Cognac as far as I am concerned.

"This is the first opportunity I have had to express to all three of you my heartfelt appreciation—and, yes, I may as well say it frankly—my reverence for the truly great and heroic work you have done for our cause through these difficult years. I am glad that, thanks to the kindness and generosity of the New York comrades, I am able to express my sentiments in this regard with something more than words.

"If I might make a suggestion as to how you could squander a small part of this money, it would make me very happy if the three of you, who have worked so long on skimpy rations, would get together and treat yourselves to the best French meal you can get in a good French restaurant. Wash it down with the best French wine the 'maison' has to offer. And then, when the Cognac is served with the coffee, you might drink a toast to my sixty years. But not a political one, in thesis form, to which you Europeans are too much addicted, but just something personal, like this: 'Here's to the old son-of-a-bitch who believes that money was made to be spent and shared with friends.'"

One day Jim said he wanted to dictate a letter to Joe. That was on March 28, 1952. For sometime prior to this, he had been preoccupied and seemed worried.

"Dear Joe:

"We are standing on a great bridge of history. Things we discuss and the decisions we make are the most important in the history of the world. Bear in mind that when I talked to Trotsky in 1935 [the year was actually 1934] about the French question, about Molinier and Naville, I said they have a great historical responsibility. He answered me: 'The greatest responsibility in the history of the world and they quarrel and split over trifles.'

"That's reported in my book *The History of American Trotskyism*.

"The thing that bothers me, Joe, is that we who have created the greatest cadre—shall they fall apart and split over trifles? Or are we strong enough to absorb the little things and still keep the cadre together? That is my will, and what I want to know is who is going to help me?

"You saw that meeting last Saturday. [The Political Committee meeting.] If I had been a willful man, I could have broken the whole thing to pieces right there, but I didn't want to do it.

"I ask you to take into consideration not only the drastic action that I took in reading my letter to the International, but my secondary action in withdrawing the letter. And not merely withdrawing it, but, as Reba will tell you, burning it up and asking her to burn her stenographic notes (which she did).

"People who are working with me—I want them to know when I give something with the left hand, I don't take it back with the right. That letter which caused such consternation to some of the comrades does no longer exist. Maybe that is a small lesson for you, Joe. When you give a concession, make a real one.

"In your future troubles and factional arguments, etc., when you make a concession, make a real one. My greatest pride, Joe, in all the bitter years we had to fight is that no man dares to come before the leading body and say he didn't get a fair deal. Pin any man down, no matter what his beliefs are, and he will admit that he can get a square deal in this party. He will not be framed up; he will not be taken advantage of and run out. If anybody wants evidence, you can tell them about yourself. When we had the dispute about the sociological designation of Eastern Europe, you were in a minority. I was on the other side, but we approached it from different angles. You were approaching it from the theoretical side; I was approaching it from the political side. I had a mortal terror of any conciliation towards Stalinism. So the discussion proceeded.

"You at the beginning of the discussion were in the minority; I was in the majority. You are in a position to tell the party, if the question arises, does a minority have a fair chance in this party? Were you hounded, persecuted, and denigrated because you disagreed with Cannon? Were all the doors of the party closed to you? Or, on the contrary, were all the doors opened and were you given the opportunity to make a national tour so that comrades all over the country could meet you and you could explain your minority opinion?

"As far as I know this dispute is still unresolved. I do not accept the decision of the world congress. I *do* accept the political conclusion that we must defend these formations, so why fight about it? Do you think for one minute that if I considered this a fighting issue that I wouldn't fight?"

Jim and Rose moved to California in September 1952. This brought to a close my working with Jim on a daily basis, but he wrote me as if the relationship still continued. His letters indicate this very clearly. They are also of great interest in showing the kind of working conditions he required in order to continue writing at full capacity. First, he told me about the location of his work space:

"We are definitely settled down as permanent tax-paying citizens of California, but I must admit that we still watch the mailbox for news from New York. It is hard for a habitual—and convinced—sinner to resist the pull of Babylon. But I suppose this, too, will wear off in time.

"My office seems like the realization of a dream. It is a good sized room in a regular office building just *one block* from our house. One flight up. They don't have many tall buildings here on account of real estate being so plentiful. (There is also the little matter of earthquakes but, as good Californians, we are not supposed to mention that.) The ground floor is occupied by a drugstore and other places of business. The second floor was originally devoted to one-room furnished kitchenette apartments with wall beds. I have one of these apartments, minus the wall bed."

Jim went into what some may consider minute detail, but he knew that I would be interested. And he got a bonus—he had the fun of describing his new office.

"In addition to the main workroom," he continued, "there is a small kitchen *and private bath*. I am getting a gas plate so that I can fix coffee and tea for the necessary mid-morning and mid-afternoon breaks when I feel myself working too hard. My workroom is well lighted by north light (two wide windows) and it is cool enough for comfort even on the hottest days. It has a pleasant view, looking out over green and tidy yards of quiet and contented neighbors. It is very quiet and secluded, ideally suited for concentration on the work in hand."

Jim described the improvements in his new setup:

"My furniture consists of a 5x4 worktable, which I seem to prefer to a desk as it has more leg room; my wonderful desk chair, all my filing cabinets with their bulging contents of half-finished material for processing; a sofa and three chairs; and a dictaphone set, better than our old one in New York but not as good as the new electronic outfit; good lights, including a gooseneck desk lamp.

"The kitchen has also a dinette space, about 6x6, looking out through a good wide window, with a built-in table and wall benches, something like a spacious booth in a joint. This space is made to order for a special private workroom for a high-powered secretary who likes to organize her work efficiently with no nonsense and without having to listen to the boss's jokes. Unfortunately this secretarial department is still vacant and that's the one little gimmick missing in the machinery. The local comrades are looking around to see what they can do for me in this respect, but they seem to be terrified and paralyzed by my specifications. I can't understand this, because my demands are so moderate and conservative—all I want is just what I had in New York, without any improvements or innovations. They say I am not realistic, that I am demanding socialism, just like in my speeches and notebook entries. But I answer: 'What's the matter with socialism?' "

One of Jim's main concerns was a secretary and for a time he hinted and suggested that I come to Los Angeles. I had a feeling, however, that a good secretary would turn up out there.

Occasionally I have been asked if I knew how Jim thought out his projects. Instead of trying to describe this process, as I saw it, I can offer the following rather lengthy letter which shows in Jim's own words how a project grew on him, sometimes reaching proportions that he could not possibly cope with.

"I have been going over the material in the files and folders, sorting it out and rearranging it, and I am continually amazed at its scope and volume. I have just about definitely decided to work on processing this material for the next period and let the daily events journalism go for the time being. I can't do both without secretarial help and a decision has to be made as to the order of importance.

"The present tentative plan—which I expect to make definitive in the next few days—is to go right to work first on a big project under the general title of 'America's Road to Socialism.' The preliminary drafts of the chapters and sections would be worked up in the form of lectures to be given to the 'Friday Night Forum' of the L.A. Local. There they would be recorded on tape or wire and transcribed. This would bring the raw ore into the second stage for processing into literary form.

"The general scope of the project would extend over the following areas:

"1)-Socialism as projected by the great Utopians.

"2)-The Marxist development of Socialism from Utopia to Science. (The points of agreement and the points of difference—the great Utopians must get their full due; for the first time in our propaganda, as far as I know.)

"3)-The *pre-history* of the SWP. (An analytical panorama of the socialist and labor movement in the U.S. and its outstanding figures who blazed the trail for us.

"4)-Concretization, elaboration and extension of the 'Theses on the American Revolution,' projecting a sweeping revolutionary development in the U.S.; why it must take place and the kind of party it will call for. (Under this head, for the first time, I think— an exposition of the points of *difference* and the points of *similarity* of the problems of the Russian and American revolutions, and how Lenin's conception of the party *will* and *must* be *adapted* and *applied* here.)

"5)-The lines of development along which the Leninist party will expand and come to power in the U.S., excluding any prospect of any kind of substitute for such a party playing a revolutionary role under American conditions, or any victory for Socialism by default through automatic collapse of capitalism, etc.

"6)-A forecast of America in the transition period between Capitalism and Socialism. The most important problems which will probably arise and how they will probably be solved.(Here all the *differences* with Russia and the other backward countries will redound in our favor, permitting the quickest and most drastic solutions. The 'specter' of bureaucratism analyzed from a *materialist* standpoint. The comparative *brevity* of the transitional period, not a historical *epoch* but a period measured at the most in *decades*.)

"7)-What Socialist America will look like. An approximate estimation of how the people will live and think and change and begin to make what Marx called 'the real history of mankind.' Here we will go back to the great *anticipators*, the Utopians, and estimate how their projects of the future society may appear to people who, having broken down all class distinctions and conflicts, can plan in real life what the Utopians could only plan in their imaginations. Why the vision of the socialist future, firmly based on scientific premises, and recognized as realizable and inevitable, is faith enough to live by under any circumstances and at any price.

"The above is just a rough outline of the project as it has leapt out at me from the notes and material already at hand in the files and folders. But I think it will give you a general idea of how my plan is shaping up in my mind. As the project gets under way there will be plenty of room and opportunity to shift around and rearrange, add and subtract, etc. The general framework, however, won't change much. The big advantage of trying the sections out in lectures, as I see it now, is the flexibility it will provide for experiment, modification and change. The questions from the audience ought to help a lot, too, in uncovering blind spots and omissions.

"What I must aim to guard against in this project is any stupid compulsion to produce a definitive or scholarly work. I value academic works but it is not my duty to produce them. My inclination, and in my opinion my best service, will be to take off in the free-wheeling style of *The History of American Trotskyism,* telling what I know and what I think, for the benefit of those who may be interested, and let the scholars—of whom there will be plenty later on—take it from there.

*　　　　*　　　　*

"You will note that points 4 and 5 in the above outline have a contemporary significance for the SWP. Murry and I are discussing the points of a separate thesis on this point for party discussion after the election. We had a talk with Farrell [Dobbs] about it when he was here. I wrote a letter to Vincent about our discussion with Farrell and will send Joe a copy as soon as I can have one typed.

"P.S. If you get time, I wish you would type out a set of onionskin copies of the part of this letter [quoted above] . . . and send them to me. They can serve as outline notes of the project. Also I can show them to others to explain what is planned better than orally."

Again in the following letter Jim tells about the big projects he visualized getting done:

"I am pretty well settled down now in my routine at the office and have been so occupied with the routine that I find myself falling behind in my reports to you.

"This office setup is like the fulfillment of a life-long dream for me. It is quiet, secluded and free from irritating interruptions, and most conducive to concentrated work. The general atmosphere of the party here is also good for me. The comrades are young in spirit, cooperative, responsive to inspiration and capable of enthusiasm. They enter into the spirit of all the big projects I have outlined and this, in turn, inspires me to enlarge their scope. I have to be careful not to let my enthusiasm run away with me and promise more than I can deliver.

"I am in the groove, however, and work on an office schedule from 9 to 5 (not counting two hours for lunch—at home—and 'coffee breaks'), and, as you know, a great deal can be accomplished in time on that kind of a schedule.

"I am working on two levels—one imaginative and the other productive. On the imaginative level I keep enlarging the prospective projects, thinking of new features and aspects and steadily making notes of ideas that come into my mind. Then, every once in a while, I gather up the loose notes, sort them out and rearrange them in a systematic outline. Then, as I go along I plan to put the different outlines together in some kind of logical order in a logical structure. It is something like building a house from general architectural plans, but more fun, as I am free to change the plans around if I feel like it, and I have the privilege of working on the roof before I finish the foundation.

"The *general* plan, which assumes more and more definite shape, is to work up a *winter program* for the L.A. Local which will center around the building up of *The Friday Night Forum* as the medium. We will begin by advertising a series of lectures by me to open the program and get sympathizers and contacts into the habit of showing up at the headquarters on Friday night.

"Since Friday night is the end of the work week for most people, another regular feature of the Forum will be a social where people can hang around and visit and have a little fun after the lecture.

"In our advertising campaign for the first series of lectures we will make a big play to the students of the several colleges in L.A., and already have a group of young students (some of them still in high school) lined up and clamoring for the program to begin.

"We are going to make a big play in our advertising on the *Open Forum* feature of the Friday Night gatherings. 'The Friday Night Forum—the only place in Los Angeles where you can ask questions and speak your mind about capitalism and socialism'— something like that.

"If we can get a couple of dozen young people with inquiring minds, who are not afraid of anything, to come around, we will surely make some new converts and get some new members and revitalize the party local. This seems to me to be a realistic prospect. We all responded to great ideals and new ideas when we were young. That's what kept the movement alive from generation to generation. Why should we think that eagerness for truth and enthusiasm to serve great ideals came to an end with us? The fact is that there are others in the present generation of youth who are just as good as we were—maybe better.

"The thing is to seek them out, teach them and inspire them as we were inspired by others. Of course, in the present situation we can't expect to get great numbers. But we can get a few, and the few will later bring the many. The witch-hunt atmosphere works against us, but in a way it may also work for us in this respect. One of the reasons the human race has kept going under all circumstances is that there are a certain number of people— especially among the young—who want to know and who are not afraid of anything. I believe there are such young people right here in Los Angeles and that we are going to find some of them and get them to come with us. Of course, one can't have much luck prospecting in this territory unless he knows what he's talking about and believes what he says. But we have no troubles of this kind."

In the same letter Jim thought out loud about a lecture series he was mulling over. While the letter is rather involved and detailed, it shows—much better than I could describe—how Jim proceeded in his work.

"The lecture program is beginning to shape up about as follows: I will begin with a lecture on the results of the elections and the prospects for labor and war and peace under Eisenhower. That will be followed (probably) by a general lecture on 'The World Prospects of Capitalism and Socialism,' an analytical review of the main events and trends of the first half of the 20th Century and the probable line of development in the second half. (This may take several lectures.)

"After this broad introduction I will go over into a series of lectures on the whole question of Socialism from the Utopians to the elaboration of Marxist theory; the testing of the theory in practice; how the workers will come to power in the United States; what will happen during the transition period of the Workers' Government; and what life will be like, and, what changes in 'human nature' can be expected, in Socialist America.

"I don't know yet how many lectures this program will take, but I am not worrying about that. My plan is just to ramble along from one lecture to another and see how it goes. The lectures will be recorded on tape and the transcriptions will be raw material to work up and elaborate in written form. I expect to have a good time on this project, and if we get a good audience and get *some new members* out of it, everything will be just right. That will be the test of whether we have found the right form and kind of activity for this period.

"The *Forum-lecture* program for L.A. goes much farther than my lectures, as I visualize it and have discussed it with comrades here. My lectures will deal with all the subjects in a *general* way, hitting only the high spots, and aiming to give a popular presentation for the benefit of new people who, first of all, need to get a general view of the whole question of socialism. After my *general* presentation, if the interest and the audiences hold up, Murry and Myra can follow with separate series of lectures expanding and elaborating the themes dealt with in my prior presentation. If this works out, the winter program will combine political agitation, propaganda and more intensive educational work, all wrapped up in one package called 'The Friday Night Forum.'

"The intensive study of Marxism through class work, already a regular feature of the L.A. local activity, will not be superseded by the Friday Night Forum. I am inclined to think, rather, that interest in the intensive class work will be stimulated by the lectures, and that some of the new people, attracted and recruited by the Forum, will be eager to pursue the subject further in classes."

My guess that a good secretary would be found in Los Angeles happened just as I expected. Jim mentioned in this letter that he had "some help now." The reference is to Jeanne Morgan. The step-up in Jim's productivity is explained by the help Jeanne gave him.

"On the productive side," Jim continued, "my work so far has consisted of thinking, making notes, and examining and sorting the voluminous material in my files. I have some help now, and we spent this past week in going over the material in the collected notes and outlines of speeches and lectures I have given at different times over many years. I am now getting paid off for one merit despite my general slovenliness in the past. For some reason or other—perhaps because of some intuition that I might use them again sometime—I saved the notes and outlines of at least a couple of hundred speeches and lectures. Now I am discovering to my great delight—because it saves a lot of work and thought—that a great deal of the material I will need for my L.A. lecture series has already been used at various times in other speeches and lectures—and there it is all ready for use with a little rearranging and expansion! This is like getting paid for work done long ago and almost forgotten. It really pays to live right, doesn't it?

"This material fills *one whole drawer* of a filing cabinet! I think we will finish sorting it out and cataloging and indexing it Monday. Then I will go to work on the notes and outlines of my first lecture on the election results."

Jim accomplished a good deal of what he worked out on the imaginative level, but his actual production was never up to what he visualized. He lacked a sufficient team of co-workers. If the party had been richer and could have assembled a larger team to work with him, his literary production would surely have been much greater.

Jim continued to count me in on his projects; at least he made me feel I was still part of them. "I was very glad to get your letter of November 17," he wrote, "which shows that you are actively participating in the project, even from afar, with the same spirit that governed all our fruitful work together. You know as well as I do that inspiration is a good half of any serious endeavor—the *motor* part—and I gratefully feel your continuing interest and help crackling from the paper of your letters like a radioactive force."

I don't think that Jim really thought my letters were a radioactive force. He was just saying that a secretary's enthusiasm can go a long way. It can help accomplish a project and sometimes lead to inspiring a new one.

"The first project (the six lectures) is rolling now," Jim continued, "but they are intended only as a tune-up for things to come. At least that's the way I feel about it. Anyway, the die is cast as far as the lectures are concerned. A four-page folder advertising the series is going to the printer tomorrow."

In his correspondence Jim kept me up to date on the details of his schedule in Los Angeles. He knew that I was interested, but at the same time he wanted a little quid pro quo. In return he expected that I would let him know what was going on in the center.

He concluded his letter with these details.

"Here are a few smaller points of information re:

"1)-If you will send me a batch of airmail stamps I will see that they don't go to waste.

"2)-If you get a chance to wander over to the West Side for a change of scenery, Rose would like you to get a prescription refill from Kem Drug Co. . . .

"3)-Anytime you want to phone us to inquire how mild the weather is here, our phone number is NOrmandy 3-5296.

"4)-We are getting a dictaphone tomorrow and I will try to use the damned uninspiring thing again.

"5)-Murry's operation was postponed for another week. We will surely keep you informed of all developments on this important front.

"6)-We are hoping to have Vincent out here for a rest and some medical treatment, and await word from the N.O.

"7)-Mark took some pictures of our office Saturday, some of them in color showing the gorgeous view from the window. If they come out OK, I will send you one or two to look at the next time you are snowed in."

As the 1952 year-end holidays approached, we were reminded that this was the first time in a long while that Jim and Rose wouldn't be in New York to oversee the traditional Christmas and New Year's festivities.

I dropped Jim a note: "The other day around the lunch table at 116 someone brought up the matter of Christmas and eggnogs. 'Who'll make the eggnogs this year?' Everybody looked at everybody else. Nobody knows your recipe, and anyway there doesn't seem to be any incentive, at this point at least."

The incentive urgently presented itself the day Kay Thorne and I were asked to make the eggnogs for the New York Local Christmas party. I sent Jim an SOS.

He came to our rescue and sent the recipe. "This is written from Palm Springs where Rose and Marsh [Jim's son-in-law] and the two kids [Lorna and Mattie] and I just arrived for a four-day vacation. I am tired out and greatly appreciate the two weeks' lull before the last half of the lecture series is resumed. I wouldn't interrupt the vacation to write to anyone but you. Knowing me as you do, you know I mean that by 50% at least."

Jim liked to kid around. He'd hand you a really nice compliment, then ask if you'd heard about blarney. "Blarney," he would say, "has some truth, maybe 50%."

Just to make sure and leave nothing to chance, I looked up the word in Webster's Third New International Dictionary. "blarney [fr. *Blarney stone*, a stone in Blarney Castle, near Cork, Ireland, reputed to bestow talent for eloquent cajolery upon those who kiss it]."

I'll go along with Jim's explanation that blarney is at least 50 percent truth, maybe.

Jim sent a copy of his fifth lecture "which represents, at last," he wrote, "the accomplishment of one of the biggest projects we had on our agenda, but didn't get a chance to finish together.

"But your work and your inspiration is in it just the same, and I want you to read it first and let me know what you think about it. When you get through with it, hand it over to Joe to check and edit. He might show it around also to some of the others who would be interested, for criticism and correction on any points that need it."

This fifth lecture, entitled "America Under the Workers' Rule," was later included in the book *America's Road to Socialism*.

When Jim wrote, he had a very definite audience in mind. This was one of the heritages of his training as a speaker and his experience as a socialist propagandist and agitator.

"I have tried to write," he explained, "with a definite reader in mind all the time—the new young worker militant who will be coming to us as the advance representative of thousands and millions of future American socialist workers—and asking as they will all do: 'What is your program and how is it going to work out?'

"I tried to write for him in language he will not consider too technical; and within the framework of legality; and at the same time without blunting or slurring any Marxist principles. Others will have to judge whether or not I have succeeded in this extremely difficult and complicated task. That's why I would welcome any criticism from that point of view before the lecture is sent to the press.

"I still have to finish the lecture number six, 'What Socialist America Will Look Like,' but I am going to postpone that for a couple of weeks until I catch up on correspondence and other stuff on the party situation.

"I would be glad to hear from you in regard to the party situation as it looks to you at this point. Of course I hear from Joe and Farrell but I am sure you see quite a few things they miss, and they are just the points I am most curious about right now. Also I would like to know how things are going with you in general, how the world looks and so forth."

I wrote Jim that I thought the reader he had in mind would be able to grasp the ideas without any difficulty; and I utilized this occasion to let him know that I was feeling a little grumpy. "As for my work, it isn't as much fun as it was when I was collaborating in the project. No more cocktails, no more talks, no 'hookie.' The young in heart are stimulating. And where there's real give and take comradeship it brings out the best in you. I miss all that."

It was time to get out of the city for a couple of days. We went to

Mountain Spring Camp where we usually went whenever city life started bugging us.

This particular weekend Connie Weissman was there too. And as was customary we went for a leisurely walk up the hill and talked of many things. At one point Connie asked if I would explain why I found so much satisfaction in my work. She thought I seemed very happy with my job.

I hadn't really given the matter much thought until then, but I supposed it was because I felt the work I was doing was important; offhand, I couldn't think of any party job that was more important. I'm sure that Jim helped generate and foster that feeling.

Rose expressed this another way in a letter about Jim when she mentioned "the robust elation he is capable of and will be to his last breath. That is what he imparts to others, stimulating and inspiring them to the best that is in them."

Jim made very clear in many ways that whatever is done for the good of the movement, no matter what the task, then *that* work is important.

If ever I showed any disgruntlement in any way—and Jim said he could tell because I would get "uppity"—he would say: "Remember, you're part of a team," and recite what he claimed to be an "old Irish proverb": "Who can say which plays the music, the bow or the fiddle?"

The Cannons moved again, this time to a house at 1902 Hyperion Avenue, which had a large basement. While Jim was in New York for the May 1953 plenum of the National Committee, Rose and some of the other comrades in Los Angeles remodeled it into a high-efficiency fifteen by twenty-five foot office.

By the time Jim returned to Los Angeles, he seemed raring to go. On June 15 he wrote me:

"I arrived in Los Angeles all rested up from the three days of loafing and sleeping on the train. The journey was as restful as a sea voyage. I had to discipline myself to take the rest of last week off before starting in to work again. Even at that I had to go into the office one day to check up and see if everything was in order and get the feel of things."

Note Jim's reference to three days in a train. He disliked planes, not only their speed but also the height they flew above ground. He never changed.

By this time Jim and Jeanne were working together as a smooth functioning team. "Jeanne showed up at 9:00 o'clock this morning," he continued in his letter, "and we are already working out our schedule of production for the next period. First thing, I wish you would send me all the information you have about your electronic dictaphone. Is it a dictaphone or an ediphone? How much did it cost? What terms did you get it on? Did you get any credit for turning in your old machine? How does it work, etc.? We want to look into the proposition, and if possible, get an outfit like this in the interests of smoother coordination and more production.

"I think we agreed that a transcription should be made of my long speech at the Plenum. I would also like a transcription of my questions to Clarke following his speech. In fact we should also have a transcription of Clarke's speech. If these transcriptions break in too much on your crowded schedule, I suggest that you send the tapes here and Jeanne can transcribe them. While you're at it I would like to have the following tapes (or copies):

"1) My concluding speech

"2) Clarke's speech and my questions to Clarke

"3) My long speech at the Plenum

"4) My speech on Internationalism and the SWP—at the caucus

"5) Myra's Plenum speech

"6) Murry's Plenum speech

"What about that letter you were supposed to write to Jeanne in which you were supposed to let her know indirectly all that I and others said in N.Y. in appreciation of her great work during the past period? You know how shy I am about saying these things directly. Or don't you know?

"Don't forget to give me your report of the membership meeting where Farrell and George spoke, and your general impression. Of course, I will get an official report but I always need the 'third dimension' to fill out the picture.

"The weather here is glorious as always, or nearly always—cooler than N.Y. with the sun shining more brightly at the same time; a steady, pleasant breeze but never any strong wind; never any fear of rain, mist or fog. If we want water we just turn on the faucet or the sprinklers.

"How is Murry getting along in his first semester in the Hansen School of Journalism, and how does he like his teacher? How is Kay getting along with her new regime of majority rule? In short, how's everything? Rose is in pretty good health and in general, as little Mattie says—the main thing he seems to have picked up from me—'Everything is lovely and the goose hangs high.'"

In July, when we returned from our vacation at Mountain Spring Camp, there was a letter in the mailbox from Jim.

"Here is a little present to welcome you back to the city after your vacation," he wrote. "After reading it yourself pass it on to Joe for the editorial mill.

"When I read your remark about what a wonderful thing it was at camp 'not to have to think about what to fix for dinner—no shopping, no dishwashing'—I sat right down and wrote a section in this final lecture on Socialist America about the revolutionary transformation of the whole housekeeping business and the emancipation of women from the kitchen. If you don't believe it really happened that way, I am sure you will believe if I hadn't already written this section I would have done so after getting your letter."

Jim is referring to his sixth lecture, "What Socialist America Will Look Like"—the final chapter in *America's Road to Socialism.*

Jim was never one to show great patience in waiting for mail. In a letter to me on July 9, he groused a bit. "I was glad to get that long-delayed letter from Tom [Kerry]. I hope the same kind of a slip-up on the mail is not happening in the case of Warde [George Novack]. I sent him a long political letter last week; and since I have received no acknowledgment, I am afraid it is also sitting in his mailbox while he and Evelyn are at camp. I wish you would check on this, as I think this letter could be useful to our people in the New York situation and around the country generally.

"I am eagerly awaiting your opinion of lecture number 6. I hope Joe is in a position now to rush through the pamphlet so that I will be put out of reach of temptation to fiddle with it some more. I am feeling fine, working on a regular schedule; and Rose's new medicine seems to effectively arrest her periodical attacks of dizziness. The weather here is wonderful, as always. Dry heat—not too hot—with salubrious breezes in the daytime; cool, crisp, sleep-inducing nights."

Jim's intense interest in the development of cadres never flagged. He wanted the cadres to be well rounded, able to organize, to speak, to write. This stands out with unusual clarity in the following letter which he wrote when Myra Tanner Weiss was getting ready to leave Los Angeles for New York:

"Myra is in a dither about her impending transfer to the big city. She takes decisions literally. We are giving her a send-off banquet this Saturday night. When it was finally decided that she could leave after the banquet she interpreted that to mean 'forthwith' and got a plane ticket for 7:00 o'clock the next morning. She takes literally my favorite axiom that leadership means the capacity for decision. It can be stated another way: Don't fool around.

"I think it would be a good idea if Joe can work out a spot for Myra to work on *The Militant* staff in her spare time. (She plans to get a part-time job.) I think it would be a good idea if, instead of assigning her a column or anything pretentious like that, he would help her to break in on all kinds of little chores and odds and ends all the way from small assignments and fillers to proofreading and makeup—so that she gets a chance to learn the trade from the ground up.

"I hope nobody gets the idea that Murry and Myra are getting some kind of special consideration or promotion. All that they are getting, as I see it, is the same chance to acquire a little experience in the Center and on the paper that all the others have had."

Jim never tired of talking about the extraordinary importance of teamwork and he expressed some additional thoughts on this in the same letter:

"My theory of the building and development of cadres is the opposite of handpicking and artificial selection. As far as it is practically feasible and means permit, I have always thought that a large number of younger comrades should be rotated from one task to another, in the Center and in the field, until they all acquire a rather thorough rounded experience and then can fill in anywhere on short notice. It is an adaptation of nature's method of turning quantity into quality, of scattering seeds in profusion to make sure that some of them will take root and sprout.

"The recent Plenum was an impressive vindication of this volume theory. The significant thing revealed by the Plenum was not so much that some talented, trained and qualified people showed up at the turning point of the party crisis, but that there were *so many* of them. That basic fact of volume, plus the no-less important supplement that a large number of people have learned how to work together as a team—that's what makes the difference between a leading *cadre* and merely a few talented individuals, who have always been found in every party.

"From this point of view we ought to value the Trotsky School more highly and resolve that from now on we will permit nothing to interrupt its annual sessions. The more people we gather up for this basic theoretical training every year and then scatter back around the country, the stronger will be our local points of support for the elementary training of local cadres, and the broadening of the party cadre as a whole, in preparation for our self-confident struggle against all other tendencies for leadership of the new vanguard in the coming time."

Jim was always testing out projects he had in mind on different comrades to get their reactions, so he asked me to write to Art Sharon. ". . . ask him to drop me a line and let me know what his plans are. I am thinking about writing a long essay on the subject of 'Bolsheviks and trade unionists'; on the qualitative difference between them, and the all-around superiority of the former over the latter; on the necessity of transforming trade unionists into Bolsheviks, and the impermissibility of Bolsheviks becoming mere trade unionists and bringing the primitive scissor-bill prejudices, habits, methods and ignorant wise-acreism, generated by the most elementary form of workers organization—the trade union—into the highest, most conscious, and most important form of workers organization—the party.

"I may take this necessary exposition of a few plain truths out on Art in the form of a letter—now that I hear he will have a long-delayed opportunity to go into direct party work. The spectacle of some people, who have had the inestimable privilege of education in the party, strutting around as 'trade unionists' and claiming special recognition and privileges on these grounds, has got me fit to be tied. I have to sound off on this question in one form or another.

"As a result of the 1940 fight with the petty-bourgeois opposition the stick got bent backward and some prejudices have been allowed to flourish as a result. We have to bend the stick in the other direction now in order to straighten it out. The task then was to *proletarianize* the revolutionists—to 'trade unionize' the party, so to speak. One of the most important tasks at present, as some of the arguments we heard at the Plenum amply demonstrated, is to *revolutionize* the trade unionists."

The faction fight that broke out in the SWP in 1953 worried Jim a great deal, particularly because of its international ramifications. He wanted information about it from every possible source and he pressed me for details about developments in New York on this front. In the following letter he disclaimed any excitement:

"I am bogged down now with preparation of a report to the majority caucus this coming Sunday. As soon as I get through with that I will write at length in answer to the recent letters. They may be irritated by my Olympian calm in the new situation. But after the results in New York—which overshadow everything else in the order of importance—and the report of the conversation with [Sam] Marcy—which is also very important—I find it difficult to get excited about the new outburst of 'frenzy.' It's not directed against me anyway, is it? Or is it? I quit, didn't I? What the hell more do they want?

"I fully agree with the procedure in the discussion with Marcy and will write about that as soon as I get a chance. I hope copies of Warde's letter to me on this subject, or the same information in another form, has been sent to all the people in the field. The reaction from Akron, from a comrade I do not seem to know, is also most heartening. At each new turn of events we have to recognize that we have more politically alert people in the rank and file than we realized. That's a great strength in time of crisis."

Jim was referring to the fact that a majority had been won in the New York Local against the faction led by Bert Cochran and that the new majority had made a bloc with Sam Marcy and the comrades in his tendency.

Later in August, and "experimenting for the first time with a new dictating mechanism," Jim decided "to try now to catch up with delayed acknowledgment of a number" of my letters.

"Your comprehensive reports on the New York Convention and pre-Convention discussion," he wrote, "helped me a great deal to get a clear and rounded picture of the whole situation there. I badly need this kind of material to supplement the official reports. I think I now have a pretty clear impression of the new situation in New York and I am very well satisfied with the way things are going.

"Don't believe that Eastern canard about the so-called 'Santana' desert wind sweeping down into Los Angeles and producing mass psychological unrest. Nothing ever disturbs Los Angeles. Everything here is 'cucumber'—cool, that is."

Cucumber cool, toastily warm—whatever the weather, Jim enjoyed it, more in writing perhaps than in actuality. And he generally commented about it in his letters.

Having reported on the weather, Jim continues:

"I have been wondering what happened to Joe. I don't see any articles by him in the paper and received no answer to a letter I sent some time ago about editing the lectures for pamphlet publication. If you have time, I wish you would hunt him up and check the situation and ask him to let me know if he received that letter about the pamphlet, and in general how he feels and what he thinks. I noticed that Murry's name is signed to articles all over the paper. What happened to the system of parcelling out pseudonyms for different staff members who can't be held down to one article per week? A lot of Militant readers think Keller is more interesting than Preis. [Keller, pseudonym for Preis.]

"I was glad and greatly relieved to get the final lecture in the first series off our hands and in the mail. Now [George] Breitman has raised the question of inserting a new section about the Negroes under socialism, and I suppose I will have to go back to it once more for this specific purpose. But when that is done, I hope Joe will get the pamphlet on the press so that I will not be tempted, or even permitted, to monkey with it any more."

This letter of Jim's was not as carefully organized as most, but, as he put it, he was trying out a dictating machine. I don't know what it is about a dictating machine that intimidates people, but something does. There are those who won't even try it out and then there are others who try it once and never try again. But Jim, although I don't think he ever learned to appreciate the machine as much as his secretary, finally got the hang of it.

"In your letter of July 13," he continued, "you mentioned that Myra had arrived and been welcomed at the airport. Since then I have heard nothing from her, and I assume the big city has swallowed her up. The same thing applies to Murry. We have all been saddened a bit by this fickle transfer of affections and try to console ourselves philosophically by recalling the proverb: 'Out of sight, out of mind.'

"I received a letter from Vincent the other day. He has now definitely set the date of September 2 or 3 to leave Minneapolis for a protracted visit here. We have made arrangements to accommodate him in the most comfortable way, and we are looking forward to a fine visit which we hope will be good for him, as it will be for all of us.

"The moving has been finished, but we are not recovered from the effects of it yet. It wore us both out, and badly disrupted my working schedule. This week, however, Jeanne and I have started again a little more seriously and systematically, and I hope that we will soon be back in the old groove and rolling along at the regular pace. I have committed myself to so many projects that I am beginning to feel nervous and crowded. The only possible way I can hope to dig myself out is to make up a schedule and try to do the various things in order.

"I hope to clear things out of the way and get to work on the projected new series of lectures for the Fall and Winter Forum. There are quite a number of things that have to come in ahead of that. For one thing I am now beginning to get nervous about the assignment I took to make a Trotsky Memorial speech at the Los Angeles Summer School and Camp, which begins here Labor Day. That will be quite a chore in itself, and the worst of it is that I won't be able to devote full time to it. At least not for another week.

"I have heard nothing about how Art Sharon is doing in his new job. I would like to get your impressions about this [Sharon had accepted the assignment of New York Local organizer]."

Because of the continuing factional atmosphere in the New York Local, branch meetings were sometimes very hectic. I made it a point to get the highlights in shorthand so that I could keep Jim up to date. He comments on this:

"I am watching with the greatest interest to see how the majority in Local New York—the rank and file as well as leadership—cope with the new situation of a virtual sit-down strike by the Cochranites. I have the impression, gained particularly from your illuminating report of the last meeting of the downtown branch, that the situation is being handled very well. The problem, as I see it, is to stick to the formal line of the Plenum resolution, offer collaboration on that basis, but if it is refused, to go right ahead with the party work anyway.

"I gained a very high respect for the caucus of the majority in New York from the great work they did in the pre-Plenum fight, and from what I was able to see for myself, during my visit there at the time of the Plenum. The new situation imposes another task which consists of combining the internal political struggle with the development of external party work in spite of factional opposition, or even sabotage. I lived through years of that kind of business in the old Communist Party. It is much more difficult than a straight-out faction fight, and ten times more difficult than the orderly development of constructive party work in a nonfactional situation. It takes a real Bolshevik to combine the two, and not to neglect either.

"Art Sharon, as the organizer, will have to be the leader of this combined activity. I personally have the impression that he is just about the right man for the job. He is poised and good-natured enough to assimilate everybody in the practical work who shows any disposition or has any capacities to take part in it. At the same time he has the necessary political understanding, knowledge and firmness not to get lost in the external work and neglect the tasks of political education and political struggle in defense of our program and position."

Jim finished his letter with a final poke at the dictating machine.

"This letter may not turn out to be a very well constructed job, as I am experimenting for the first time with a new dictating mechanism. I am dictating into a tape recording machine and am still somewhat intimidated by all the gadgets, and terrified by the prospect that I may have pushed the wrong button and that everything I have dictated will turn out to be a blank. Once I get the hang of this new mechanism, however, I feel that it is going to aid production. So I am going to stick to it and keep cucumber until I acquire the necessary facility. Then I'll be real gone— 'nervous,' that is.

"P.S. I see from *The Militant,* which just arrived, that you have finally decided to teach the editors, by example, how to lighten up and brighten up the paper and to convey the most basic socialist ideas at the same time. I enjoyed your article immensely. It reads easy and smooth, tells an interesting story and then nonchalantly drops a fundamental socialist conception about the changeability of human nature into the reader's lap like a ton of bricks. Where did you learn these crafty journalist tricks, and why have you been keeping them under cover so long?"

The article Jim mentions caught his attention for several reasons. One was that it violated a basic rule of the *Militant*; it didn't deal with people. It took up the cause of a monkey in a laboratory. To earn her bananas she had to put coins in a slot machine and the coins became harder and harder to get, leading to a lot of complications. The mad scientists were trying to get the poor ape to go to work. Laura Gray drew a wonderful sketch of the animal to illustrate the article.

After an unusually long silence, Jim wrote on February 2, 1954: "Don't jump to the impatient conclusion, just because it took me two months to acknowledge your letter of December 4, that I am in any way negligent of correspondence in general or indifferent to your communications in particular. The only trouble is that I am a bit slow. Also, when I get absorbed in some single task, as you know, I go into a sort of coma and don't seem to hear or understand anything that is being said on any other subject. But now that I have finished with Deutscher for the time being, and haven't yet started again on the interrupted articles on other aspects of the international question, I am trying to answer all neglected correspondence, to take an interest in all the general affairs of the world, and in the people who are especially interesting to me, and in general to be my normal half-normal self."

Jim's reference is to a polemical article he wrote—"Trotsky or Deutscher?"—that was printed in the Winter 1954 issue of *Fourth International*. For a time Jim considered that Deutscher's attacks against the Fourth International could offer a bridge for splits from the Trotskyist movement into the camp of Stalinism. Later—after Khrushchev's speech in 1956 confirming many of Stalin's crimes—he decided that the danger was not as acute as he had feared. In some instances, in fact, "Deutscherism" proved to be a bridge for splits from the Stalinist movement toward Trotskyism.

Although Jim was generally very considerate of the comrades he worked with, he insisted on accuracy and neatness in everything we did. This wasn't just because he was fussy but because, he said, the material that went out of the national office provided an important part of the party's image. Very often it is first impressions that stick in people's minds. So, he reminded us more than once, everything we did must show that we are serious, efficient people who know what we're about, people who show even in small things their efficiency and capacity to do things right. And, believe me, we tried; we really worked at getting everything letter-perfect in the national office.

How two typographical errors got through in one of the internal bulletins I still don't know. But Jim caught them and sent a couple of paragraphs in his February 2 letter:

"By the way, I did a little detective work when I read the Internal Bulletin containing my report on the November Plenum and found two typographical errors. That caused consternation here in Los Angeles. There were excited demands from numerous comrades for an explanation of such an unprecedented occurrence, which I have told everybody, with absolute assurance, could not possibly happen in any material coming out of the National Office apparatus administered by you and Kay. In a flash of insight, which only Sherlock Holmes and I could be capable of, I finally deduced the reason and explained this fantastic faux pas as follows to a wide circle of believing listeners:

" 'New York, as you know, has a very inclement climate. It snows heavily, and then fierce winds from even farther north blow down and pile the snow up into huge drifts. Both Reba and Kay simply got caught in a snow bank on the day that bulletin went to press, and couldn't get to the office in time to make their customary final check for the complete elimination of all possible errors. The fault,' I said, 'is not with them. Just blame the New York weather, and keep believing that everything that comes out of the National Office will be letter-perfect—except in case of snowdrifts.'"

Some may think that Jim was just kidding. That could very well be, but both Kay and I got the point. Actually, how could such a thing happen in the national office?

One day I read an article in a daily newspaper about the death of John Rust. Jim had told me about this man and his cotton-picking invention. I sent the clipping to Jim and he wrote me:

"I was very sad to receive the clipping about the death of John Rust, the inventor of the cotton picker. I knew him since 1919. I first encountered him as a young World War I soldier still in uniform, in a radical veterans organization of that time, known as 'World War Veterans' with headquarters in Minneapolis, which as far back as then was a center of labor radicalism. I invited John to attend a class I was conducting in the ABC of communism. Then he attended another class of mine in public speaking. After he had broken through his first shyness, which is the main obstacle for most beginners, he became a good public speaker.

"This undoubtedly served him in good stead in later years when he had to tour around, speaking to organizations wherever he could, in the effort to raise money to promote his great invention. He joined our movement in 1919. Later, when we were expelled in 1928 he was in Texas beginning his experimental work on the cotton picker. 'Shorty' Buehler of Kansas City, who was in correspondence with him, put him on the mailing list of *The Militant,* and he became one of the original Trotskyists. I was in communication with him from time to time ever since.

"He visited me in New York in the early thirties. He told me then that his dearest ambition was to make enough money out of his invention to be able to help our movement. He was still struggling along in 1938, when we visited him and his family at Memphis on our way to our meeting with Trotsky. He received us very warmly, and asked us to tell the Old Man that he was an ardent Trotskyist and that he still hoped to make some money which would be useful for our movement.

"His 25-year battle with the farm implement companies

consumed his life. They tried to steal his invention, or to manufacture it for him with a small royalty. This ran up against his stubborn determination to promote it himself, so that all the profits beyond what he would need to live on, could be devoted to good causes. He finally died before he was able to realize his full ambition in this respect. But from all accounts, his cotton picker has revolutionized the production of cotton. Vincent saw him in 1948 in Missouri somewhere, and found him still friendly and still hopeful that he would be able to do something for us. Well, John is dead now, like a lot of other good people I've known. I'm glad I knew him."

This letter about John Rust was very interesting to me. It showed how fresh Jim's memory remained of the old-timers in the movement and how each one was first won to the Communist and later to the Trotskyist movement. Also the letter contained a bit of information about Jim's early activities—that he taught a class in the ABCs of communism and another in public speaking. With Rust, of course, Jim had a special relation; I heard him speak of him on more than one occasion at social gatherings in his home. Jim was especially interested in the cotton picker because Rust's dream was to make a fortune through which he could help finance the party. It didn't turn out that way because of Rust's death.

Jim was worrying about the staff in the center and wrote on April 6, 1954, stressing the importance of letting up a little after a period of intensive work and tension.

"When I saw your note to Rose about Kay being off sick and how rushed and crowded you were, I felt very sorry that I had added additional chores to your calendar by my numerous requests. I'll try to slow down on this business until you catch your breath. And even after that, in the future I will be satisfied if you just put such requests in the bottom of your drawer to be attended to when you get time.

"From the looks of things Murry and I may be able to go out to the desert for a few days before he heads back to New York. If the trip works out, I will personally hand-pick some dates from the wild palms of the desert for you and Kay to nibble on some afternoon when you are taking a breather, if and when you get a chance to do such a thing."

By "desert," Jim meant Desert Hot Springs, about 120 miles from Los Angeles. Jim claimed that the desert air was conducive to thinking. And when some of his comrades or friends from out of town visited him, he would often recommend going to the desert for a few days to mull things over.

Jim did send us some dates. I doubt he handpicked them, but many stands in the area do offer dates that taste like they've just been picked.

Jim's letter continued:

"I have been painfully aware that the whole staff in the Center has been overworked in recent months. At the same time, however, I have sensed that there was present an element of psychological pressure not justified in the new situation. There may be as much work to do, or even more than before the Plenum. But the general atmosphere of uncertainty should have been removed by the Plenum decisions and, with that, the feeling of strain and tension on the part of the comrades involved. I have felt that way here, and as a result have been able to do more work without getting tired than before the Plenum. As for the strain and tension, that was entirely eliminated for my part, when the basic decisions were made last November.

"The whole party situation is qualitatively different now. The great decisions have been made; the national fight is finished in good shape; the international fight is three-fourths over, and the favorable final outcome is clearly indicated. We don't have to worry about uncertainties on that front unless we worry ourselves into it. In these new circumstances the work routine ought to be carried through each day without strain or pressure. I would like to suggest that you and the other members of the staff think over this aspect of the new situation and psychologize yourselves accordingly.

"See what a smug little psychological preacher I have become?"

Not too long after Rose and Jim settled in California, Jim started writing about his "little black dog," named appropriately "Blackie." When they went to Desert Hot Springs to "bake out," Blackie was always getting "hooked with another cactus bur."

In Los Angeles, Blackie could not be depended on to stay in the yard. Rose wrote for instance: "Jim says 'tell Reba about Blackie.' He means for me to say that after eight days away, without his collar, Blackie found his way back and appeared on the doorstep just a day or so before we left for camp."

In the middle of December, Jim used Blackie to make a point about the weather: "How's the weather in New Jersey? It's tough out here too. Our little dog got sunburned yesterday."

The story is that Blackie came in off the highway and adopted Jim at one of the West Coast Vacation Camps. Jim was very fond of dogs; middle-size dogs, that is. He didn't like big dogs too much and had an antipathy for bulldogs, as I mentioned in telling about our vacation with Jim and Rose in Maine. Jim called his distaste for bulldogs a "phobia." When he was very young, in Rosedale, one used to rage at him from the other side of the fence when Jim passed, and the small boy's imagination did the rest.

His fondness for dogs did not extend to cats. However, cats were fond of Jim. If there was a cat in the house, it would invariably select Jim out of a roomful of people to lavish its affection on. Our orange-colored Persian, normally quite standoff-ish with strangers, took to Jim this way, leaping from a bookshelf and landing on Jim's lap, much to his disgust. Cleo looked up at Jim as if she was trying to remind him of a previous incarnation and I could hardly peel her away.

One time at Mountain Spring Camp, Jim was sitting comfort-ably with his pipe in the shade of a big tree on the lawn, when one of the camp cats trotted out of the shrubbery with a baby rabbit in its jaws, evidently proud of its catch and wanting a little praise for a job well done. Jim saw the poor little rabbit give a kick and he went after the cat, brandishing his cane, and shouting bloody murder.

The cat made a split-second decision, dropped the rabbit, and went up the tree under which Jim had been sitting. If Jim wanted the rabbit all that bad, he could have it. The rabbit sought safety, too—scurrying back into the shrubbery.

The incident showed how the plight of the weak and the helpless automatically triggered a response in Jim.

Early in 1956, agreement was reached among the leading comrades in New York for Joe and me to transfer to Los Angeles to work with Jim, and specifically to help him on an autobiogra-phy. That was our objective.

There was some skepticism as to whether we would succeed. Even on Jim's part, I'm sure. This was expressed in several letters from Rose. In one she writes: ". . . Jim is not set against the project. He is merely 'modest' about the value of his life as a person. Yet he is an omnivorous reader of biography—that is, of course, of men and women who were socially minded. In recent days he has brought up the subject at [the] supper table. Always in the form of a question, but a question that expressed interest and even a hope that perhaps something of value for the future generations may come of such a book."

In another letter Rose refers to the project: "Jim. . . . fears that he has said most of what he has to say politically, and he cannot visualize a personal biography that could be of any value to the movement; besides, he is not one to give out regarding purely personal anecdotes, feelings or reactions. So you also have the job of convincing him of the need for the book. . . . As for me, I am with you."

I already knew of Jim's reluctance to talk about himself, but thought the project well worth a try.

To keep travel expenses within our means, we made a trade, loaning Duncan Ferguson our hi-fi components for his small English-built automobile, and started across country in June 1956. We stayed with Rose and Jim until we could find an apartment. Sharing their home with Blackie the dog and our two Siamese cats was an experience!

During the next year we made a little progress on the autobiographical project, but it never really seemed to jell. Jim talked freely about his early days in the movement, but dummied up when his personal experiences might become involved.

In the spring of 1957, when the comrades in New York shifted *International Socialist Review*, the party's theoretical magazine, to Los Angeles where printing costs were lower than those in New York, both Joe and I had a busier schedule. We made it a point to spend a part of each day with Jim, however, still hoping—at least I was—that the biography would materialize.

As it became increasingly clear, however, that we hadn't been able to convince Jim to really go to work on a biography of himself, the pressure mounted to return to New York where the staff was shorthanded. By the spring of 1958 we were again settled in New York.

In 1962 I was asked to take charge of a nationwide tour that Joe was to make on the situation in Latin America. We had just returned from a four-month trip and Joe was to give an eyewitness account of what we had learned.

I mentioned this to Jim, who wrote back immediately. In his letter he gave me a lot of advice about how to organize the tour which as a greenhorn in this field I appreciated a lot. But aside from that aspect, I think the letter is of some value in what it shows about Jim's experience in such matters. If the specific tour involving Joe is left aside, Jim's advice on organizing tours will be appreciated by everyone who has ever been involved in this arduous work where attention to detail is at such a premium. For this reason I think the entire text is worth putting in the record, even though it's rather long.

". . .This is a big step forward in two respects: first, a national tour is a big party action and, like the fund drives and other special actions, should always be placed in charge of a director who can specialize and concentrate on it and leave the national secretary free for his many other pressing duties; two, your appointment to this important task is a guarantee that it will be handled with businesslike precision and careful attention to every detail. (As you know, I ain't kiddin' and I ain't whistlin' Dixie, whatever that means.)

"The proper organization of tours is a specialty in itself as I well know from past experience. At one time in the early days of the CP I was in charge of the organization of speaking tours and put in a lot of time on it. There is a general pattern to this business that somehow or other seems to have been lost in recent years. If you can set the pattern again with Joe's tour it can be a guiding line for the organization of all future tours. Here are a few tips:

"1. Take time to think out a good title for the subject of the speeches. The one announced for Joe's tour "What Makes Latin America Explosive" is lousy. It suggests a professorial analysis calculated to scare people away. The big feature of this tour is that we have somebody fresh back from an extensive investigation of the Latin American situation on the spot and that he has come back to make a *report*. You need a positive title something like this: 'The Latin American Explosion—An Eyewitness Report,' or something like that.

"2. The tour must be publicized from week to week just like the Fund Drive and preceded by a couple of articles giving a build-up for it. You're a bit late on this, but there's still time to catch up. You need a couple of publicity articles announcing the tour as a big event, and telling who Joe is and where he's been and what he has seen and why he is qualified to give his audience the lowdown on an explosive situation south of our border which is not reported in the commercial press.

"3. Every week there should be a report of Joe's meetings as he goes along to whip up the appetite of the readers of *The Militant* in cities where he is yet to appear.

"4. Every week, without exception, either following the report of his latest meeting or in a special box the paper should carry Joe's complete unfilled itinerary as a reminder to *The Militant* readers of the date when Joe will be coming to their town so that they will begin to look forward to it. (It is not adequate at all to send the itinerary merely to the branch organizers. Print it in the paper for the benefit of *Militant* readers who don't get to branch meetings and don't have access to the local organizer's files.)

"5. Don't hesitate to print Joe's picture along with the story of his great nationwide tour.

"6. Fire out plenty of special letters to local organizers, not merely mimeographed circulars which usually attract little attention. Even short personal letters with a little news and gossip about the way the tour is going and how much it means to the party help a lot to keep the local tour organizers on their toes.

"7. I don't need to tell you the importance of getting press conferences and radio and TV appearances for Joe. But quite a few local organizers haven't mastered this technique yet. Some detailed tips on how to go about this can be very useful in such cases.

"8. Don't assume that all local organizers know enough about the special appeal this tour will have to Spanish-speaking elements in the population. Spell it out for them.

"9. Ask all local organizers to fire in reports, first, about their preparations for Joe's meetings and then later about the success of the meetings themselves for use in your weekly column boosting and booming the tour."

There it is, a nine-point manual on how to organize a tour. It can probably be enlarged and brought up to date with suggestions concerning modern-day technological devices, but the essence is in Jim's letter.

In 1966 when Jim was seventy-six years old, the question of the role of the Control Commission in the Trotskyist movement came up for discussion in the leadership of the SWP. I became involved in it for two reasons: one was that I was a member of the Control Commission and second, I was one of a committee of three designated to review the party constitution and report back to the National Committee on any recommendations to change it. Since Jim was responsible for founding the institution of a control commission in the SWP, his opinion was of prime interest in relation to a proposal to change the constitution with respect to the norms used in selecting members of the Control Commission.

I wrote a brief letter to Jim which among other things said:

"You will see from a copy of the letter enclosed that it will be very helpful to us on the Constitution Committee to get your recollections concerning the Control Commission.

"Nobody here that I've talked with can recall the details, only that you initiated the idea, that you motivated the necessity for a Control Commission, etc."

Jim utilized the occasion to make some pedagogical points. This way of teaching was quite characteristic of him. He often used seemingly small proposals or incidents to drive home a lesson. In this instance he perhaps felt that his concept of control commissions and how they should function, which he had learned from Trotsky, might not be sufficiently well understood by the party. Thus he went to some lengths to once again explain his concept.

When I received Jim's response I again felt how seriously he took such matters. It was the same feeling I had throughout my working with him. Underlying the friendship in our association was a hard political relationship in which I was able for a time to help him in an effective way in his job of leading the party and building for the socialist future that guided him.

For this reason I would like to offer the entire letter despite its length. To me his response seems to epitomize the special relationship I had with him. In addition it may be of particular interest because of certain debates on the role of control commissions which have been going on in the world Trotskyist movement in the recent period.

Here is Jim's reply:

"This answers your letter of November 2 with which you enclosed a copy of the comrade's letter of October 12. I was surprised and concerned by the proposals to change the constitutional provisions providing for an independent Control Commission elected by the Convention, and making it a mere subcommittee of the PC. This would be the *de facto* liquidation of the Control Commission as it was originally conceived.

"As far as I can see all the new moves and proposals to monkey with the Constitution which has served the party so well in the past, with the aim of 'tightening' centralization, represent a trend in the wrong direction at the present time. The party (and the YSA) is too 'tight' already, and if we go much further along this line we can run the risk of strangling the party to death.

"As I recall it, the proposal to establish a Control Commission, separately elected by the Convention, originated at the Plenum & Active Workers' Conference in the fall of 1940, following the assassination of the Old Man. The assassin, as you will recall, gained access to the household in Coyoacan through his relations with a party member. The Political Committee was then, as it always will be if it functions properly, too busy with political and organizational problems to take time for investigations and security checks on individuals.

"It was agreed that we need a special body to take care of this work, to investigate rumors and charges and present its findings and recommendations to the National Committee.

"If party security was one side of the functions of the Control Commission, the other side—no less important—was to provide the maximum assurance that any individual party member, accused or rumored to be unworthy of party membership, could be assured of the fullest investigation and a fair hearing or trial. It was thought that this double purpose could best be served by a body separately elected by the convention, and composed of members of long standing, especially respected by the party for their fairness as well as their devotion.

"I can recall instances where the Control Commission served the party well in both aspects of this dual function. In one case a member of the Seamen's fraction was expelled by the members of the Los Angeles branch after charges were brought against him by two members of the National Committee of that time. The expelled member appealed to the National Committee and the case was turned over to the Control Commission for investigation. The Control Commission, on which as I recall Dobbs was then the PC representative, investigated the whole case, found that the charges lacked substantial proof and recommended the reinstatement of the expelled member. This was done.

"In another case, a rumor circulated by the Shachtmanites and others outside the party against the integrity of a National Office secretarial worker was thoroughly investigated by the Control Commission which, after taking stenographic testimony from all available sources, declared the rumors unfounded and cleared the accused party member to continue her work. There were other cases in which charges were found after investigation to be substantiated and appropriate action recommended."

The secretarial worker Jim refers to was Sylvia Caldwell. Rumors like that one, proved by the investigation of the Control Commission to have been unfounded, were periodically circulated by sources interested in disrupting the SWP.

Jim's letter continued:

"All these experiences speak convincingly of the need for a separate Control Commission of highly respected comrades to make thorough investigations of every case, without being influenced by personal or partisan prejudice, or pressure from any source, and whose sole function is to examine each case from all sides fairly and justly and report its findings and recommendations. This is the best way, not only to protect the security of the party, but also to respect the rights of the accused in every case.

"As far as I know, the only criticism that can properly be made of the Control Commission in recent times is that it has not always functioned in this way with all its members participating, either by presence or correspondence, in all proceedings—and convincing the party that its investigation was thorough and that its findings and recommendations were fair and just.

"It should be pointed out also that the idea of a Control Commission separately constituted by the convention didn't really originate with us. Like almost everything else we know about the party organizational principles and functions, it came from the Russian Bolsheviks. The Russian party had a separate Control Commission. It might also be pointed out that after the Revolution the new government established courts. It provided also for independent trade unions which, as Lenin pointed out in one of the controversies, had the duty even to defend the rights of its members against the government. Of course, all that was changed later when all power was concentrated in the party secretariat, and all the presumably independent institutions were converted into rubber stamps. But we don't want to move in that direction. The forms and methods of the Lenin-Trotsky time are a better guide for us.

"I am particularly concerned about any possible proposal to weaken the constitutional provision about the absolute right of suspended or expelled members to appeal to the Convention. That is clearly and plainly a provision to protect every party member against possible abuse of authority by the National Committee. It should not be abrogated or diluted just to show that we are so damn revolutionary that we make no concessions to 'bourgeois concepts of checks and balances.' The well-known Bill of Rights is a check and balance which I hope will be incorporated, in large part at least, in the Constitution of the Workers Republic in this country. Our constitutional provision for the right of appeal is also a 'check and balance.' It can help to recommend our party to revolutionary workers as a genuinely democratic organization which guarantees rights as well as imposing responsibilities, and thus make it more appealing to them.

"I believe that these considerations have more weight now than ever before in the 38-year history of our party. In the present political climate and with the present changing composition of the party, democratic-centralism must be applied flexibly. At least ninety per cent of the emphasis should be placed on the democratic side and not on any crackpot schemes to 'streamline' the party to the point where questions are unwelcome and criticism and discussion stifled. That is a prescription to kill the party before it gets a chance to show how it can handle and assimilate an expanding membership of new young people, who don't know it all to start with, but have to learn and grow in the course of explication and discussion in a free, democratic atmosphere.

"Trotsky once remarked in a polemic against Stalinism that even in the period of the Civil War discussion in the party was 'boiling like a spring.' Those words and others like it written by Trotsky, in his first attack against Stalinism in 'The New Course,' ought to be explained now once again to the new young recruits in our party. And the best way to explain such decisive things is to practice what we preach."

My memories of Jim also include one of my closest comrades and friends, Bea Hansen, who became one of his secretaries. She was a Trotskyist woman leader, well-known in left-wing circles in the auto plants in Detroit. She died in Los Angeles in March 1969.

When Bea agreed to work as Jim's secretary, she spent days asking me about the different aspects of working with him, what it was like, what was required. I briefed her on everything with complete frankness, even about those times when Jim could become quite difficult, also about the compensations of working with him.

Jim appreciated Bea and mentioned her in the following letter February 27, 1967:

"Bea showed up here suddenly at 10 o'clock last Wednesday morning and said, 'Let's go.' Before I could recover my balance we had started to work on our first book. After reading and discussing some of the material, we have finally come to an almost definite conclusion that the first book will be *Letters from Prison*. They were typed up by Sylvia [Caldwell] 22 years ago but I had never read them over again since they were written.

"In the last few days we have been going through them and have come to the conclusion that they will probably be more suitable for publication than anything else as a starter. Although formally composed as letters, they are in reality a day by day *prison diary* recording all the thoughts and impulses that come to a rebel in prison day after day. They deal with virtually all the problems of the party and party politics of that time which later broke out and came to the front in party struggles and discussion.

"Bea tells me that the printshop is well set up now and that it is important to supply them with copy to keep them out of mischief. You can tell all concerned to take a deep breath and wait for the first batch of manuscripts which will probably be coming along in the very near future.

"The manuscript, as I see it, may be sent to you in installments to facilitate an early start on the printing. As a whole it will amount to a full-sized book. And if my personal judgment is worth anything, it will contain some of the best writing I ever did.

"Take it easy. The worst is yet to come."

Jim was now seventy-seven years old and despite his determination to keep going, his production inevitably declined. His health became fragile. With Rose's death in 1968, he lost one of his main sources of inspiration. His mind remained keen, however, and he continued to follow politics very closely, particularly developments in the Fourth International and the Socialist Workers Party.

Most of Jim's contributions during this period came through discussions and occasional tape-recorded interviews. His home became a kind of commune as young comrades moved in to help him. Such secretarial assistance as he needed was always at hand.

I saw Jim several times in these final years and he seemed unchanged, except things had become difficult for him physically. He kept up with world events, followed the radical press, and read enormously, even increasing the flow of books that attracted his interest. He contended that reading, too, was an activity. And it showed in his political conversations, where his observations were right up to date.

Those who met Jim in this final period will probably remember him sitting in his easy chair wearing a green eyeshade and looking a little grouchy as he read. If they talked politics with him, they will remember some of the sharp things he said, or his ironic look if he was in a kidding mood. That is the way I remember him, too, except that it was with my notebook and shorthand pen at the ready and Jim working over some paragraph orally, or striking out sentences, or adding new ones to a manuscript that we had been working on together. Or maybe reading it out loud to see if I thought it was any good.

Index